THE PUBLIC INTEREST ON EDUCATION

THE PUBLIC INTEREST ON EDUCATION

edited by

Nathan Glazer

Abt Books
Cambridge, Massachusetts

Library of Congress Cataloging in Publication Data
Main entry under title:

The Public Interest on Education.

1. Education—United States—Aims and objectives—addresses, essays, lectures.   2. Education and state—United States—Addresses, essays, lectures.   3. Education equalization—United States—Addresses, essays,
lectures.   I. Glazer, Nathan.
LA210.P82   1984   379.73   83–21548
ISBN 0–89011–590–7

Printed in the United States of America.

Contents

Acknowledgements

The articles in this volume originally appeared in the following volumes of *The Public Interest*.

"Black Excellence—The Case of Dunbar High School", No. 35, Spring 1974.

"Patterns of Black Excellence", No. 43, Spring 1976.

"Career Education—Reforming School Through Work", No. 46, Spring 1976.

"Moral Education in the Schools", No. 50, Winter 1978.

"The 'White Flight' Controversy", No. 51, Spring 1978.

"A Response to 'The White Flight Controversy' ", No. 53, Fall 1978.

"What Do You Mean When the Supreme Court is Wrong?", No. 57, Fall 1979.

"Crime in American Public Schools", No. 58, Winter 1980.

"The Mandate Millstone", No. 61, Fall 1980.

"Christian Schools Versus the I.R.S.", No. 61, Fall 1980.

"The Conflict in Moral Education: An Informal Case Study", No. 63, Spring 1981.

"Public Schools, Private Schools, and the Public Interest", No. 64, Summer 1981.

"Power to the Parents?—The Story of Education Vouchers", No. 48, Summer 1977.

Introduction

SINCE 1954, at least, education seems to have become a key focus of all the major issues and tensions in American life. The *Brown* decision made issues of race and equality central for American schools. Then, issues of quality and international competition were brought to national attention by the Russian success in launching the first space rocket. These issues have regained centrality with startling rapidity in 1983, as the pre-eminence of the United States in science and technology has weakened in the 1970's and 1980's. The moral revolutions of the 1960's and after also had their consequences in the schools—sex education, moral education, crime in the schools have all become burning issues locally, and to some extent nationally. The growth of government and of the power of the federal government specifically became national issues in the 1980 presidential election and the schools were one key area in which many felt that the federal government was too intrusive, local government too bureaucratic, and non-state alternatives more effective than state efforts. Throughout, questions of "excellence," of the quality of American education, contended with the alternative of more equality, of a democratic education open to all.

All these issues, and others, were raised in *The Public Interest* during the past ten years. This current selection of articles is drawn from twice or three times as many dealing with these matters. Thomas Sowell raises the key question of what makes a school good, in the context of a study of successful black schools. Black students and black schools raise some of the most difficult issues in education. Yet there are successful black schools, and a close analysis of them teaches us what makes any school good. Eleanor Farrar McGowan and David Cohen address the problem of how one can better relate schools to jobs and work, a major concern of recent years. William J. Bennett and Edwin Delattre, and Martin Eger, deal with the question of moral education in the public schools, and how, or whether, a system that reflects a diverse society can teach morality. One of the key issues in the struggle over desegregation—white flight—is analyzed by Diane Ravitch. Senator Daniel P. Moynihan raises the troubling question of Supreme Court interventions in education, particularly in defense of the clause forbidding an establishment of religion, interventions which have sharply limited public aid to non-state schools, and asks what one can do when one is honestly convinced the Court is wrong. Mayor Edward Koch of New York City describes how the federal government has imposed endless and costly requirements on the public schools, and raises the question of the proper limits of federal requirements on local schools. Jackson Toby deals with crime in the public schools— certainly one reason why private schools retain their popularity. Peter Skerry describes one type of private school which has shown remarkable growth in recent years, the Christian schools, and tries to estimate the causes of their growth, and its relation to the changing moral temper of public schools and the efforts to desegregate public schools. David Cohen and Eleanor Farrar describe one major experiment designed to give greater power to parents, vouchers giving parents freedom to choose. This remains a major public issue. In a concluding article, James Coleman describes his controversial research on the effectiveness of private and public schools, a key question in the debate over government assistance to non-state schools.

Nathan Glazer

Black excellence
—the case
of
Dunbar High School

THOMAS SOWELL

Social pathology has held an enduring fascination for researchers, and nowhere more so than in the study of black Americans. Isolated "successes" or "heroes" receive occasional attention, but large-scale or institutionalized progress and excellence seem almost to be shunned, except for passing references to the "middle-class" end results. With all the voluminous outpourings on black educational pathology, there has been an almost total neglect of one of the most remarkable black educational success stories: Dunbar High School.

For a period of 85 years (1870-1955) Dunbar was an academically elite, all-black public high school in Washington, D.C. As far back as 1899, Dunbar students came in first in citywide tests given in *both* black and white schools. Over the 85-year span, most of Dunbar's graduates went on to college, even though most Americans—white or black—did not. Most Dunbar graduates could afford only to attend the low-cost local colleges: either federally-supported Howard University or tuition-free Miner Teachers College. However, those Dunbar graduates who attended Harvard, Amherst, Oberlin, and other prestigious institutions (usually on scholarships) ran up an impressive record of academic honors. For example, it is known that Amherst admitted 34 Dunbar graduates between 1892 and 1954; of these, 74 per cent graduated, and more than one fourth of these graduates were Phi Beta Kappas.

In their careers, as in their academic work, Dunbar graduates excelled. The first black general (Benjamin O. Davis), the first black federal judge (William H. Hastie), the first black Cabinet member (Robert C. Weaver), the discoverer of blood plasma (Charles Drew), and the first black Senator since Reconstruction (Edward W. Brooke) were all Dunbar graduates. During World War II, Dunbar graduates in the Army included "nearly a score of majors, nine colonels and lieutenant colonels, and one brigadier general"[1]—a substantial percentage of the total number of high-ranking black officers at that time.

Almost as astonishing as Dunbar's achievements has been the ignoring of those achievements—which might, after all, conceivably have some bearing on questions about educating black children. No scholarly study of the school has yet appeared, and almost the entire literature on the subject consists of one slim volume, *The Dunbar Story*, printed privately at her own expense by Mary Gibson Hundley, a retired Dunbar teacher. Where Dunbar has been noticed at all, it has been brushed aside as a "middle-class" black school, and local tradition in Washington suggests that its students were predominantly light-skinned Negroes, many scarcely distinguishable from whites. The facts do not support either assertion, but the attempt to dismiss the Dunbar experience is a significant phenomenon in its own right.

History

What are the facts and factors in the Dunbar story? First of all, Dunbar High School, as it existed from its founding in 1870 to the school reorganization following the Supreme Court's integration decision in 1954, is no more. The name and the building are still there, but it is now just another ghetto school—in appearance, atmosphere, and statistical profile. It is more fortunate than most in having a dedicated principal, but she is clearly struggling against the odds. Alumni who refer to "Dunbar when it *was* Dunbar" do not help her, or today's students, but they are expressing a bitter historical truth.

The unique educational phenomenon that was Dunbar High

---

[1] Mary Gibson Hundley, *The Dunbar Story* (New York: Vintage Press, 1965), p. 57.

School occurred between 1870 and 1955. The experience began in a basement school, changed locations and names,[2] but maintained institutional continuity and high academic standards. It was the first black high school in the United States, and it was an academic school from the beginning—fiercely resisting recurrent pressures upon it to become vocational, commercial, or "general." It taught Latin throughout this period, and in some early years Greek as well. It was never "relevant" to the passing fads, but it instilled individual and racial pride. In the building it has occupied since 1916, the auditorium is dominated by a verse by black poet Paul Laurence Dunbar:

> *Keep a-pluggin' away,*
> *Perseverance still is king . . .*

Why this particular school—and why Washington, D.C.? There is no ready answer. Certainly there was nothing radically distinctive about the Washington black community through most of the 20th century, and since Dunbar was unique from the outset, the elements of that uniqueness are probably best found in history and in the traditions generated by its early success.

Back in 1870, the Washington black community was in fact unique. Although slavery had ended just five years earlier, the Washington Negro community was much older than that. As far back as 1830, half the Negroes in Washington were free. Before the Civil War started, 78 per cent of the blacks in Washington were free. As the slave states of the South progressively tightened up their restrictions on the "free persons of color" in the decades preceding the Civil War, Washington became something of a Mecca for those free Negroes seeking a better life. The federal government's presence made Washington less oppressive than the Southern slave states and also opened employment opportunities in government jobs better than those open to black people elsewhere.

The Washington black community was thus more than a generation ahead in freedom and acculturation. Moreover, Dunbar was not a neighborhood school, but drew upon the entire black community of Washington for its students. It was in a similarly favorable position in recruiting its teachers and principals. Given the extreme scarcity of educated Negroes in 1870, Dunbar's performance could not be readily duplicated elsewhere within any reasonable span of years. The first black woman to receive a college degree in the United States graduated from Oberlin in 1862—and taught at Dunbar. The

---

[2] Rather than keeping track of a variety of changing names, we will use "Dunbar" throughout to denote each of the successive institutions continuously deriving from the high school established in 1870.

first black man to graduate from Harvard received his degree in 1870 and became principal of Dunbar in 1872. For decades to come, Dunbar would have its choice of teachers with outstanding academic credentials. Four of its first eight principals graduated from Oberlin and two from Harvard. Some had graduate degrees as well. Dunbar had three Ph.D.'s on its teaching staff in the 1920's, due to the almost total exclusion of blacks from most college and university faculties. (It was 1942 before there was a black senior faculty member at any major university—and he was a Dunbar graduate.)

In short, as the first black high school, Dunbar had its pick of potential teachers and principals. By its early reputation for excellence, it continued to attract them. Segregation and discrimination gave it a captive market of both students and teachers. But though these may have been necessary conditions for Dunbar's success, they were hardly sufficient. What Washington also had was a black community that demanded academic excellence even in 1870, and continued to fight tenaciously for it over the years. As early as 1807, the approximately 500 "free persons of color" in the District of Columbia built a small school house for their children. Over the next several decades they sent their children to private schools before they were allowed in the public schools. When the "colored trustees" of the D.C. public school system established the first high school in 1870, they were planting it in fertile ground.

The founders

The achievements of Dunbar no doubt also reflect the personal qualities of individual leaders during the institution's formative years. A special kind of confidence and courage must have been required for a black man or woman to pioneer at Oberlin or Harvard in the middle of the 19th century, when the very capacity of the race for education was openly questioned, even by liberals opposed to slavery. The early Dunbar principals had to be individuals not easily discouraged, frightened, or inclined to compromise about quality. This is how historical accounts describe them. Certainly this became the dominant tradition of the school.

The head of the group which founded the first high school for Negroes was a remarkable man named William Syphax. He grew up as a free man, having been freed in infancy in 1826, and became a civil rights activist in the Washington Negro community in the mid-19th century. He was described as a man of "dauntless courage and unwavering integrity" who "dared to demand what was due his race, fearing no man regardless of position or color." The substance and tone of his messages to municipal and federal officials clearly support this description. He was hard-headed on education. While the group he led preferred Negro teachers for Negro children—other things being equal—they were not prepared to compromise quality for the sake of racial representation, for they deemed it a "violation of our official oath to employ inferior teachers when superior teachers can be had for the same money." Syphax was equally frank in telling the black community that it would have to send its children to school with respect for teachers and a willingness to submit to discipline and hard work, if their education was to amount to anything.[3]

The early principals were equally remarkable people. Mary Jane Patterson not only was the first black woman in the United States to earn a college degree, she did it by spurning the usual courses for women at Oberlin, and taking instead a program of Greek, Latin, and higher mathematics designed for "gentlemen." As principal, she was "a strong, forceful personality," noted for "thoroughness," and for being "an indefatigible worker." She was principal for a dozen years in the formative period of the school.[4]

A successor as principal, Robert H. Terrell, "devoted most of his time out of school to preparing boys for college," with the result that "a goodly number" later "completed their education at Harvard"[5]—and this at the turn of the century. The tradition continued as the school changed principals and buildings. In the period 1918-1923, Dunbar graduates earned 15 degrees from Ivy League colleges and universities, and 10 degrees from Amherst, Williams, and Wesleyan.

Throughout the period of its academic ascendancy, Dunbar was characterized by the *esprit* of its students, the dedication of its teachers, and the strong support of the community, both in everyday chores and in episodic crises. Special efforts were made to get college scholarships for bright but poor youngsters. Indeed, special efforts were often needed to get the parents of such youngsters to keep them in high school, instead of sending them to work to bring home some much needed help for family finances. One concrete indicator of student attitude is the record of attendance and tardi-

---

[3] E. Delorus Preston, Jr., "William Syphax, A Pioneer in Negro Education in the District of Columbia," *Journal of Negro History* (October 1935), pp. 462-64.

[4] Mary Church Terrell, "History of the High School for Negroes in Washington," *Journal of Negro History* (July 1917), pp. 255-56.

[5] *Ibid.*, p. 259.

ness. A spot check of old Board of Education records in both categories shows Dunbar's record to have been superior to the average of its white counterparts, both around the turn of the century (1901-1902) and around mid-century (1952-1953).

Dunbar I.Q.'s

The argument has often been made that I.Q.'s have little relationship to performance as far as black people are concerned; however, there is already a considerable literature indicating that I.Q. and similar tests are equally accurate predictors of black and white academic performance. Dunbar provides a somewhat different kind of test of this hypothesis, based on a black group with outstanding performances in both academic and career terms. Are Dunbar I.Q.'s significantly different from the national average I.Q. of 85 for black Americans? The table below answers that question:

TABLE 1. *Mean I.Q. of Dunbar Students*

CLASS OF	ALL STUDENTS	GRADUATES ONLY	NON-GRADUATES ONLY
1938	105.5	111.6	97.1
1939	111.2	114.0	101.9
1940	108.5	111.1	100.9
1941	109.3	111.7	101.7
1942	105.2	107.8	101.4
1943	101.3	102.6	98.5
1944	106.0	109.8	97.5
1945	98.8	101.6	93.5
1946	102.1	105.7	102.1
1947	102.6	108.4	94.9
1948	105.3	106.5	98.2
1949	106.1	106.1	104.0
1950	110.9	111.3	99.4
1951	102.7	103.4	98.1
1952	103.1	104.7	94.3
1953	101.3	102.7	93.5
1954	101.7	102.6	98.8
1955	99.6	100.8	96.4

Dunbar students' average I.Q.'s were substantially higher than those of other blacks as reported in numerous surveys, and usually were above the national average as well. Even the Dunbar dropouts scored higher than the average of other blacks. It should be noted that Dunbar students were *not* selected on the basis of I.Q. tests. Indeed, admission to Dunbar was a matter of individual self-selection. No one was automatically assigned to Dunbar, because it was not a neighborhood school during the 1870-1955 period. Nor was it likely that anyone merely happened to enroll there, since its reputation and standards were well-known throughout the local black community. Indeed, some black youngsters from nearby Maryland and Virginia were known to give false D.C. addresses in order to attend.

The high I.Q.'s at Dunbar were hardly the whole story, however. An equal number of black students scattered elsewhere with equal I.Q.'s might not have produced an equal number of high academic and career performances, because certain other factors would have been lacking: (1) the *motivational* element associated with self-selection for such a school; (2) the benefits of mutual association with high-quality students and with teachers attracted to teaching such students; and (3) the school traditions, including distinguished alumni who were constantly being held up as examples to the students. Certainly, the kind of personal interest, counseling, and extracurricular tutoring which Dunbar students received is extremely rare for black students today, whether in all-black or in integrated schools. A recent Ford Foundation study, for example, has reported the quality of counseling available to black students to be "markedly inadequate" in both North and South, and the testimony of college recruiters paints an even grimmer picture of neglect or distorted "guidance" given to black students.[6]

Clearly *not* essential to the Dunbar performance was racial integration, outstanding physical facilities, or generous financial support. It had none of these. Except for a few white teachers in its early days in the 1870's, Dunbar was an all-Negro school, from students to teachers to administrators, for generation after generation. Moreover, it was located in a segregated city, where as recently as 1950 Negroes were not admitted to most downtown movie theaters or restaurants. The physical facilities of Dunbar were always inadequate; its lunchroom was so small that many students had to eat lunch out on the street, and it was 1950 before the school had a public address system. Dunbar was part of a segregated school system, administered by whites at the top and perennially starved for funds. Internally, there were class-conscious and color-conscious cliques among students, and resentment of administration favoritism among the teachers. In short, the list of "prerequisites" for success in which educators indulge themselves was clearly not met at Dunbar.

I.Q.'s and sex

There is evidence that Dunbar was at its peak some time *before* the period when I.Q. scores were recorded. The slight downward

---

[6] See Thomas Sowell, *Black Education: Myths and Tragedies* (New York: David McKay Co., 1972), p. 143.

drift of I.Q.'s over the 1938-1955 period is in keeping with the impression that this was the declining phase of its academic prime. The 1938-1955 period was studied statistically because this is the only period during Dunbar's academic prime for which I.Q. scores are available. Over the 18-year span, girls outnumbered boys every year—usually by about two to one, but by as much as three to one in the class of 1952. This conforms to a general predominance of females among high-I.Q. American Negroes—a baffling phenomenon, difficult to explain by either hereditary or environmental theories or by the cultural bias of the tests. Black males and females obviously draw upon the same pool of genes. They are also raised in the same environment. True, this environment creates sex role differentiation, but I.Q. tests are so structured as to produce virtually identical averages for males and females in the general population. Nevertheless, higher female I.Q.'s remain a persistent phenomenon among American Negroes, even though different tests are used in different times and places. I.Q. results from an all-male and an all-female junior high school (J.H.S. 139 and J.H.S. 136, respectively) serving the same neighborhood in central Harlem for a 20-year period (1941-1960) show the female school to have had a higher average I.Q. for all but one of the years for which such data were available. The particular I.Q. test used varied, but the relative standings of the sexes were virtually constant.

The higher I.Q.'s of black females might be a cultural peculiarity (along the lines of the Moynihan thesis, for example) or they could be a clue to the lower black I.Q. in general. Among human beings as a whole, and even among other mammals, males vary more (physically, emotionally, and mentally) with the environment than do females. If the generally low I.Q. scores of black Americans (or any other group) are due to environment rather than to heredity, it should also be expected that the lower average I.Q. would be accompanied by a degree of sex difference in I.Q. not found in the general population. This is almost invariably the case in studies of black American I.Q.'s. It is also true of studies of working class I.Q.'s in Britain, so it is hardly a racial characteristic.

Class and color

Given the general predominance of mulattoes among the "free persons of color" and their descendants, it seems probable that the light-skinned mulatto stereotype was applicable to the early Dunbar students and teachers. This group continued for many years to be over-represented among Dunbar students and teachers—but this is not to say that it constituted a majority. A study of old yearbook photographs at Dunbar High School shows the great bulk of the students to have been very much the color of most American Negroes. Any bias in the photography of that period—before black was beautiful—would be toward printing the pictures lighter than in life. My impression from visiting a Dunbar reunion also accords with the conclusion that most Dunbar students were not unusually light in complexion.

A study of class records for the period 1938-1955 also confirms that most Dunbar students' parents were *not* middle-class professionals. Among those students whose parents' occupations could be identified and categorized, the largest single category was consistently "unskilled and semi-skilled," and the median job index was at about the level of a white-collar worker. Perhaps more significantly, the differences in mean I.Q. were relatively slight between students whose parents fell in different occupational categories. For the classes of 1938-1955, the mean I.Q. of students whose parents were in the "unskilled and semi-skilled" category ranged from 96.1 in 1945 to 113.3 in 1950. The mean I.Q. of students whose parents were "professionals" ranged from 102.1 in 1942 to 124.2 in 1950. Moreover, even the academic exclusiveness of Dunbar should not be overstated. Figures available for the period 1938-1948 show that approximately one third of all black students enrolled in D.C. high schools were enrolled in Dunbar.

Although the local stereotype of Dunbar was that it was where the doctors' and lawyers' children went to school (as it probably was), the percentage of Dunbar students whose parents' occupations could be identified as "professional" never exceeded six per cent for any of the 18 years surveyed. Since only about half of the parental occupations were identifiable and categorized, this should be regarded as a high of about 12 per cent of the occupations known and classified—exceptionally large for a black school, but still a long way from predominance. Former Dunbar principal Charles S. Lofton refers to the middle-class stereotype as "an old wives' tale." "If we took only the children of doctors and lawyers," he asked, "how could we have had 1400 black students at one time?" Similarly, former Dunbar teacher Mary Gibson Hundley wrote: "A large segment of the students had one or more government employees for support. Before the 1940's these employees were messengers and clerks, with few exceptions."[7]

---

[7] Hundley, *op. cit., p.* 31.

Time and tradition

It is true, however, that the history and traditions of the school were to a large extent shaped by members of a few prominent families in Washington's Negro community. These were, typically, descendants of the antebellum "free persons of color," light-skinned in general, and in particular cases physically indistinguishable from whites. This group was not numerically dominant, and did not intermarry with the mass of blacks during most of the period under discussion, so it had little *biological* effect on the rest of the Negro population. (In fact, this small group of families married among themselves to such an extent that it became noted for birth defects.) But it did have a major and enduring cultural impact on the Dunbar community. For example, as late as the 1950's there was a dedicated Dunbar teacher of many years' service who had herself graduated from Dunbar, whose mother had graduated in the class of 1885, and whose grandfather had headed the group that set up the original school in the basement of a church in 1870. She is still active in alumni affairs today.

The history of Dunbar High School places in sharp relief the importance of time and tradition. Not only did the institution have a decisive head start as the first black high school in the country; the community from which it came had a similarly decisive head start in freedom, combined with stable employment opportunities in the federal government, even before the Civil War. These circumstances in turn drew into Washington a nucleus of like-minded and highly qualified Negroes, as well as a larger mass of less favored but also ambitious blacks receptive to their leadership. The individuals who founded and shaped the early history of the institution which became known as Dunbar High School were remarkable people, as is evidenced by their achievements as well as by accounts and descriptions of them. They were not narrow education careerists. Most went on to achieve distinction in other fields—as lawyers, judges, and, in one case, U.S. Consul in Vladivostok. The children and grandchildren of these individuals also went to Dunbar and often became teachers there as well, bringing a tradition and dedication that could not be bought on the open market.

A 20th-reunion survey of the class of 1940 indicates that Dunbar graduates apparently shared a striking characteristic of the black elite: fertility rates too low even to replace themselves. The married members of the class of 1940 averaged 1.6 children. This is typical of middle-class Negroes: They not only have far fewer children than lower-class Negroes, they have fewer children than whites of the same income or education as themselves. This demographic peculiarity means that a great part of the struggle from poverty to middle-class status has to be repeated in the next generation, for very few black children are born to parents who could start them off with the benefits won by their own struggle.

Decline and fall

The Supreme Court desegregation decision of 1954 set in motion a series of events which in a few years destroyed all that had been built up over several decades at Dunbar High School. The whole dual school system in Washington had to be reorganized. In this reorganization, all D.C. schools became neighborhood schools. The neighborhood in which Dunbar was located was one of the poorest multi-problem areas of the Washington ghetto. For years it had been the pattern that most youngsters who *lived* near Dunbar did not *go* to Dunbar. Now, suddenly, they did—and the character of the school began to change drastically. As an interim measure, existing Dunbar students were allowed to continue in the school until graduation, regardless of where they lived, and most elected to do so. This postponed the inevitable, but not for long.

Teachers used to bright, eager students began to find learning problems and then disciplinary problems in their classrooms. Advanced courses in mathematics faced dwindling enrollments which finally forced their cancellation, while remedial math courses appeared for the first time. Similar trends were apparent in other subjects as well. The Dunbar teaching staff at that time was somewhat advanced in years, and many began retiring—some as early as the minimum age of 55, whereas in the past it had been common for Dunbar teachers to stay on until the mandatory retirement age of 70. Equally qualified replacements were hard to find, with Dunbar now rapidly becoming a typical ghetto school. Ironically, the drastic changes forced upon Dunbar in the reorganization that followed the 1954 Supreme Court decision had virtually no desegregation effect, given the virtually all-black neighborhood in which the school was located.

Today, the present principal of Dunbar, Mrs. Phyllis Beckwith, spends much of her time dealing with discipline problems: roaming the halls to maintain order, receiving police reports on truants loitering on the streets during school hours, and otherwise struggling to achieve the kind of learning atmosphere earlier Dunbar principals could take for granted. In addition, Mrs. Beckwith spends a considerable amount of her own after-school time maintaining contacts with the still active Dunbar alumni groups—attending class reunions and trying to elicit concern from the old Dunbar graduates for today's very different students. Her dedication is virtually the only reminder today of the Dunbar tradition. To an observer, her efforts seem heroic but largely unappreciated—either by the current students or by the old alumni, who show little sympathy for the students who to them represent the destruction of their school.

The Supreme Court's desegregation decision, as such, did not doom Dunbar High School. Theoretically, Dunbar could have remained an academically elite high school, not tied to neighborhood boundaries, and could have simply opened up to students without regard to race. There have been public schools of this sort in New York, Boston, and other cities. But in the emotionally charged atmosphere of the time, under the strong legal and political pressures to "do something" in the nation's capital, such a resolution was never a realistic possibility. "Neighborhood schools" was the rallying cry of whites resisting total desegregation; "integration" was the battle cry of black leaders. The maintenance of educational quality at a black elite high school had no such emotional appeal or political clout. The school reorganization plan gave something to both sides —a measure of integration and the maintenance of neighborhood schools—and so was a political success. For Dunbar, however, it was an educational catastrophe.

The Board of Education which promulgated the reorganization plan of 1954 that destroyed Dunbar High School seems to have had no appreciation of or concern about this possibility. In the lengthy and bitter debates recorded in the Board of Education minutes, almost every conceivable problem was argued, other than the effect of the reorganization on Dunbar High School. This is all the more remarkable because the Board's most vocal critic of the school superintendent's plan was a Dunbar alumna. Yet even today she cannot recall saying a word about Dunbar High School at the time, even in executive sessions not reported in Board minutes. Integration was the cry of the hour and the fight of the hour.

The conditions of achievement

Although Dunbar High School was the product of unique historical circumstances, its educational and social achievements have continuing relevance. First of all, it showed what could be done with black children, including substantial numbers from low-income backgrounds. The question of *how* it was done needs more exploration. It was not done by teaching ethnocentric "relevance," nor was it achieved with generous financing or even with adequate plant and equipment.

What Dunbar had was a solid nucleus of parents, teachers, and principals who knew just what kind of education they wanted and how to produce it. They came from one of the oldest and largest urban black middle classes in the nation. But the beneficiaries of this situation were not exclusively, or even predominantly, middle-class students. Because the knowledge and educational values of the black elite were institutionalized and traditionalized, they became available to generations of low-income black students. Despite the fashionable (and sometimes justified) criticism of the old "black bourgeoisie," they were a source of know-how, discipline, and organization otherwise virtually unavailable to lower-class blacks. The possibilities of transmitting this sophistication from a fortunate segment of the race to a wider range of receptive individuals may now have declined with the exit of the black middle class to the suburbs and with the rise of ideological barriers insulating "militant" black youth from such influences.

The I.Q. scores of Dunbar students averaged very much higher than those of black students in general, indicating that I.Q.'s and achievement are correlated among blacks as among whites. Note that "achievement" here means the *subsequent* accomplishments of students, rather than the socioeconomic background of their parents. Dunbar students from homes of low socioeconomic status also had substantially higher I.Q.'s than the black population at large. Special efforts were made by Dunbar teachers and counselors to tutor promising students from such backgrounds and to see that both they and their parents understood the importance of a college education, and the numerous practical details to be taken care of in order to secure college admission and financial aid. Most black high school students today get nothing resembling this kind of preparation, whether they are in all-black or in "integrated" schools.

Patterns of black success

Dunbar developed and thrived during its period of academic ascendancy in almost total isolation from whites. Even as a subject of research, Dunbar was as remote from whites as if it were on Mars. It was part of a dual school system ultimately controlled by whites, but the white officials took little interest in what was going on at Dunbar, and such interest as they did manifest took such forms as trying to get the school to move in a non-academic direction and resisting the demands of Dunbar parents for calculus courses and better chemistry labs. They casually destroyed the institution as an incidental by-product of their reorganization of the Washington school system in 1954. Ironically, white liberals noticed Dunbar only *after* it became a typical ghetto school with all the usual problems—and even then its previous history remains wholly unknown to them. Considering the general effect of white liberals on black education, it may be that the absence of such people and their "innovative" programs should be counted among Dunbar's major advantages.

The Dunbar experience is by no means an argument for either externally imposed segregation or self-imposed separatism—and in fact the school fought against both these ideas. The founders of the school first tried to secure equal access to all public schools for all students, and only when this failed did they set about producing the best school they could for black youth. Down through the years, Dunbar teachers sought to break through the imposed insularity of a segregated society by bringing both black and white speakers, entertainers, and other cultural attractions to the school. While Dunbar promoted racial pride, it was pride in the achievements of outstanding Negroes as measured by universal standards, not special "black" achievements by special "black" standards.

There is a tendency among some white critics of the American Negro to point to particular black "success" models and ask, "Why can't the *others* do it?" If racial barriers and cultural handicaps did not stop men like Ralph Bunche and Edward Brooke, how can they provide a blanket excuse for welfare recipients and hell-raisers? It is no answer to say that Bunche, Brooke, and others were just "exceptions," for that amounts to nothing more than rephrasing the question. What the Dunbar history shows is the enormous importance of time, tradition, and institutional circumstances in providing the essential setting in which individual achievement can flourish. If such achievements were wholly or predominantly a matter of personal ability, so many outstanding individuals would not have come from one institution.

This concentration of black achievement in a few special settings is not limited to Dunbar. As rare as black doctorates are, empirically they are not *isolated* phenomena. A study of 609 Ph.D.'s awarded to Negroes in 1957-1962 showed that, while these black Ph.D.'s had attended 360 different high schools, 5.2 per cent of these high schools had produced 20.8 per cent of the Ph.D.'s. (Dunbar was first among these high schools.) A more relevant comparison would have included the vast number of black high schools whose alumni earned *no* Ph.D.'s during that period—but this would only have made the concentration still more extreme. Another study examined those black families in which someone had earned a doctoral degree of some sort (M.D., Ph.D., etc.) and found that the average number of doctorates per family was 2.25. If the family setting permitted someone to earn a doctorate, it generally permitted more than one to earn a doctorate. Impressionistic evidence on the backgrounds of historic black figures also suggests that black achievements have come out of circumstances very different from those which the majority of Negro Americans experience. W. E. B. DuBois grew up with aristocratic New England whites, Ralph Ellison grew up on frontier territory, George Washington Carver was raised by a German couple, and even Booker T. Washington, though "up from slavery," was in his youth the protegé of a succession of wealthy, educated, and influential whites. This in no way demeans the achievement of these men, for ultimately they had to have the ability to do what they did. But it does underline the importance of the special circumstances necessary for individuals to realize their potential—and the remoteness of these circumstances from the lives of most American Negroes.

The problem of discipline

Despite the emphasis on small classes in the educational literature, Dunbar had large classes. As far back as 1877, there were 40 students per teacher, and a survey in 1953 showed Dunbar's student-teacher ratio to be higher than that of any white senior high school in Washington. This was not a matter of principle but of necessity, given the inadequate financial support the school received from the white-controlled Board of Education. Obviously, class size is less of a handicap with self-selected and highly motivated students than with average students or with students lacking self-discipline. But while the Dunbar experience is not directly generalizable to ghetto schools, it does indicate where the problem lies. There is no inherent reason why large classes cannot be educationally effective, or even psychologically inspiring. The class size at which learning breaks down and disorder sets in is a function of the attitudes brought to the situation by students and teachers.

Much contemporary discussion of teaching methods, educational philosophies, and organizational principles in the school system seems unreal in the context of the "blackboard jungle" atmosphere in many ghetto schools. While more classroom time is often devoted to trying to maintain order (or contain disorder) than to teaching, more educational literature is devoted to philosophy, politics, "black English," and in fact almost anything other than the overriding problem of reducing the chaos, disruption, and fear which can prevent *any* teaching method or philosophy from being effective. Yet it is not considered politic, much less chic, to discuss such things.

Although Dunbar, when it was an elite high school, had few discipline problems, its history is not wholly irrelevant here. The importance of parental attitudes and parental involvement was recognized literally from the inception of the school. Although Washington in 1870 had many Negro families who were ready and eager for a first-rate school, it also had many who were not. The recent abolition of slavery had swelled the black population of Washington with many new arrivals from Southern and border states. As of 1868, only about one third of the Negro children of the District of Columbia were attending any school. In this setting, William Syphax's admonitions to black parents to send their children to school with respect for learning and a readiness to work were very much to the point.

Black schools that have been educationally successful generally have *not* shared a common teaching method or educational philosophy. They *have* almost invariably had a high level of parental involvement. This was true throughout the ascendacy of Dunbar High School. It was also true of successful Harlem schools studied by Charles E. Silberman.[8]

The importance of parental involvement

I found a graphic example of this in a ghetto school I visited in Cincinnati. Although Frederick Douglass School did not attain the erstwhile academic achievements of Dunbar, it was striking because its ancient building stood in the midst of a run-down slum, with no fence around it, no bars on the windows, no graffiti, quiet halls, and an atmosphere of human relations among the staff that would have been a credit to a middle-class private school. Board of Education statistics showed its staff morale indicators (turnover, etc.) and student performance to be well ahead of what should have been ex-

[8] Charles E. Silberman, *Crisis in the Classroom—the Remaking of American Education* (New York: Random House, 1970).

pected according to the socioeconomic profile of its neighborhood. Principal Tom Murray mentioned in passing that the school had corporal punishment, and added: "The staff resisted the idea, but the parents insisted upon it." When a white principal in a black school is given the authority to administer corporal punishment at the insistence of the parents, there is clearly more here than meets the eye—particularly in an era when the very appointment of a white principal in a black school is often opposed by the community (as Murray's appointment had been). Yet, by visiting the homes of hundreds of students, by talking "straight" (even bluntly) to the parents, by involving himself in the community, this man had been able to involve the community in the school. The important question here is not whether corporal punishment is good or bad, any more than the important question about Dunbar was whether Latin was really needed. The point is that certain human relations are essential to the educational process, and when these conditions are met, then education can go forward—regardless of methods, educational philosophy, or physical plant.

Parental involvement is particularly important in black schools, for the black culture is not a permissive culture. If black kids raise hell, it is because their parents don't know or don't care, but *not* because of any philosophy that youths should "do their own thing." Where black parents have become involved in a school, they have sometimes urged a stricter discipline than the school was prepared to impose. Parental involvement does not mean making "community control" either an ideological dogma or a public relations ploy. Where a community has a high rate of residential turnover, "community control" can mean the unchallenged dominance of a handful of activists not accountable to any lasting constituency. What is important is the widespread involvement of individual parents as such.

The importance of individual parents is often ignored or slighted. Schemes for "open enrollment," voucher systems, or any other form of free choice by black parents of public school children invariably run into the argument that uneducated ghetto parents cannot make informed educational choices. Yet the history of Dunbar High School shows that only a relative handful of people need to understand the complexities involved in creating a first-rate education. Once they have created such an education, the others need only be able to *recognize* it. Generations of *non*-middle-class youngsters were sent to Dunbar for just this reason. Today, thousands of other non-middle-class black youngsters are being taken out of dreadful ghetto schools (created by those who presumably do understand education) and enrolled in local Catholic schools by Protestant black families. The cost of such schools is typically very low compared to other private schools, but still very high compared to ghetto incomes—and yet many black families are making this sacrifice in cities across the country. But this widespread phenomenon remains a non-event for intellectuals, just as Dunbar High School was a non-event for 85 years. To admit the possibility of widespread individual initiative on the part of those at the bottom of the socioeconomic ladder would be to threaten a whole conception of the world and of the intellectuals' own role in it.

The Dunbar example

During the 1870-1955 period, the self-selection of students freed Dunbar from the incubus of disinterested and disruptive students. After such students began entering, following the school reorganization of 1954, they destroyed the school within a few years. Various forms of self-selection can free other institutions from the hard core of disruptive and violent students, but all plans that involve freedom of choice (vouchers, open enrollment, etc.) are damned by critics as inhibiting racial integration. It is an empirical question, however, whether black youngsters will gain more educationally by separation from a hard core of hell-raisers or by integration with whites. Studies of the educational effects of integration show few gains. Yet the shibboleth of integration is still powerful enough to thwart fundamental educational reform.

The combination of historical circumstances that created Dunbar High School can never be recreated. Some of those essential circumstances *should not* be recreated—for example, the racial barriers which led a scholar like Carter G. Woodson to teach at Dunbar High School, when he should have been conducting graduate seminars at a major university. Yet such historical experiences contain important lessons for the present. Dunbar did not seek "grass-roots" teachers who could "relate" to "disadvantaged" students, even though a substantial part of its students were the children of maids, messengers, and clerks. Dunbar's faculty included many "overqualified" people, in today's parlance. Almost all of its principals during its 85-year ascendancy held degrees from the leading colleges and universities in the country—not teacher's college degrees or education degrees from other institutions. They had been trained in hard intellectual fields and had been held to rigid standards, and this was reflected in the atmosphere and standards of Dunbar.

While the Dunbar experience provides some empirical refutation for currently fashionable statements about the "necessary" ingredients of good education for black children, it is not itself a universal model. Part of Dunbar's strength was that it did not try to be all things to all people. The founders of the school intended it to be an institution solely devoted to preparing black students for college and in that special role it was unsurpassed. It showed what could be done and some of the ways that it could be done; it also demonstrated that some of the presumed "prerequisites" of good education are not really essential. What *is* essential is to create and sustain an atmosphere of academic achievement.

Dunbar High School provides no instant formulas for use by "practical" planners. Its example suggests that instant formulas by "practical" planners may not be the way to quality education. What is needed, above all, is *a sense of purpose,* a faith in what can be achieved, and an appreciation of the hard work required to achieve it. As the many flaws of Dunbar indicate, it is not necessary to find ideal people or an ideal setting, but it does require a dedicated nucleus of people in a setting where their dedication can be effectual.

Patterns
of
black
excellence

THOMAS SOWELL

THE history of the advancement
of black Americans is almost a laboratory study of human achievement, for it extends back to slavery and was accomplished in the
face of the strongest opposition confronting any American racial or
ethnic group. Yet this mass advancement is little discussed and seldom researched, except for lionizing some individuals or compiling
a record of *political* milestones. But the story of how millions of
people developed from the depths of slavery—acquired work skills,
personal discipline, human ideals, and the whole complex of knowledge and values required for achievement in a modern society—is
a largely untold story. A glance at the mass of human misery
around the world shows that such development is by no means an
automatic process. Yet how it was accomplished remains a matter
of little concern—in contrast to the unflagging interest in social
pathology.

One small, but important, part of the advancement of black
Americans has been educational achievement. Here, as in other
areas, the pathology is well known and extensively documented,
while the healthy or outstanding functioning is almost totally unknown and unstudied. Yet educational excellence has been achieved
by black Americans.[1] Current speculative discussions of the "pre-

---

[1] Thomas Sowell, "Black Excellence: The Case of Dunbar High School," *The
Public Interest*, No. 35 (Spring 1974), pp. 1-21.

requisites" for the quality education of black children proceed as if educational excellence were only a remote possibility, to be reached by futuristic experimental methods—indeed, as if black children were a special breed who could be "reached" only on special wave lengths. When quality education for black youngsters is seen, instead, as something that has *already* been achieved—that happened decades ago—then an attempt to understand the ingredients of such education can be made on the basis of that experience, rather than as a search for exotic revelations. The problem is to assess the nature of black excellence, its sources, and its wider implications for contemporary education and for social policy in general.

There are a number of successful black schools in various cities that exemplify this educational excellence—for the purposes of this study, six high schools and two elementary schools were selected. The high schools were chosen from a list, compiled by the late Horace Mann Bond, which shows those black high schools whose alumni included the most doctorates during the period from 1957 through 1962. The two elementary schools were added because of their outstanding performance by other indices. Some of the schools were once outstanding but are no longer, while others are currently academically successful. The schools were researched not only in terms of such "hard" data as test scores but also in terms of such intangibles as atmosphere and school/community relations, as these could be either observed or reconstructed from documents and from interviews with alumni, former teachers, and others. On the basis of this research, several questions were raised:

1. Is black "success" largely an individual phenomenon—simply "cream rising to the top"—or are the successes produced in such isolated concentrations as to suggest powerful forces at work in special social or institutional settings? Strong and clear patterns would indicate that there are things that can be done through social policy to create or enhance the prospect of individual development.

2. Does the environment for successful black education have to be a special "black" environment—either culturally, or in terms of the race of the principals and teachers, or in terms of the particular teaching methods used? Are such conventional indices as test scores more or less relevant to black students? For example, do these top black schools have average I.Q. scores higher than the average (around 85) for black youngsters in the country as a whole? Are their I.Q. scores as high as white schools of comparable performance by other criteria?

3. How much of the academic success of these schools can be explained as a product of the "middle-class" origins of its students? Have most of the children taught in these schools been the sons and daughters of doctors and lawyers, or have they represented a cross section of the black community?

4. How important was the surrounding community as an influence on the quality of education in these schools? Did this influence come through involvement in school decision-making or through moral support in other ways?

5. How many of the assumed "prerequisites" of quality education actually existed in these outstanding schools? Did they have good facilities, an adequate budget, innovative programs, internal harmony, etc.?

6. What kind of individual was shaped by these institutions? More bluntly, was the black excellence of the past an accommodationist or "Uncle Tom" success molded by meek or cautious educators, or the product of bold individuals with high personal and racial pride?

Although these questions will be treated in the course of this article, the first question is perhaps the easiest to answer immediately. Black successes—whether measured by academic degrees or by career achievement—have not occurred randomly among the millions of black people scattered across the United States, as might be expected if individual natural ability were the major factor. On the contrary, a very few institutions in a few urban centers with a special history have produced a disproportionate share of black pioneers and high achievers. In Horace Mann Bond's study, five per cent of the high schools produced 21 per cent of the later Ph.D.'s.[2] Four of the six high schools studied here—McDonough 35 High School, in New Orleans; Frederick Douglass High School, in Baltimore; Dunbar High School, in Washington, D.C.; and Booker T. Washington High School, in Atlanta—produced a long list of black breakthroughs, including the first black state superintendent of schools (Wilson Riles, from McDonough 35), the first black Supreme Court Justice (Thurgood Marshall, from Frederick Douglass), the first black general (Benjamin O. Davis, Sr., from Dunbar), the first black Cabinet member (Robert C. Weaver, from Dunbar), the discoverer of blood plasma (Charles R. Drew, from Dunbar), a Nobel Prize winner (Martin Luther King, Jr., from

---

[2] Horace Mann Bond, "The Negro Scholar and Professional in America," *The American Negro Reference Book* (Englewood Cliffs, Prentice-Hall, 1970), p. 562.

Booker T. Washington), and the only black Senator in this century (Edward W. Brooke, from Dunbar). From the same four schools, this list can be extended down to many regional and local "firsts," as well as such national "firsts" as the first black federal judge (William H. Hastie, from Dunbar), the first black professor at a major university (Allison Davis, from Dunbar, at the University of Chicago), and others. All of this from just four schools suggests some systematic social process at work, rather than anything as geographically random as outstanding individual ability—though these particular individuals had to be personally outstanding, besides being the products of special conditions.

The locations of these four schools are suggestive: Washington, D.C., Baltimore, New Orleans, and Atlanta. Baltimore, New Orleans, and Washington were the three largest communities of "free persons of color" in the Southern or border states in 1850.[3] None of these schools goes back to 1850, and some of them are relatively new; but the communities in which they developed had long traditions among the old families, and historical head starts apparently have enduring consequences. New Orleans had the most prosperous and culturally advanced community of "free persons of color" and the largest number of high schools on H. M. Bond's list—all three of which are still outstanding high schools today.

Atlanta: Booker T. Washington High School

When Booker T. Washington High School was founded in 1924, it was the first public high school for Negroes in Atlanta and in the state of Georgia, and one of the first in the nation. However, the black community of Atlanta had had both primary and secondary education for its children long before that. In 1869, the American Missionary Society—which greatly influenced quality education for Southern blacks—established in Atlanta several "colleges" and "universities," whose initial enrollments were actually concentrated in elementary and secondary study, with only a few real college students.[4] The first principal of Booker T. Washington High School was, in fact, a man who had been in charge of the high school program at Morris Brown College.

Professor Charles Lincoln Harper was principal of Booker T.

---

[3] E. Franklin Frazier, *The Negro in the United States* (New York, Macmillan, 1971), p. 74.

[4] Henry Reid Hunter, *The Development of the Public Secondary Schools of Atlanta, Georgia: 1845-1937* (Office of the School System Historian, Atlanta Public Schools, 1974), pp. 49-52.

Washington for its first 19 years, and a major influence on the shaping of the institution. By all accounts, he was a man of great courage, ability, and capacity for hard work. Far from being middle-class in origin, he came from a black farm family living on a white-owned plantation. As a child, he attended the only available school, which was 10 miles away and which held classes only three months of the year. Somehow Harper managed to educate himself and go on to college, and later to graduate work at the University of Chicago and Columbia. In addition to becoming a principal, Harper was a civil rights activist at a time when economic retaliation, lynchings, and Ku Klux Klan violence were an ever-present threat. The times were such that many blacks gave money to the NAACP *anonymously* through Harper, who bore the onus of converting it into checks to mail to the NAACP headquarters in New York. Thurgood Marshall said that Harper "stood out head and shoulders above many others because of his complete lack of fear of physical or economic repercussions." [5]

As principal, it was common for Harper to work Saturdays, and to spend part of his summer vacation taking promising students to various colleges and universities, trying to gain admission or scholarships for them. A contemporary described him as a man of "utter sincerity" who "lives on the job." Though he was a man who drove himself, with teachers he was "affable" and "easy to approach," and he showed "vast stores of patience" with students. A man of modest means—he owned only one suit—he nevertheless gave small sums of money to poor children in his school when they needed it. Yet for all his dedication to black people, he was not uncritical of black institutions. As late as 1950, he said, "There is not a single first-class, accredited college in the state for the education of Negro students." [6] To say that must have required considerable courage in Atlanta, home of Morehouse, Spelman, and Morris Brown colleges, and of many proud alumni.

The cohesion of the Atlanta black community and the political sophistication of its leaders were directly responsible for the building of Booker T. Washington High School. A public high school for Negroes was unprecedented in the state of Georgia, and some members of the all-white school board considered it an outrageous demand. Black voters enforced their demand by turning out in sufficient numbers—in the heyday of the Ku Klux Klan—repeatedly to

---

[5] "They Knew Charles L. Harper," *The Herald* (October 1955), p. 19.
[6] Quoted in V. W. Hodges, "Georgians Join Atlantans in Tribute to Mr. Harper," in *The Atlanta World* (June 14, 1950).

defeat school bond issues until it was agreed that the high school would be built. But the board of education did not go one step beyond its grudging agreement: The school building alone was built on bare land. Harper conducted a fund-raising campaign in the community to provide landscaping and to build a statue of the school's namesake in front of the entrance. The board of education's tightfistedness continued to be a problem for the school for decades. Classes were large in the early years: 45 to 50 pupils per class was not unusual. The students received hand-me-down textbooks discarded after years of use in white schools.

Extra efforts by Harper, the staff, and the community overcame these obstacles. The community contributed money for the building of an athletic stadium and helped support school athletics out of their own pockets. The board of education provided no money at all for athletic uniforms, or for athletes to travel. However, the coach obtained uniforms from a local sports store and drove the teams in his own car, with gas supplied free by a gas station in the community. The team ate hot dogs donated by a black drugstore. On their own time, teachers drove students to cultural events during the spring vacation. The teachers of this era also maintained closets full of second-hand clothing and shoes for needy pupils—all brought to school in paper bags, so that no one would ever know whose old clothes he was wearing.

The atmosphere in the school during this era was a blend of support, encouragement, and rigid standards. One alumnus described it as a "happy school" with "hard taskmasters." Of one teacher it was said: "She did not tolerate sloppy work any more than a Marine sergeant tolerates a coward on a battlefield." Another teacher "threw homework at you like you were in college instead of the sixth grade." Those who did not learn on the first try in school stayed after school for as many days as it took to learn. Yet the students found the teachers inspiring rather than oppressive. A sense of individual worth and pride of achievement were constantly sought. "You couldn't go wrong," an alumnus said: "The teachers wouldn't let you."

Racial and political awareness were part of the early curriculum but traditional subjects—including Latin—dominated. Racial pride was developed by example as well as by words. Many teachers refused the indignity of riding in the back of segregated buses, which meant that some of them had to walk during years when cars were rare.

In the 50 years of its existence, Booker T. Washington has had only five principals: C. L. Harper for 17 years (1924-1941), C. N. Cornell for 20 years (1941-1961), J. Y. Moreland for eight years (1961-1969), before being promoted to area superintendent, and A. A. Dawson for four years (1969-1973), also before being promoted to area superintendent. The present principal, Robert L. Collins, Jr., assumed the post in 1973. He is a graduate of the school, and his daughter is the third generation of his family to attend.

The school has undergone some metamorphoses in the half-century of its existence. It is no longer the only black high school in the city, and the neighborhood in which it is located is run down —both factors tending to lower academic performance—while there are such offsetting tendencies as better financial support and better physical equipment. The available records do not go back far enough to permit comparison with the performance of the early years, but the current academic performance of Booker T. Washington is far from that of an elite school. On a variety of tests, its students scored significantly below the national average, and below the average of other Atlanta high schools. The demeanor of its students also seems much more in keeping with that of a typical urban ghetto school than a school with a distinguished past. Black Atlantans seemed defensive about discussing these changes, though one characterized the school as "a little thuggish" today. It is not unusual for a school which loses its monopoly of black high school students and is located in a declining neighborhood to have difficulties maintaining standards. Other schools in this study have suffered similar fates. But the justifiable pride of Atlantans in the school's past makes it difficult to trace the process by which the present uninspiring situation came about. Certainly it is clear that the present financial resources and political clout—a black superintendent of schools and a black mayor of the city—are no substitute for the human resources that enabled earlier generations to overcome heavy handicaps.

Interestingly enough, the current principal is not as defensive as other Atlantans inside or outside the school system. While he will not openly concede a decline in academic performance, he freely acknowledges a number of factors which make it a harder job to get good performance from students of a given level of ability. Chief among these is less parental support and cooperation: Parents may be more "involved" in school decisions today, but they are less cooperative than in earlier decades. In particular, parents are less willing to take the side of the school teacher or principal who wants an able student to take more demanding courses instead of following the path of least resistance. Even when the parents understand the long-run educational need, they are often not willing to risk immediate problems in relations with their children. Discipline problems are also more numerous and more difficult, and there are fewer methods available for dealing with them. Corporal punishment was still permissible in the mid-1940's, when Collins was a student, but it is no longer an option. Moreover, whatever discipline is imposed is less likely to have parental support or reinforcement, and more likely to provoke parental indignation. Still, Collins works at it—12 hours or more a day. It is too early to tell if he can turn the situation around, especially since the general problem extends well beyond Atlanta, is not limited to black schools, and has had a varying impact on schools across the country.

Atlanta: St. Paul of the Cross

A very different school in many ways is St. Paul of the Cross. Its openness was the first of many contrasts. Records just received from a testing organization were taken straight from the envelope and spread out on the table for inspection. This confidence was based on years of solid performance. A sample of I.Q. scores for this Catholic elementary school shows them consistently at or above the national norm of 100—which is to say, significantly above the national average of about 85 for other black children. This school came to our attention as a result of an earlier research project surveying I.Q. scores. The mean I.Q. of the St. Paul student body for the years surveyed (1960-1972) ranged from 99 to 107.

St. Paul is located in a middle-class black suburban area of Atlanta, but its students are drawn from various parts of the city. Of all the schools in this study for which we were able to obtain the data, St. Paul has the highest proportion of white-collar and professional occupations among its students' parents. For the period 1960-1972, 40 per cent of the parents were either white-collar or professional. Our breakdown shows 33 per cent white-collar and seven per cent professional, but that is based on counting school teachers in the white-collar category, and the two categories are presented together simply to avoid needless (and endless) debate over where the line should be drawn. For the other schools in this study, this internal breakdown is of little significance, since the two categories together usually add up to no more than 10 per cent. But although St. Paul has a substantial proportion of white-collar and professional parents for a black school, it is still not predominantly middle-class, in the usual sense of having children whose parents are doctors, engineers, or professors, or are in similar occupations.

Quiet, calm, and orderliness prevail in St. Paul's modern building, even during the changing of class. Yet the students do not seem either repressed or apprehensive. There was talking during the change of classes, but no yelling or fighting. Corporal punishment is one of the disciplinary options, but it is seldom used. Discipline is usually maintained through individual discussions between the teachers—half nuns and half laity—and the children. For example, a little boy who had spilled his soda in the hall without cleaning it up was told that the cleaning woman works hard to keep the school nice, and it was suggested that he apologize to her for making her job harder—but all this was done very gently without burdening him with guilt. This calm, low-key approach is made possible by small classes (about 30), small student body (about 200), and an automatically self-selective admissions process, since hardcore troublemakers are unlikely to apply for admission to a private school.

Instruction is highly individualized. Instead of the classic picture of the teacher standing in front of the class lecturing, the more usual scene in the classroom at St. Paul was a teacher very much engaged with an individual student or a small group, while the other members of the class worked intently on their respective assignments. This individualized approach extended even to allowing students to go to the library on their own. The child's self-confidence is built up in subtle ways. However, there was no single teaching method or formula imposed from above. The usual bureaucratic paperwork was absent at St. Paul. Records were well kept and complete, but not cluttered with trivia. Administrators had time to circulate through the school and get to know the students, rather than being stuck at their desks behind piles of paper. Morale is high enough to attract lay teachers at lower salaries than they receive elsewhere.

St. Paul has had only four principals in its 21-year history. Three of these were nuns of the Sisters of St. Joseph, and the other was a black layman appointed in the 1960's at the height of the emphasis on "blackness." However, the initiative for a black lay principal came from whites in the religious order, rather than from either the black community or black parents. The current principal is a white nun.

The children are encouraged to take pride in their black heritage, but the curriculum is heavily oriented toward the basics of education—especially reading. There is also religious instruction, but the student body is about 70 per cent *non*-Catholic, though it was initially predominantly Catholic. Black non-Catholic students in Catholic schools are common in cities around the country, as black parents seek the education, the discipline, and the sheer physical safety which the public schools often cannot offer. The tuition is modest—about $450 per year for non-Catholics and $360 for Catholics—and the school runs a deficit, which is made up from general church funds.

Though quite different from Booker T. Washington High School in many ways, St. Paul has one problem in common with it: Some parents think that the school is *too* intellectually challenging for their children. Interestingly, this view is more common among those parents who are public school teachers.

Baltimore: Frederick Douglass High School

As of 1850, the 25,000 "free persons of color" in Baltimore were the largest number in any city in the United States, so it is not surprising that Baltimore's high school for black children was among the earliest founded, in 1892. Like many other black schools throughout the United States, Frederick Douglass High School survived for decades with inadequate financial support, was located in a succession of hand-me-down buildings that whites had discarded, and was stocked with old textbooks used for years before by white students, refinished desks from white schools, second-hand sports equipment, and so on. Douglass was for many years the only black high school in Baltimore. The school contained academic, vocational, commercial, and "general" programs. Because the surrounding communities had no high schools for Negro children, black students from outside Baltimore also came to Douglass—some legitimately, through stiff tests given to outsiders, and many others by the simple expedient of giving false addresses in Baltimore, often the addresses of relatives or friends.

Although pupils from Baltimore faced no tests for admission, there was a self-selection factor at work. Those without sufficient interest or skills would have dropped out before high school, in an era when students left school at earlier ages and when substandard students repeated grades, instead of today's automatic promotion. In short, while Frederick Douglass in its early decades was formally an all-inclusive black high school serving Baltimore and vicinity, in practice there were automatic selection factors which screened out the wholly uninterested or negative student. These were not high academic admission standards, such as elite private schools imposed, but even this wholly informal screening was sufficient to keep the school free of "discipline problems."

The teachers included men and women trained at the leading colleges and universities in the country. An alumnus of the 1930's recalls that his principal, Mason Hawkins, had a Ph.D. from the University of Pennsylvania and his teachers included individuals with degrees from Harvard, Brown, Smith, and Cornell. They were trained in content rather than educational "methods"—and their teaching styles approximated those of rigorous colleges: discussions rather than lectures, reading lists rather than day-by-day assignments, papers rather than exclusive reliance on "objective" tests. But there was no single teaching method imposed from above. The teachers often put in extra time, without pay, especially to work with promising students from low socioeconomic backgrounds.

Students were given pride in their achievements as individuals, but no mystique of "blackness." Negro history week was observed, and there was an elective course in black history, but it was not a prominent element in the curriculum. Although formal guidance counselling was minimal, the individual teachers actively counselled students on their own. But the teachers' concern for the students took the form of getting them to meet standards, not of bringing the standards down to their level of preparation. In reminiscing about her 40 years as teacher and administrator at Douglass High School, former principal Mrs. Edna Campbell said of her students, "Even though you are pushing for them, and dying inside for them, you have to let them know that they have to produce."

The interest of the teachers in the students was reciprocated by the interest of the parents in supporting the teachers and the school. "The school could do no wrong" in the eyes of parents, according to alumni. Parental involvement was of this supportive nature rather than an actual involvement in school decision-making. "Parent power" or "community control" were unheard-of concepts then.

Most of the whites in Baltimore were relatively unaware of Frederick Douglass High School—they did not know or care whether it was good or bad—and this indifference extended to the board of education as well. Under the dual school system in the era of racial segregation, the lack of interest in black schools by the all-white board of education allowed wide latitude to black subordinates to run the black part of the system, so long as no problems became visible. "Benign neglect" is perhaps the most charitable characterization of this policy. In short, Douglass High School's achievements were not a result of white input, at either the administrative or the teaching levels.

Color differences within the black community were significant in the school as well. Light-skinned alumni tended to minimize this factor, but darker-skinned alumni sometimes still carry bitter memories. One man, now an official of the Baltimore school system, recalls being maneuvered out of the honor of being class valedictorian at Douglass, in favor of a lighter-skinned student from a socially prominent family.

Like several of the schools studied, Douglass' days of glory are past. A decline began with the building of other black high schools in Baltimore and became precipitous in the wake of the Supreme Court's desegregation decision in 1954. While the mean I.Q. in the academic program at Douglass ranged from 93 to 105 for the 20 years before the 1954 decision, it fell immediately below 90 in 1955 and remained in the 80's from February 1955 through February 1958. This reflected the exodus of more capable students to white high schools. A concerted effort was made to reverse this trend in the 1960's, especially from 1965 to 1973, when Mrs. Edna Campbell was the principal. Our sampling of test scores for this period indicates some success. I.Q. scores went back into the 90's from 1965 through 1971, the last year for which we have a sample of 20 or more scores.

Today, in its decline, Frederick Douglass High School has better physical facilities, some integration of the faculty, and more parental input into the decision-making process, as well as a Baltimore school system dominated by black officials. There is little evidence that this compensates for what it has lost. Indeed, some knowledgeable people in Baltimore believe that it is precisely the growth of "student rights" and "parent power" that is responsible for declining discipline in schools. There certainly was evidence of such discipline problems at Douglass. A researcher collecting data for this study had her purse snatched in the school building itself, and some weeks earlier there had been a shooting there. This was a far cry from the school that had once been second in the nation in black Ph.D.'s among its alumni, and the only black school to produce a Supreme Court justice.

New Orleans: McDonough 35 High School

New Orleans has had a unique role in the history of American race relations, and so it is not surprising that the city has had not one, but three outstanding black high schools on Horace Mann Bond's list—and all three are *still* outstanding. Long before the Civil War, the free Negro community in New Orleans had rights, privileges, and economic success well in advance of its counterpart in any other American city. By 1850, "free persons of color" owned *$15 million* worth of taxable property in New Orleans—one fifth of the total taxable property in the city.

The pattern of race relations in New Orleans had been established before the city became a part of the United States as a result of the Louisiana Purchase in 1812, and it was—and largely remained—the pattern common to Latin America, rather than the pattern of Anglo-Saxon slave societies in the Western Hemisphere. For example, the "free colored" population of Latin America had a far wider range of occupations open to them than did American Negroes, and they often dominated the skilled artisan trades in Latin countries—simply because there were just not enough whites. The French, Spanish, and Portuguese who colonized the Western Hemisphere did not bring women, families, or a working class with them to the extent that the Anglo-Saxons did, and so were both economically and sexually more dependent upon the indigenous populations and those of African descent. This dependency led to a greater relaxation of racism in practice, even though the Latins subscribed in principle to the same "white supremacy" doctrines as the Anglo-Saxons.

New Orleans, as a former French (and Spanish) colony, reflected the Latin pattern in the skills of "free persons of color," few of whom were laborers, many of whom were small businessmen, some of whom were wealthy, and a few of whom were even commercial slave owners. New Orleans also reflected the multicolored caste system characteristic of Latin American countries, in contrast to the stark black/white dichotomy of Anglo-Saxon nations. The celebrated "quadroon balls" of antebellum New Orleans were but one aspect of this system.

Segments of the "free colored" population of New Orleans had been giving their children quality education (sometimes including college abroad) for more than a century before the first black public high school was founded in 1916. This school—McDonough 35 High School—was for many years the only public high school for New Orleans Negroes, but it was preceded by, and accompanied by, private black secondary schools, including Catholic schools—again, reflecting the Latin influence. Two Catholic high schools—St. Augustine and Xavier Preparatory—and McDonough 35 make up today's three outstanding black high schools in New Orleans.

So many schools in New Orleans are named for philanthropist John McDonough that numbers are added to distinguish them. McDonough 35 High School is outstanding among these. It has had only four principals in its nearly 50-year history. The first principal, John W. Hoffman, was a well-traveled man with a cosmopolitan outlook. The second principal, Lucien V. Alexis, was a graduate of Phillips Exeter Academy ('14) and Harvard ('18), and was an "iron-fisted" ex-Army officer. The third principal, Mack J. Spears, was a more diplomatic man with considerable political savvy—which proved to be decisive in saving the school from the physical or educational extinction which came upon other outstanding black high schools during the time when "integration" was regarded as an educational panacea. The current principal, Clifford J. Francis, is a quiet, thoughtful man who accepts overtime work as a normal part of his job. He runs a smoothly operating, high-quality school which, for the first time, has a good physical plant and a good racially-integrated staff.

When McDonough 35 was opened in 1917, it was housed in a building built in the 1880's. As late as 1954, this building was heated by potbellied stoves, with the students keeping the fires going by carrying coal. When a hurricane passed through New Orleans in 1965, the ancient building simply collapsed. At this point, the all-white board of education decided to disband the school and assign its pupils to other schools in New Orleans. But, unlike other outstanding black schools which were destroyed by white officials who were unaware of their quality, McDonough 35 fought back. Principal Mack Spears organized community support to save the school, lobbied Congressmen, and ultimately obtained the use of an abandoned federal court house to house the institution until a new school building could be constructed.

The institution he saved was one which was an inspiration to its students, as well as a leading producer of later black Ph.D.'s. By chance, I happened to encounter Wilson Riles, the California State Superintendent of Schools, the day after my first visit to McDonough 35, and the very mention of the school's name caused his face to light up and provoked a flood of warm memories of his student days there. He credited the school with taking him and other black youngsters from an economically and culturally limited background, and giving them both the education and the self-confidence to advance in later life. Mack Spears, a student and later a principal at McDonough 35, told a very similar story. Spears was the son of a poor farmer, but he remembers vividly how his teachers promoted the idea of the worth of the individual—how they always called the boys "Mister" and the girls "Miss," emotionally important titles denied even adult Negroes throughout the South at that time.

Although the school had few counsellors in its earlier days, the teachers acted as counsellors, and as instructors and role models. But with all the psychological strengthening that was an integral part of the educational process, there was no parochial "blackness" in McDonough 35. Cultural expansion was the goal. Questions about "black English" in McDonough 35 brought a "hell no!" from Spears. The current principal more gently observed that this was a recent and minor matter, of interest to only a few young white teachers.

Like some other outstanding black high schools, McDonough 35 suffered a decline in quality as other black high schools were built in the same city and as neighborhood changes left it in a less desirable part of town. At one point in the 1950's, there was a controversy over the right of its teachers to carry guns for self-protection. The academic deterioration of this period matched the deterioration in social conditions and morale. The median I.Q. of the school population in the mid-1950's was in the low 80's; but under the new policies introduced when Spears became principal in 1954, I.Q.'s began to rise, to a peak of 99 in the 1965-1966 school year; and they have remained in the mid-to-upper 90's since then. Unfortunately, there are no I.Q. data available for the earlier period of the school's academic excellence—the period during which the Ph.D.'s studied by H. M. Bond would have been high school students there. The present I.Q. scores—at about the national average, and therefore significantly above the average for black students—must be interpreted in the context of a city where private Catholic schools attract large numbers of both white and black students with higher educational aspirations and achievements. McDonough 35 median I.Q.'s have consistently been above the city-wide average for public school students—white and black—for the past decade.

The policies introduced in the mid-1950's which reversed McDonough 35's decline included keeping neighborhood derelicts out of the school, ability-grouping, or "tracking," to deal with the variation in student capabilities and interests, and a widening of school boundaries beyond the immediate neighborhood. Spears, a former football player, was perfect for keeping the derelicts out of the school—for even though he spoke softly, the big stick was implicit in his very presence. Instead of explaining away low test scores by "cultural deprivation" or dismissing them as "irrelevant," Spears used those scores to demonstrate to parents and to the black community the full depth of the problem and to get support for educational change, including ability-grouping to deal with the wide range of scores and a self-selection admissions system to supersede neighborhood boundaries.

All was not harmony in McDonough 35, even in its heyday. The internal class differences within the black community—which revolved around color differences going back to the era of slavery —were more pronounced in New Orleans, just as intra-group color differences in Latin cultures generally exceeded those in Anglo-Saxon cultures. However, light-skinned Negroes were *not* noticeably overrepresented among students, faculty, or administrators. And darker Negroes, such as Riles and Spears, were nevertheless accepted by the school, even though the larger community was divided socially along internal color lines.

Whites were, at best, a negligible factor in the development of McDonough 35 High School. According to former principal Spears, the all-white board of education "did not give a damn—and we took *advantage* of that to build academic excellence."

New Orleans: St. Augustine High School

St. Augustine High School is a school for boys founded in 1951 by the Josephite Fathers. Its first principal was a young priest, Father Matthew O'Rourke, with neither experience nor training in education. Keenly aware of these gaps in his preparation, Father O'Rourke began a crash program, taking education courses at a local university—but found them "empty" and "a big zero." He and the other similarly inexperienced young priests and laymen on the faculty proceeded by trial and error—and dedication.

One of the first issues to arise came with the introduction of corporal punishment. In an era of growing racial sensitivities, some white priests outside the school were disturbed by the thought of white men (even in priestly garb) beating black youths. But Father O'Rourke and the other priests felt no guilt—the Josephite Order had been founded in the 19th century to serve blacks—and viewed the problem in purely pragmatic terms. Their options were to allow disruptive students to undo their work with others, to save the school by expelling such students, or to attempt to save both the students and the school by an occasional paddling. They elected to try the last. Despite the misgivings of some outside priests, the black parents backed the teachers completely, and the system worked. It has remained a feature of St. Augustine to the present—strongly believed in, but infrequently used. The student/teacher relations in St. Augustine are more relaxed and warm than in most public schools, where corporal punishment is usually forbidden by law.

The school was neither wedded to tradition nor seeking to be in the vanguard of "innovation." It did whatever worked educationally, and abandoned what did not. The wide range of student preparation led to ability-grouping, and to the jettisoning of the traditional English courses for the least prepared students in favor of an emphasis on reading, at virtually any cost. *Time* magazine was found to be an effective vocabulary tool for many students, and hundreds of St. Augustine students subscribed, at the urging of their teachers. A special summer course featured speed reading, with assignments of a novel per week, including reports.

The teachers' inexperience and lack of familiarity with educational fashions paid off handsomely. The first Southern Negro student to win a National Merit Scholarship came from St. Augustine. So did the first Presidential Scholar of any race from the state of Louisiana in 1964, and 10 years later, St. Augustine had produced 20 per cent of all the Presidential Scholars in the history of the state. In the National Achievement Scholarship program for black students, St. Augustine has produced more finalists and semi-finalists than any other school in the nation. In 1964—*before* the big college drive to enroll black students—St. Augustine's students won more than $100,000 in college scholarship money. This is all the more remarkable since the total enrollment is less than 700.

The pattern of I.Q. scores over time at St. Augustine shows a generally upward movement, beginning at a level very similar to the average for black students and reaching a level at or above that for the United States population as a whole. In its early years, St. Augustine had mean I.Q.'s as low as 86; but during the period from 1964 through 1972, I.Q.'s were just over 100 for every year except one.

The reasons for the rising I.Q.'s at St. Augustine cannot be easily determined. Father O'Rourke is reluctant to claim credit for the school itself. But in recalling his years as principal, he cited a number of instances where students with potential, but without cultural development, had improved after extra attention—improved not only on achievement tests, but also on I.Q. tests, "though that's not supposed to happen." Test scores were never used as a rigid admissions cutoff at St. Augustine. Our sample includes individual I.Q.'s in the 60's, as well as many others more than twice as high.

Father O'Rourke was succeeded as principal in 1960 by Father Robert H. Grant, one of the other young priests teaching at St. Augustine. Where Father O'Rourke had been universally liked, Father Grant tended to have both enthusiasts and detractors. Under Father Grant's administration, a heavy emphasis on academic achievement and tighter discipline brought Merit and Presidential scholars, school-wide I.Q.'s averaging over 100—and murmurs of discontent in the community. The discontented usually were *not* parents of students at St. Augustine. The rise of racial militancy raised questions about a white principal of a black school and brought demands for a "black" orientation of the curriculum. In retrospect, Father Grant describes his administration as "benignly autocratic" and himself as "blunt." "We didn't spend much time hassling, debating, or dialoguing." The teachers and principal had their meetings, but once an agreement had been reached, they did not "waste time" with "parent power" or "student rights," but relied instead on parental trust and on student achievement as a vindication of that trust. He met the demands for "black studies" by establishing an elective course on the subject—meeting at a time that was otherwise available as a study period. Only six students enrolled, out of more than 600 students in the school.

Although Father Grant fought a legal battle to integrate Louisiana's high school athletics, and was sympathetic to the civil rights movement in general, he was also opposed to the introduction of "extraneous elements, issues, and concerns" into the school itself. Keenly aware of both the students' cultural disadvantages and the need to overcome them, he felt that "we absolutely could not do the two things well," though both were important. It was a matter of time and priorities: "Don't consume my time with extraneous issues and then expect me to have enough time left over to dedicate myself to a strong academic program where I will turn out strong, intelligent, competent kids."

In 1969, Father Grant accepted a post in Switzerland and was replaced by a black lay principal—just what the doctor ordered politically, but apparently not administratively or educationally. He was replaced after a few years. The current principal, Leo A. Johnson, is also a black layman and, in addition, the first alumnus of St. Augustine to head the school. His term began in 1974, and it is too early to assess his impact on the school.

Teaching methods at St. Augustine are traditional, and both its academic and behavioral standards are strict. Students must wear "a dress shirt with a collar," and the shirttail "must be worn inside the trousers at all times." The general atmosphere at St. Augustine is relaxed, but serious. Its halls are quiet and its students are attentive and engrossed in what they are doing, as are the teachers. Yet it is not a wholly bookish place. Its athletic teams have won many local championships in football, basketball, and baseball. At lunch time, the students were as noisy as any other high school students, and the boys in the lunch room were visibly appreciative of a shapely young woman who was part of our research team. One of the real accomplishments of St. Augustine has been to give education a masculine image so that black youths need not consider intellectual activity "sissy."

The achievements of St. Augustine cannot be explained by the usual phrase of dismissal, "middle-class." Although it is a private school, its modest tuition ($645 per year) does not require affluence, and about 15 per cent of the students pay no tuition at all, while others pay reduced tuition because of their parents' low income. The school runs a chronic deficit, despite the low pay scale for those teachers who are clergy. Despite the color/caste history of New Orleans, the students at St. Augustine are physically indistinguishable from the students at any other black high school. Their demeanor and their work are *very* different, but their skin color is the same. Our statistical tabulation of parents' occupations covers only the years from 1951 through 1957, but in each year during that span more than half of the known parental occupations were in the "unskilled and semi-skilled" category, and the parents with professional or white-collar jobs added up to less than one tenth as many. While the students are seldom from the lowest poverty level, there is only occasionally the son of a doctor. Many come from families where the father is a bricklayer, carpenter, or other artisan, and has only a modest educational background. They are not middle-class in income, career security, culture, or lifestyle. Many are ambitious for their children and send them to school with attitudes that allow the education to "take." But such attitudes are not a monopoly of the middle class, despite sociological stereotyping. If such attitudes were in fact a monopoly of the middle class, neither blacks nor other ethnic minorities could ever have risen.

New Orleans: Xavier Prep

Xavier Prep is an all-girl Catholic school run by the Sisters of the Blessed Sacrament. It was founded in 1915, and was coeducational until 1970. It had 18 graduating seniors in 1918, and the enrollment increased to about 500 in 1940. It has about 350 students today, after the male students were phased out in the 1960's. Even when it was coeducational, it had more female than male students. One of the reasons for the difficulty of maintaining a masculine image for education among black youths is that, throughout the country and down through the years, Negro girls have outperformed Negro boys by a wide margin on grades, tests, and virtually every measure of intellectual ability. Studies of high I.Q. black students have consistently found the girls outnumbering the boys, by from two-to-one to more than five-to-one.

Over 90 per cent of the graduates of Xavier Prep go on to college. Until the 1960's, almost all went to Xavier University in New Orleans, run by the same order of nuns. Today about 60 per cent of the graduates go to either Xavier University, Loyola, or Tulane —all in New Orleans—even though their academic preparation would make them eligible for many other colleges and universities in other parts of the country.

I.Q. scores and other test scores vary considerably among Xavier students, but the average score of the school as a whole has fluctuated around the national norm—which is to say, higher than for Southerners of either race, higher than for black students nationally, and considerably higher than for black Southern children from the modest socioeconomic backgrounds of Xavier students. The mean I.Q. of the school as a whole ranged from 96 to 108 during the 1960's, and has been at or above 100 for each year surveyed during the 1970's.

In the earliest years of Xavier Prep, many of the students were from Creole backgrounds. But today the colors and conditions of the students represent a cross section of black America. Over the years, about 40 to 50 per cent of the students have come from low-income families, many entering with serious educational deficiencies, requiring remedial work. More than 60 per cent of its students are eligible for the free lunch program. While Xavier is a private school, its tuition is only $35 a month. Our statistical tabulation of parental occupation shows that from one half to four fifths of the parents' occupations have been in the "unskilled or semi-skilled" category, in the period from 1949 to 1972 for which we have data. Parents in professional or white-collar occupations put together added up to only seven per cent of the total during that same span. The principal, Sister Anne Louise Bechtold, recalls "one dentist" this year and "one lawyer last year" among the parents, but no engineers or college professors, and a small percentage of public school teachers—and otherwise parents of very modest socioeconomic backgrounds, with some of the mothers being domestics or store clerks and the fathers in similar occupations.

Unlike middle-class parents, the parents of Xavier students tend to be very cautious about their input into the school—even when invited and encouraged to participate. They seek discipline and an emphasis on basic education, and seem particularly pleased when their children's teachers are nuns. The caution of the parents is also a factor in the narrow range of colleges which most Xavier graduates attend. Ivy League and other Northern colleges attempt to recruit Xavier graduates, but the parents are reluctant to have their daughters exposed to strange influences in faraway colleges. In some cases, the teachers or counsellors fight a losing battle to get a promising student to accept an offer from a top-level college or university. This is not all the result of the limited cultural horizons of the parents. Economic pressures make it difficult for many of the parents to finance the travel involved, much less the living expenses, even if the student has a full scholarship.

Classes at Xavier Prep in the past tended to be large (35-40 students), but since boys were phased out in the mid-1960's, classes have been reduced to about 25 to 30 students. These students are "tracked" by academic ability. The less prepared students are given intensive and imaginative remedial work. Unlike St. Augustine, Xavier Prep has neither corporal punishment nor an emphasis on athletics. But the general atmosphere—described by one nun as "reserved but informal"—is very similar. Nuns and lay teachers are about equally represented on its faculty, and its principal is a nun. It is a quiet, low-key place where the changing of classes produces swarms of black teenagers in the halls, but little noise. The classes in session have students and teachers absorbed in mutual endeavor, but with a certain relaxed geniality. Discussions with Xavier teachers indicate that they put much thought and work, on their own time, into the preparation of their classes. Although subject to the guidance of superiors both inside and outside the school, the teachers seem to have more scope for personal initiative than do public school teachers. Among alumni of the school, their teachers' personal interest in them is a factor often cited as having given them the inspiration and self-confidence that came before the educational achievements themselves.

Brooklyn: P.S. 91

Perhaps the most remarkable of all the schools in this study is P.S. 91, an elementary school in a rundown neighborhood of Brooklyn. Here, where over half the students are eligible for the free lunch program and a significant proportion are on welfare, *every grade approximates or (usually) exceeds the national norms* in reading comprehension. A tour of the ancient school building is even more surprising than these statistics. Here, in class after class, the students—overwhelmingly ghetto youngsters—work quietly, intently, and pleasantly under the direction of obviously intelligent and interested teachers and teacher aides who represent a wide range of ages, races, and personal styles. The sheer silence of the school was eerie to one who had attended elementary school in central Harlem and had recently researched similar schools elsewhere.

In class after class, discussion periods brought lively exchanges between teachers and pupils—the children speaking in complete sentences, gramatically and directly to the point, and returning to the subject if the teacher's response was not clear or satisfactory to them. To see this happening with children identical in appearance and dress to those who are dull, withdrawn, or hostile in untold other ghetto schools can only be described as an emotional experience. After leaving one classroom where a lively discussion was still in progress, the principal said matter-of-factly, "That was our slow learners' class. They are doing all right, but I think there is need for improvement."

That was the remarkable attitude of a remarkable man. Martin Shor, the principal, is white and was principal of the school when the school was white. As the Crown Heights section of Brooklyn changed its racial composition and the socioeconomic level fell, the school population reflected these changes. Now there are only a few white or oriental children in P.S. 91. But unlike other schools whose academic standards have fallen along with the socioeconomic level of their neighborhoods, P.S. 91 has had a *rising* proportion of its students scoring above the national norms in reading. In 1971, just over 49 per cent of its students exceeded the national norms, in 1972 it was 51 per cent, in 1973 it was 54 per cent, and in 1974 it was 57 per cent. To put these numbers in perspective, *none* of the 12 other schools in its district had even 40 per cent of their students above the national norms, even though some of these other schools are in higher-socioeconomic-status neighborhoods. The highest percentage in the whole borough of Brooklyn —with more than 600 elementary schools—is 60 per cent above the national norms.

The handicaps under which P.S. 91 operates include a very high turnover rate, characteristic of ghetto schools. There was a 34 per cent turnover in just three months. This means that the school loses many of the good students it has prepared in the early grades and receives from other ghetto schools badly prepared youngsters whom it must reeducate in later grades. This is apparently a factor in the pattern of scores whereby the lower grades at P.S. 91 exceed the national norms by wider margins than the higher grades (see the table below). However, it should be noted that other black schools in other cities also tend to score relatively higher in their earlier grades—sometimes even exceeding the national norms in the early grades, in schools far below the national norms overall. How much of the later disastrous decline in scores in ghetto schools is the result of high turnover and how much is the result of the negative effects of the school itself, or the development of negative attitudes by the students toward the school (or life), is a subject which has scarcely been explored. Indeed, the phenomenon itself has hardly been recognized. It is well known that black children tend to fall progressively further behind as they go through school systems, but just how well they do in the first or second grades—even in school systems with dreadful overall results, such as in Chicago or Philadelphia—is a largely unrecognized phenomena.

Martin Shor puts heavy emphasis on teaching the P.S. 91 pupils to read well in the first grade. Indeed, half of the P.S. 91 children can read when they have finished kindergarten. While the school

Reading Scores, P.S. 91, Brooklyn [1]

GRADE	NATIONAL NORMS	P.S. 91 MEDIAN
2	2.7	3.5
3	3.7	4.1
4	4.7	4.5
5	5.7	6.3
6	6.7	6.7

[1] Source: Compilation from District 17, Brooklyn.

bears the imprint of his own special methods and approach, Shor argues that none of these methods would work unless the students first knew how to read. A disproportionate amount of the school's money and teaching talent goes into preparing the first-graders to read, write, and express themselves orally.

The higher grades use a variety of self-teaching materials, including programmed books, teaching machines, and tape recorders. Many of these materials are *a year or more ahead* of the "age" or "grade" level of the students using them. Students are separated into small groups by ability within each class as well as between classes, and each group has its own assignment. "This may look like an 'open' classroom," Shor said. "But it's not. Every group is working on its own *assigned* task." When asked if this "tracking" system did not originally lead to certain racial imbalances in classes within the school, Shor pointed out that initially disadvantaged students advanced enough to produce more racial balance eventually.

"But if other schools followed your system," I asked, "wouldn't that mean that, in the interim, a multi-racial school would have the appearance of internal segregation, which would lead to a lot of political flack?" "Then you just take the flack," he said. He had taken flack during the period of racial transition at P.S. 91, but the educational results silenced critics and gained parental support. How many other white principals in a ghetto neighborhood have that kind of courage is another question. A study of unusually successful ghetto schools by the Office of Educational Personnel Review in New York concluded that "the quality and attitude of the administrator seemed to be the only real difference" between these schools and less successful ones. A few hours with Martin Shor reinforce that conclusion. He is a quietly confident, forceful man, with an incisive mind, much experience and resourcefulness, and the implicit faith that the job *can* be done. His talk is free of the educational clichés and public relations smoothness normally associated with school administrators. He comes to the ghetto to do a job, does it well, and then goes home elsewhere—contrary to the emotional cries about the need for indigenous community leadership in the school.

P.S. 91 does not teach "black English" or black studies, though its many books and other materials do include a few items of special interest to black children. The school tries to *expand* the students' cultural horizons: Several hundred of these elementary school pupils study foreign languages. P.S. 91 students also read excerpts from translations of the classics of world literature, such as Cervantes or Aesop. They are constantly exposed to material that allows their minds to see beyond the drab school building, the decaying tenements, and the area that caused a friend to tell me, "You sure are brave to park a car in *that* neighborhood." The usual "middle-class" label used to dismiss black educational achievements is only a bad joke when applied to P.S. 91.

Washington, D.C.: Dunbar High School

The oldest and most illustrious of the black elite schools was Dunbar High School in Washington, D.C., during the period from 1870 to 1955. Over that 85-year span, most of its graduates went to college—rare for whites or blacks, then—and many went on to outstanding academic achievements and distinguished careers. Back at the turn of the century, Dunbar was sending students to Harvard, and in the period 1918-1923, Dunbar graduates earned 15 degrees from Ivy League colleges, and 10 degrees from Amherst, Williams, and Wesleyan. During World War II, Dunbar alumni in the Army included "nearly a score of Majors, nine Colonels and Lieutenant Colonels, and a Brigadier General"—a substantial percentage of all high-ranking black officers at that time.

Dunbar was the first black public high school in the United States. Its unique position allowed it to select some of the best of the educated blacks in the country for its teachers and principals. Of its first nine principals, seven had degrees from either Harvard, Oberlin, Dartmouth, or Amherst. Of the remaining two, one was educated in Glasgow and London, and the other was a Phi Beta Kappa from Western Reserve. The principals included the first black woman in the United States to receive a college degree (from Oberlin, 1862) and the first black man to graduate from Harvard (in 1870). Clearly they were remarkable people even to attempt what they did, when they did.

So too was the man who spearheaded the drive that led to the founding of the school which ultimately became Dunbar High School (after several changes of name and location). William Syphax was a "free person of color," born in 1826 and active in civic affairs and civil rights issues, "fearing no man regardless of position or color." As a trustee of the Negro schools in Washington, Syphax preferred to hire black teachers, but only when their qualifications were equal to those of white teachers—for the trustees "deem it a violation of our official oath to employ inferior teachers when superior teachers can be had for the same money." He addressed demands not only to whites in power, but also to his own people, exhorting them to send their children to school with discipline, respect, and a willingness to work hard. These became hallmarks of Dunbar High School, as did the academic success that flowed from them. As early as 1899, Dunbar scored higher in city-wide tests than any of the white high schools in the District of Columbia. Down through the years its attendance records were generally better than those of the white high schools, and its rate of tardiness was lower. Dunbar meant business.

The teachers at Dunbar usually held degrees in liberal arts from top institutions, not education degrees from teachers colleges. The scarcity of alternative occupations for educated Negroes allowed Dunbar to pick the cream of the crop. As late as the 1920's, its staff included individuals with Ph.D.'s from leading universities, including the distinguished historian Carter G. Woodson. The teachers were as dedicated and demanding as they were qualified. Extra-curricular tutoring, securing scholarships for graduating seniors, getting parents of promising students to keep them in school despite desperate family finances—all these were part of the voluntary work load of Dunbar teachers and principals. In a city that remained racially segregated into the 1950's, there were also constant efforts to bring cultural attractions to the school that were unavailable to black youngsters in theaters, concert halls, or other cultural and entertainment centers. While individual pride and racial awareness were part of the atmosphere at Dunbar High School, cultural expansion was the educational goal. Latin was taught throughout the period from 1870 to 1955, and in the early decades, Greek was taught as well. In the 1940's, Dunbar fought a losing battle with the superintendent of schools to have calculus added.

Throughout the 85-year period of its academic ascendancy, Dunbar never had adequate financial support. At its founding it was allowed to draw only on taxes collected in the black community. While this arrangement eventually gave way to drawing on the general taxes of the city, so too did the separate administration of Negro schools by black trustees give way to city-wide administration by an all-white board of education, which never provided equal support. Large classes were the norm from the 1870's, when there were more than 40 students per teacher, to the 1950's, when Dunbar's student/teacher ratio exceeded that of any white high school in Washington. The school was in operation more than 40 years before it had a lunch room, which then was so small that many children had to eat lunch out on the street. Blackboards were "cracked with confusing lines resembling a map." It was 1950 before the school had a public address system.

The social origins of Dunbar students were diverse. For three decades, Dunbar was the only black high school in Washington, D.C., and for three more decades it was the only black academic high school in the city, so it drew on a broad cross section of students. As late as 1948, one third of all black high school students in Washington were enrolled in Dunbar. Nevertheless, the "middle-class" label has been stuck on Dunbar, and no amount of facts dispels it. According to a *Washington Post* reporter, the one word "Dunbar" will divide any room of middle-aged black Washingtonians into "outraged warring factions." Some are fiercely loyal to Dunbar as a monumental educational achievement, while others see it as snobbish elitism for middle-class mulattoes who either excluded poor blacks from the school or ostracized them if they attended. A look through old yearbook photographs will disprove the myth of mulatto predominance, and our statistical tabulation of parental occupations from 1938 through 1955 shows 38 per cent of known parental occupations to have been "unskilled and semi-skilled" (including many maids), while "white-collar" and "professional" occupations together added up to only 17 per cent.

Unquestionably, almost all middle-class Negroes in Washington sent their children to Dunbar during the period from 1870 to 1955, and for historical reasons, middle-class Negroes tended to be lighter in color—but that is very different from saying that most Dunbar students were either middle class or mulattoes. Former Dunbar Principal Charles Lofton calls it all "an old wives' tale." "If we took only the children of doctors and lawyers," he asked, "how could we have had 1400 black students at one time?" Yet the persistence and power of the myth suggests something of the depth of the hurt felt by those who either did not go to Dunbar because of fear of social rejection or did go and did not feel accepted. To this day, one Dunbar alumna has a policy at social gatherings in Washington of never mentioning where she went to high school.

Dunbar alumni claim that the school was at its academic peak in the 1920's or earlier—in particular that the "M Street School," which was the name prior to 1917, was superior to "Dunbar," which was the name attached to the building constructed that year. There is some inconclusive evidence—graduation years of distinguished alumni, numbers of graduates attending top colleges, etc.—supporting this view, but no standard tests were given in both eras that would permit a direct comparison. The earliest I.Q. records available are for 1938, so that our data cover only its supposedly declining years. Nonetheless, for this 18-year period, the average I.Q. in the school was below 100 for only one year (when it was 99) and was as high as 111 (in 1939).

There is general agreement that Dunbar declined precipitously and catastrophically after the school reorganization of 1955 made it a neighborhood school for the first time in its history. Its neighborhood was one of the worst in the city, and as its new students entered, advanced elective courses gave way to remedial math and English, and its quiet building now became the scene of "discipline problems." The past excellence of the school had caused many teachers to stay on past the retirement age, and now many of them began to retire at once. By the 1960's a newspaper story on the school was titled "Black Elite Institution Now Typical Slum Facility." It remains a typical slum school today—its past recalled only in the heat of a bitter controversy over the tearing down of the old building standing alongside a modern school bearing the same name. One of several city councilmen who favored demolition said that Dunbar "represents a symbol of elitism among blacks that should never appear again." But a Dunbar alumnus wondered if the real problem was that the new school fears the "silent competition" of the old building and the achievement it represents.

Educational "law and order"

Contrary to current fashions, it has not been necessary (or usual) to have a special method of teaching to "reach" black children in order to have high-quality education. Teaching methods used in the schools studied here have varied enormously from school to school, and even in particular schools the variation from teacher to teacher has been so great as to defy general characterization. Everything from religious principles to corporal punishment has been used to maintain order. The buildings have ranged from the most dilapidated wrecks to a sparkling plate-glass palace. The teachers and principals have been black and white, religious and secular, authoritarian and gentle, community leaders and visitors from another social world. Some have had a warm "human touch" and others would have failed Public Relations I. Their only common denominators have been dedication to education, commitment to the children, and faith in what it was possible to achieve. The institutional common denominators of these schools are a larger and more complex question.

In general, test scores have been significantly higher at these schools than at black schools in general, and have been highest at the most elite and oldest—Dunbar High School in Washington, in its academic heyday. Yet their I.Q. scores have not been as high as those at white high schools of comparable achievement, and all of the schools studied have included students well below national test score norms. In short, test scores are not "irrelevant" for black achievement, but neither are they the be-all and end-all. One of the tragedies in the wake of the Jensen controversy is that many schools and school systems avoid giving I.Q. tests for fear of political repercussions, when in fact much useful information can be obtained from this imperfect instrument, once its limitations are understood. Even where I.Q. tests are used, the results are often handled in a politicized way. For example, the Austin (Texas) public school system refused to release data on a school being considered for inclusion in this study because of "legal" reasons—but only after a lengthy cross-examination on my personal beliefs about various issues involved in the I.Q. controversy. Sometimes the data are suppressed for more directly institutional political reasons—as in the case of a large metropolitan black school on the West Coast whose outstanding performance is kept quiet for fear of citizen demands to know why the other black schools in the same city cannot produce similar results.

Perhaps the most basic characteristic of all these schools could be called "law and order," if these had not become politically dirty words. Each of these schools currently maintaining high standards was a very quiet and orderly school, whether located in a middle-class suburb of Atlanta or in the heart of a deteriorating ghetto in Brooklyn. Schools formerly of high quality were repeatedly described by alumni, teachers, and others as places where "discipline problems" were virtually unheard-of. "Respect" was the word most used by those interviewed to describe the attitudes of students and parents toward these schools. "The teacher was *always* right" was a phrase that was used again and again to describe the attitude of the black parents of a generation or more ago. Most Negro students of that era would not have dreamed of complaining to their parents after being punished by a teacher, for that would have been likely to bring on a second—and worse—punishment at home. Even today, in those few instances where schools have the confidence of black parents, a wise student maintains a discreet silence at home about his difficulties with teachers, and hopes that the teachers do the same. The black culture is not a permissive culture. But in more and more cases, "student rights" activists among adults—particularly adults with an eye to political exposure—create a more contentious environment in which it is the teacher or the principal who maintains a discreet silence for fear of legal or physical retaliation. The sheer exhaustion of going through "due process" for every disruptive student who needs to be suspended is enough to discourage decisive action by many school officials.

The destruction of high-quality black schools has been associated with a breakdown in the basic framework of law and order. Nor did it require mass violence to destroy these or other black schools. Again and again those interviewed who were working in the field of education pointed out that only a fraction—perhaps no more than one tenth of the students—need to be hard-core troublemakers in order for good education to become impossible. Another way of looking at this is that only a small amount of initial selectivity (including student self-selection) or subsequent ability to suspend or expel is necessary to free a school of a major obstacle to education. At one time this small amount of selectivity was provided automatically for black (and other) high schools, because most uninterested students did not go on to high school. Those whose educational performances were substandard in the lower grades were left back often enough to reach the age to leave school before reaching high school. Moreover, that legal age was lower then; and, in addition, those utterly uninterested in school were unlikely to be zealously pursued by attendance officers in the era before the "dropout" problem became an emotionally important political issue.

Formal selectivity, in terms of entrance examination cutoff scores, was the exception rather than the rule for the schools studied here. Most of these were public schools serving all students in a given area; and for some period of their history, that area has included all black children in the city, in the cases of Dunbar, Douglass, and Booker T. Washington High Schools. The private schools—St. Augustine, Xavier, and St. Paul—have entrance examinations, but these do not automatically admit or exclude, and the wide range of student test scores in these schools indicates that such scores are far from decisive in admissions. In short, no stringent "elitism" is necessary to achieve high-quality education. It is only necessary to select, or have students self-select, in such a way as to exclude the tiny fraction who are troublemakers.

At one time, it was a relatively simple matter to suspend, expel, or transfer a disruptive student to some "special" class or "dumping ground" vocational school, allowing the rest of the educational system to proceed undisturbed. Now this has become more difficult with the growth of "student rights" and "parent power"— and, more generally, with an agonizing preoccupation with the question of what can be done for the disruptive student to "solve" his "problem." This mass projection of the academic paradigm of problem-solving to the whole society is part of the general spirit of the times, but it overlooks the vital question whether there is, in fact, a solution—whether we have it within our grasp today, and whether we shall allow the "problem" to take its fullest destructive toll before such indefinite time as we have it "solved." Recent campaigns to "get the drunk driver off the road" suggest that there are cases where the primary concern is to protect society, and where whatever remedies can be offered the individual are secondary. The enormous toll of a few destructive students on black education is one of the tragic untold stories of our time—perhaps because there is no political gain to be made by telling it, and much political capital to reap from championing "student rights."

Recovering the past

While order and respect have been universal characteristics of the schools studied here, other ingredients have also been necessary to create academic excellence. Chief among these have been the character and ability of the principals. Some of these principals have been of heroic dimensions—fighters for civil rights at a time when that was a dangerous role—and others have been simply dedicated educators. The number of these principals who have trained at top colleges and universities in the country suggests that investments made in promising Negro youths more than half a century ago have paid off large and continuing dividends.

Ability grouping has been a prominent feature of most of these schools during their periods of academic excellence—contrary to the "democratic" trends in contemporary education. For many reasons going back into history, there are very wide ranges of educational preparation and orientation among black children, and accommodating them all in one standard curriculum may often be impractical. Among Dunbar students in the period from 1938 to 1955, it was not uncommon to find individuals with I.Q.'s in the 80's and individuals with I.Q.'s in the 140's in the same grade. In P.S. 91 today, the ability-grouping principle includes not only several different classes in the same grade but also several different ability groupings within each class—all told, perhaps two dozen ability levels in a single grade. This may not sound plausible as an educational policy, but it works—and it works in an unpromising social setting where many more popular ideas fail to show any results.

Perhaps the most disturbing aspect of contemporary education is the extent to which the very process of testing ideas and procedures by their actual *results* has been superseded by a process of testing them by their consonance with existing *preconceptions* about education and society. Father Grant, even after his remarkable successes as principal of St. Augustine, found no receptivity at the Ford Foundation either to his appeals for money for the school or to his ideas about education. He was out of step with the rhetoric of his time and did not use the "innovative" methods that were preconceived to be necessary or beneficial to black students. Xavier Prep, even after more than half a century of demonstrable results, is still looking for a modest sum of money to improve its library, but libraries are not "exciting" or "imaginative"—as "black English" or "black studies" are.

The social settings of the schools studied here are also significant. Every one of them was an urban school. This is remarkable because during the academic heyday of most of these schools most American Negroes lived in rural and small-town settings. This suggests that the rise of such prominent blacks as those who came from these schools—which is to say, most of the top black pioneers in the history of this country—seems a matter less of innate ability and more of special social settings in which individual ability could develop; and that the settings from which such black leadership arose were quite different from the social settings in which the mass of the black population lived. The second point needs emphasis only because of the recent mystique surrounding "grass roots" origins and/or the faithful reflection of "grass roots" attitudes by leaders. Much of this is nothing more than brazen presumption and reckless semantics: No one ever applies labels like "middle-class" to Angela Davis or LeRoi Jones (or others of their persuasion), though that is in fact their origin, while those with a more moderate philosophy are often condemned as "middle-class" —no matter that they may actually have come from desperate poverty, and no matter how many polls show that their opinions are shared by the masses of blacks.

The particular cities in which the high-quality black schools arose were distinctive as centers of concentration for the "free persons of color" in the antebellum era. Except in the case of Dunbar High School in Washington, there was no unbroken historical line traceable back to the free Negroes of the early 19th century, but it seems more than coincidence that these schools took root in places where there had been schools for black children (usually private schools) 50 or 100 years earlier. That is, an old black community with a demand for good education existed even before good schools became an institutional reality. It is not that the bulk of the Negroes in these cities necessarily wanted quality education, but that there was an important nucleus that understood what was needed, and that the others recognized and respected good education when it appeared.

Apparently the great bulk of black children who benefited from these schools were *not* descendants of "free persons of color" or of middle-class Negroes in general. But the knowledge, experience, and values of the more fortunate segment of the race became their heritage. While the black educated classes were not angels—they could be as snobbish and insufferable as any other privileged group —they were a vital source of knowledge, discipline, and competence. They opened a window on a wider world of human history and culture. They did not glorify provincialism or tribalism, in the manner of some of today's black middle-class radicals who attempt to expiate their own past by being "blacker-than-thou." Those white officials who have successfully run high-quality black schools have, without exception, been men and women who were neither impressed nor intimidated by the militant vogues of the 1960's.

Whatever is the objective importance of social history in any final assessment of black education, that history must be dealt with—if only to counter the *fictitious* history that has become part of current stereotypes. Messianic movements of whatever place or time tend to denigrate the past as a means of making themselves unique and their vision glorious. Recent black messianic movements, and white messianic movements speaking in the name of blacks, have been no exception. The picture that emerges from these visions is of an inert, fearful, and unconcerned black leadership in the past— leaders only recently superseded by bold men of vision, like themselves. This is a libel on the men and women who faced up to far more serious dangers than our generation will ever confront, who took the children of slaves and made them educated men and women, and who put in the long hours of hard work required to turn a despised mass into a cohesive community. In many ways, those communities had far more cohesion, stability, mutual respect, and plain humanity than the ghettos of today.

"Career education"— reforming school through work

ELEANOR FARRAR MCGOWAN

AMERICANS have tried to solve a number of problems with public education. A recurrent worry has been that primary institutions—family, church, and community—were so weakened by modernization that they could no longer transmit a common culture. Since the 1840's, it has been hoped that schools could do the job instead. If children seemed to be the hapless victims of their families' poverty, nationality, criminality, or bad manners, schools would save them. If the decline of apprenticeship, the growth of large-scale industry, and the development of technology seemed to leave adolescents with no way of learning a trade or finding a job, schools seemed the obvious answer. They would teach vocational skills, test aptitudes, sort students into programs, and counsel them into careers. For more than a century, American educators and school reformers have sounded the alarm: The "natural learning" adequate for a simpler society could no longer be trusted. Formal schooling would have to replace informal education if Americans were to enter the modern age.

These attitudes were hopeful, but ambivalent as well. Americans since Horace Mann have been certain that only schooling could suffice, but they have also idealized a simpler time in which youngsters learned trades at their parents' knees—or in close apprenticeship to journeymen. Industrialism and technology struck Americans as demanding more—and more rigorous—formal education. But they also mourned the loss of an earlier and more harmonious community, in which learning to work was merely part of growing up. In their ambivalence, Americans saw schools as a way to reconstruct things. Life in classrooms would compensate for the deficiencies of life outside them.

Education and the "real world"

All this now seems to be changing. To judge from recent developments, America's long romance with schooling is on the wane. In the late 1950's and early 1960's, reformers attacked schools for not trying to do the things they should—integration, better science education, and compensatory training for the poor. The schools then took on these tasks, but by the late 1960's the reformers complained that they were not executing the reforms properly. Critics and social scientists questioned the efficacy of schooling, Ivan Illych became the darling of the intellectuals, and his ideas about the destructive power of schools took hold. "Deinstitutionalization" had become a fad in treating delinquents, criminals, and the mentally ill, and the idea soon washed over to education. Formal education, formerly regarded as the solution to so many social problems, came to seem a major social problem itself. Schools, the critics argued, were an obstacle to learning.

These ideas fermented in the literary and intellectual culture of the late 1960's, and by the early 1970's they had bubbled over into officialdom. Several government and professional commissions announced that there was a serious "youth" problem.[1] By collecting adolescents in boring and frustrating surroundings segregated from the real world of work and adults, secondary schools supposedly reinforced a pathological youth culture that was "spinning

---

[1] The reports and studies mentioned in this article include: *Youth: Transition to Adulthood,* Report of the Panel on Youth of the President's Science Advisory Committee, June 1973 (Chicago, University of Chicago Press, 1974); *The Reform of Secondary Education,* National Commission on the Reform of Secondary Education, July 1973 (New York, McGraw-Hill, 1973); Ruth Weinstock, ed., *The Greening of the High School* (New York: IDEA-EFL, March 1973); *Secondary Schools in a Changing World: This We Believe,* Report of the Task Force on Secondary Schools (National Association of Secondary School Principals, 1975); Willard Wirtz and the National Manpower Institute, *The Boundless Resource* (Washington, D.C., New Republic Books, 1975). An informative review of these ideas is presented in *Youth Policy in Transition* (The Rand Corporation, 1976).

out of control," posing a serious threat to social integration. The reports called for a raft of changes, many of which sought to get adolescents out of school: reducing the age of compulsory attendance, lowering the minimum wage to encourage the employment of adolescents, and creating school programs that allowed students to work. Some reports also tried to figure out ways of using schools to legitimize "experience"—everything from making people with "real experience" into teachers to giving students academic credit for work or community service outside of school.

This represents quite a change in notions about schooling. For generations schools had been seen as a protected culture, an island where children could be safe from the problematic pressures of their environment. Some had thought schools would insulate children from cultural or class inadequacies in poor neighborhoods. Others had thought schools would train children in the skills that were required for social survival and economic progress, but were no longer taught at home or at work. Still others had thought schools would protect children, giving them the opportunity to play, grow, and enjoy learning. But rather than picturing schools as a refuge, the current wisdom portrays them as pathologically isolated products of the failure of primary institutions to socialize the young and of economic pressures to keep youth out of the work force. School children are said to be walled off from healthy social realities by irrelevant compulsory attendance and school-leaving laws, and by an unwise professional devotion to book learning. According to these reports, schools prevent students from learning; the answer to the barrenness of formal schools is real experience.

The contrast between current doctrine and inherited dogmas concerning work and school is striking. For generations schools have been regarded as the indispensable preparation for work: They would provide the skills and connections that once were handed down informally on the job or in the family. This idea underlay the earliest manual training programs, the later movements for vocational education, and the turn-of-the-century torrent of high-school and trade-school specializations in everything from accounting to veterinary medicine. It is also the inspiration for the more recent flood of post-secondary white- and blue-collar training programs.

But if schooling once seemed a prerequisite for the vicissitudes of work, it is now pictured as a barrier to learning about it. Schools, it is argued, teach things that are useless for jobs or careers; they are unresponsive to the vital curiosity that would arise in real-life situations; they keep adolescents in an artificial environment that prevents them from learning career skills. According to the recent rush of reports, the solution lies in getting adolescents out of schools into work situations; or bringing work into schools so they become more like real life; or somehow combining work and schools so that labor and learning can go together. While schools used to be regarded as a better way of preparing to work, work is now seen as a better way of preparing to learn.

The "career education" movement

This new reform movement has gathered substantial momentum since the early 1970's, spreading into thousands of schools. But it is not very easy to pin down the concept of career education, which by design or uncertainty remains vague. The United States Office of Education (USOE) defines the reform majestically as the "totality of experiences through which one learns about and prepares to engage in work as part of her or his way of living." Others call it a "renewal and expansion of vocational education aimed at reducing [students'] expectations, limiting aspirations, and increasing commitments to the existing social structure."[2]

Advocates of career education propose to reach young people from kindergarten through college with lessons and experiences designed to help them make "more informed" career choices when the time comes. These lessons vary with the students' ages. Grade-schoolers are exposed to adults working and information on different kinds of work. Junior-high-school students engage in "career exploration," presumably following their interests and aptitudes to learn more about jobs that appeal to them. High-schoolers either continue exploring careers or begin working in specific areas to graduate with a marketable set of skills. At the same time, teachers "infuse" career information into all aspects of the school curriculum at every grade level, thereby teaching students how everything they study—from art to zoology—has some bearing on the world of work. The goal of career education is to teach students about life by letting them into the workplace, putting them in close contact with adults, and giving them real-life, hands-on experience. Career education aspires to an annual crop of high-school graduates with immediately salable skills, whether or not they choose to go to college.

---

[2] Norton Grubb and Marvin Lazarson, "Policy 'Round the Workplan: Continuities and Fallacies of Career Education," *Harvard Education Review*, 45 (1975).

The idea of career education is not to dispense with but to add to what schools currently do—and to shift the focus to work.

This conceptual looseness may help to explain the popularity of career education. Educators can make of it what they want without easily doing violence to the reformers' intent. Little specific information is available on the array of programs, but at last count, 9,200 of the nation's 16,200 school districts offered career-education programs to their students. At the state level, nearly every department of education has a career-education officer, and many states are mandating programs, or considering it. Nor is enthusiasm limited to public-school officials. Pronouncements of support are broad, coming from most business and labor groups, and virtually every major education establishment has endorsed the reform.

Money is in good supply, as well. Largely through the efforts of former United States Education Commissioner Sidney Marland, career education has grown from a series of pilot projects launched in 1971 with $9 million of USOE discretionary funds, to a bewildering assortment of programs, projects, and studies expected to cost $110 million by 1978. In addition, USOE's sibling, the National Institute of Education, budgets more than $24 million annually for career-education research and development. Both will spend considerably more if Congress approves the Perkins Bill (HR 11023), which will earmark $100 million annually to the states specifically for career education. On the coattails of this bounty, new curricula have been churned out; new school programs are being developed and disseminated; and education professionals are producing a profusion of books and articles. Career education is not just a collection of novel ideas, but a reform movement of considerable proportions enjoying widespread popularity.

The new romance of work

It is easy to see its appeal. For some years now the press has given front-page attention to research that seemingly showed a decline in the income value of college degrees. This news accompanied rising educational costs at all levels, prompting rather brisk questions about the value of formal schooling. These doubts were reinforced by other studies asserting that high-school dropouts did just as well in the job market as similarly situated high-school graduates. And all of this fell in with the findings of James Coleman and Christopher Jencks that schools had little or no differential impact on the academic achievement or adult success of their students. If schools were not a particularly effective way of getting better jobs for students later on, why bother going? Why not get jobs right away? Or at least train for them in school?

It isn't hard to see how such questions would occur to state legislators contemplating increases in aid to public education, or to parents contemplating college tuition fees that escalate rapidly every year. But these questions have had added force for public school administrators—who, after all, must manage American high schools. The building boom that began in the Eisenhower years produced large secondary schools in cities and suburbs all over the country. These large, comprehensive facilities became some of the leading wonders of the education world, the pride of the school boards and administrators who passed the levies and pushed the plans.

Or at least so it was before vandalism, school crime, easy drugs, and the youth culture's vocal anti-intellectualism swept over the urban scene. Those large buildings quickly appeared less like monuments to opportunity and learning than corrals for the unruly, inviting disaster. One after another, administrators concluded that the main effect of large high schools was to create a "critical mass" that stimulated crime, dope, and hostility to school. One answer was increased expenditures on police and school security. Another was getting students out of school.

The latter had once been nicely achieved by the draft, by suspension and expulsion, and by dropping out. But the draft was abolished; civil-rights reformers made suspension and expulsion complicated procedures; and dropping out always goes out of style when the job market is tight. By the early 1970's, students who didn't like school had fewer ways to avoid it. And to make things worse, by that time many school professionals had begun to believe the ideas preached by John Dewey and brought up to date by Paul Goodman: that school often *was* boring; that experience *was* livelier; that real apprenticeships *were* preferable to make-work shop courses; that contact with the real thing was better than embracing a standardized text. Connecticut's Education Commissioner, Mark R. Shedd, claimed in a news conference last year that getting all high school students out of the classroom and into the community for at least a year would not only aid teenagers, but also help teachers and administrators cope with problems of discipline and poor attendance.

All this is partly responsible for the currency and popularity of career education, but its real intellectual glue is the new romance of work. The reports and programs suggest that work is lively, while school is boring. Work is a preparation for adult life, while school simply reinforces an irresponsible youth culture. Work will stimulate curiosity and provoke learning, whereas school stultifies them. Work will provide meaningful contact with adults and help integrate youth into society, while school prevents socialization. The common thread in career education is the notion that work is authentic, real, and healthy, that it can solve problems created or unmanaged by the dull world of compulsory classrooms.

But this is reminiscent of the old idea that formal education would make up for the inadequacies of modern families, communities, and churches. And because much of the career-education movement rests on grand ideas about the saving power of real experience, we can expect that many of its aspirations will be frustrated. Career education rests on an appealing set of ideas about work and school, but these ideas are at odds with reality. As a result, efforts to implement them have perverse and unexpected results. For the most part, new programs aimed at getting children out of school only seem to succeed in keeping them in; the idea of providing children with the real experience of work has been transformed into programs that make work a formal subject of school studies; the notion of exposing students to real adults in the real world seems to result mostly in exposing them to adult professionals in the school world. Ideas designed to weaken the power of schools and expand students' experience have been captured by the education professionals. Somehow, experiencing work on the job has been turned into learning about it in the classroom.

One reason for this may be that work is not what reformers would like to believe. A great deal of work seems to suffer from just the same defects that reformers bemoan in schools; indeed, at exactly the same time they are trying to liven up education by making it more like work, other reformers are trying to liven up the workplace to make it more humane, stimulating, and relaxed —in a word, more like school. But more important, the social division of labor in America creates powerful barriers to any serious reallocation of responsibility among business, education, and labor.

Business barriers

One serious obstacle is the business world that is supposed to employ youth. The reports on work and school all suggested that new programs should involve business as an equal partner of the schools. The notion was that both employers and educators would design the innovations, manage the programs, and educate the students. Former Labor Secretary Willard Wirtz wrote that this partnership was essential to make the ventures work, the only way to prevent the programs from becoming variations on vocational education.

But as sensible as the notion of an equal partnership seems, there is little evidence that business agrees. A federally funded feasibility study of the idea in 1971 revealed that business was willing to get involved in these programs, but not on an equal footing with schools. Employers are willing to help as they have in the past—as information resources about different kinds of work, or as employers of a few students in work-study or cooperative-education programs. But they don't want to be responsible for designing programs and teaching. And they don't want to assume responsibility for students away from school.

This reality has gradually been incorporated into career-education programs. When asked what business is doing, one federal official mentioned the APAR Program in Portland, Oregon, and the Skyline Career Development Program in Dallas, Texas—both considered first-rate examples. But neither involves a new distribution of responsibility between business and schools. Rather, a consortium of local employers has sent representatives to advise schools in developing career-education curricula, to serve as a conduit between employers and schools seeking job-placements for teenagers, and to arrange site visits for classes of students. One federal official called such programs "traffic control devices."[3] Their chief function is to match school needs with business availability, "to avoid multiple requests to one business when another business could fill the bill." Without this sort of clearinghouse, he said, many employers would soon be overwhelmed and refuse to participate at all.

Visiting businesses hardly seems like a dramatic reform, or one designed to help youth reevaluate work. But USOE increasingly seems concerned with the logistics of proliferating career-education programs. "Some schools now have 40 to 50 per cent of their students visiting plants around the city, or in job-placements," one advocate of career education said, "but the goal is to spread these

---

[3] To protect the confidentiality of federal education staffers whom we interviewed, no names have been cited. Notes on our interviews are in our personal files.

programs throughout the system, and when 2000 kids are knocking on employers' doors, we're going to have real problems. Employers won't be able to handle the numbers." Concern with visits seems central, but if one idea is to ease student access to the workplace, another is to protect business against a flood of youth. This is at best a somewhat ambiguous sign of business' commitment, and certainly shows no evidence of structural change in the relationship between work and school.

Beyond the local level, business and industry have been noticeably quiet on the subject of career education. From the "Fortune 500" firms, for example, which employ about 20 per cent of the American work-force, hardly a word has been heard. The one exception is General Motors (GM), which recently issued a policy statement on career education, committing the company to hire education coordinators in each of its assembly plants. But the policy limits GM's involvement to "cooperating," "advising," and "supporting the career-education effort." GM intends to help schools meet their objectives by providing classroom speakers and materials, and permitting students to visit plants. This doesn't differ much from what many employers—including GM—have been doing for years now, and staff at USOE agreed: "What's going on in career education consists mainly of career curricula delivered in the classroom, plant visits, and visitors invited into the school to speak about different kinds of work." Another federal official summed up business' role more succinctly: "Business isn't really doing anything different—it's just that some of the old programs have been relabeled 'career education.'' Even businesses that support the programs carefully select a familiar, limited role.

This isn't surprising, since work in America is structured to minimize the need for teaching and learning on the job. Both are cost-ineffective, and seem to clash with profitability. Nearly 70 years ago, business seized on Frederick Taylor's ideas about work efficiency and economy, and since then jobs have been increasingly fragmented and simplified to permit rank novices to be productive from the day they are hired. Skills that can't be instantly acquired are taught in the least obtrusive ways—in public or private vocational schools, apprenticeship programs, or in company-oriented classrooms set apart from the shop.

This is not to say that most businesses couldn't be restructured for teaching, and incentives devised to encourage it. Indeed, given the slack labor market and some workers' demands for job enrichment, restructuring with federal subsidies might meet a variety of needs. Some workers not needed in production might be employed as teachers, or an educational dimension might be added to some jobs that are narrowly defined. But supporters of career education tried to interest business in the idea a few years ago and were flatly rejected. Employers, it seems, feel neither qualified nor inclined to become more involved in schooling. As a result, the concept of equal partnership was abandoned. "No one talks about equal partnerships anymore," one federal career education official told us: "If you assume rational behavior, the investment just isn't worth the cost to business. People still toss the word 'partnership' around, but nobody knows exactly what that means. And for political reasons, no one is in any hurry to define it. Anyway, business shouldn't be involved in such things as evaluation, certification, and curriculum development. That should be left to school people —who know how to do it best."

It should hardly be a surprise that other education professionals agree with this. The National Association of Secondary School Principals (NASSP) issued an enthusiastic report about using business facilities and resources to spruce up schooling. But NASSP was quite clear that control of these programs must remain firmly in the hands of professionals. Providing students with out-of-school programs is one thing, but sharing authority and responsibility with business is quite another.

So one central idea in these work-and-school proposals has been quietly laid to rest: There will be no joint partnership. The hope was to dilute the influence of educators and standard school practices, expose students to work rather than school, and provide a better idea of what the adult world is like. As it turned out, however, nobody but the authors of the reports seemed interested. Employers are not prepared to become more involved in schooling: They feel they lack the training and organizational requirements, and they feel their major business is productivity and profits. Since professionals certainly don't want to share responsibility for education and weaken their control, employers will continue to help local schools in the same ways they have for years, and educators will control the curriculum and orchestrate students, as usual.

The resistance of labor

A similar problem underlies organized labor's response to career education. Labor leaders don't think that work is the solution to the problems of school; they are more attached to the old idea

—that school will help solve the problems of work. This notion is the basis of recent efforts to democratize the workplace, to make it more open and humane—as school is thought to be. And it is the basis for labor's support of more formal education for more people. Labor leaders take a dim view of letting youth out of school and into the workplace any sooner. They think this can't possibly serve youth well; they think it will only work to the advantage of business; they fear it could be a union-busting or wage-cutting tactic.

One theme in labor's complaints is the movement's pro-employer bias. According to John Sessions, assistant director of the AFL-CIO Education Division, employers have most to gain from the career-education movement: "The emphasis is on getting kids out of school faster and on the job sooner. That goes hand in hand with cutting the compulsory school age, as well as the minimum wage. Well, over our dead bodies will we go along with a cut in the minimum wage [which has been proposed to compensate students for productive work]. If kids work, employers should be willing to pay them the full minimum wage."

The argument that different wage scales were designed to encourage youth employment, not rate-busting, is greeted by labor with some skepticism. But even the idea of students working at the full minimum wage isn't much more appealing. Students will still be an economic threat to adults holding entry-level jobs. And, Sessions says, students won't learn very much for all the trouble they cause: "The most available kinds of work for kids are educationally the least productive—work in hamburger palaces and laundermats. Lots of these places are small; some employ only two people. If a student works, he puts one adult out of a job. And at that, the person is probably a marginal worker, who will end up on unemployment. And what does the student learn about work in a laundermat? He won't learn anything about management—he'll probably never even see the owner!"

Labor officials do say they are "theoretically committed to the notion of work experience for teenagers." But when asked what sorts of union work students might perform, they become somewhat vague: "There are jobs kids could do—assembly-line work, for example. And students could do some apprentice work, such as bringing in stock, or working as helpers to journeymen." But it isn't clear how carrying supplies is more educational than flipping hamburgers; nor is it certain that unions using apprentices now would welcome a new pool of students seeking apprenticeships.

All this has had a considerable impact on career-education programs. It has closed off a wide range of work to youth, and limited the jobs they can sample. An official at USOE underlined the point: "It's easier to put teenagers in non-union shops, but much of what they want to experience is unionized work. It bothers us to tell students that there are apprenticeable jobs out there, but that we just aren't going to touch them."

One way advocates of career education have tried to deal with labor's resistance is to limit the amount of time students spend on any job. "As long as students don't become productive," we were told at USOE's Office of Career Education, "they can work in the shop without pay, and there is no resistance from labor. The Department of Labor's rule of thumb is that people become productive after 13 days' work. So we can get around the non-pay issue by moving youngsters around a lot." This flies in the face of the notion that students should experience the deeper dimensions of work, developing relationships with workers and learning as much about adults as about jobs, or the tasks they involve. Worse yet, labor has other objections to this no-pay shortcut. According to John Sessions, labor is "utterly opposed" to placing students in a job for two or three weeks at a time. "In fact, it's an insidious idea," he said: "Many youngsters could outperform seasoned workers for just a few weeks, and go away thinking the job was great. They would form their conception of the work based on their short-term performance. But it's one thing to work on an assembly line for three weeks, or even three months. And it's another to work on that job for 30 years or more."

The irony is that some of labor's fears are self-fulfilling. Rather than providing deep or extended introductions to work, career-education programs can generally provide access only to marginal jobs, or jobs for which there is little demand. Labor resistance is one reason for this. As a result, students can learn little useful for career development, and the jobs seem unlikely to promote novel attitudes about work or adulthood.

Professional ambivalence

Ambivalence about these reforms is most apparent among school professionals. Many teachers like the idea of getting some youngsters out of school early, because they are troubled by difficult students. But most educators are also troubled about declining enrollments that put more and more teachers out of work. Professionals and their organizations thus oppose new programs that threaten to reduce enrollments deliberately. It is surprising that federal officials didn't anticipate this; as far back as 1967 it was no secret that the teacher shortage was over, and demographers were already offering gloomy predictions of steadily declining school enrollments. But several of the career-education reports that appeared at the turn of the decade cheerfully proposed reducing the time youth spend in schools, with nary a thought about teachers.

This naiveté may be understandable, for some of the reports were written by non-educators, and teachers' views don't usually find their way into heady proposals for reforming school. In addition, many of the reformers were motivated by the anti-teacher ideas of the late 1960's. In any event, the ideas for reform have provoked a major conflict within the profession that has had a considerable negative impact on the new programs.

One effect has been to weaken career-education programs in high schools and shift the focus of activity to the intermediate and elementary grades. "All the action is at the elementary level," we were told at USOE. A Peat, Marwick, and Mitchell study commissioned by USOE last year reported an inverse relationship between grade level and the amount of career education students receive. But this has had perverse results. Elementary-school children are furthest away from career choices, and work appears more abstract to them. But teenagers, for whom work is a more salient consideration, seem to be more interested in each other than in what they see on plant tours. The Packard Electric Company in Warren, Ohio, has had six years' experience giving tours and half-hour stints on the assembly line—mostly to sixth-graders, because older children are a problem. The director of this work-exploration program at Packard told us that they began with teenagers, but soon turned to younger children because "as they get older, kids are less interested in work, and fool around too much." USOE staff are concerned about this downward drift to younger children, but don't know what to do. One concluded that high schools, in fact, may be too early: "Career education programs really work best at the junior college level. Students there are closer to work, and take job exploration more seriously." That, of course, was what educators said of vocational training in high schools, from 1920 to the 1960's.

Several theories have been advanced to explain the failure of career-education programs to take hold in high schools. The current favorite—an old one for explaining school-reform failures—places the blame on teachers. "High-school teachers are discipline-oriented," we were told: "They are philosophically opposed to infusing career information into their mathematics, or English, or chemistry curricula." Many of them think students get too little of intellectual substance as it is, and they are hostile to the idea of giving any more time to "soft" subjects.

In any case, it is not easy to work career education into the curriculum. We asked one USOE official how teachers might infuse career information into Algebra II or American History, and his response was, "Darned if I know." He observed that an English teacher might use Dickens to teach "work values" and to show how much work has changed. But that isn't likely to help students make career choices now, or to learn about work in the computer age. Supporters of the idea are aware of this problem and know that retraining veteran teachers is often a fruitless pursuit. But even efforts to promote career-education training have met with little response. Teacher-training institutions are lukewarm, partly because their programs are also contracting, and partly because the remaining faculty are committed to their "disciplines."

Among the more serious professional opponents to career education, high-school guidance counselors may be the most intransigent. One reason is their long struggle to legitimize and dignify their specialty by working mostly with college-bound youth. "Now," we were told at USOE, "career education has come along, and guidance staff are back working with blue-collar kids. In the first place, most guidance people don't know the first thing about jobs; secondly, they're not particularly interested in learning. But they are usually the people drafted for career-education counseling, and they don't have much choice given the tight job market. So how do they deal with it? They resist—and spend most of their time managing logistics rather than counseling kids about job placements."

Logistics may be a safe refuge for now, but it probably won't be for long. Transportation is a vulnerable item on school budgets, and funds for moving students around have been shaved in the past year. Staff at USOE think plant trips will diminish as a result, and alternatives are being developed. One device gaining in popularity is the use of video tape to record career-education activities that students can't experience individually. Some districts, we were told, make tapes of the plant visits of one class and show them to others unable to make the trip. And students are also filmed "shadowing" workers who can't be followed by everyone. The reasons for this may be economic, but the effect is to transform career education into a familiar, vicarious school activity. Films and career curricula, not real work experiences, become the rule.

Project Discovery, a career-education program developed by the Iowa State Department of Education, is another example of this. Ray Morley, a consultant to the program, says, "Project Discovery is designed to get students actually doing things." This "hands-on career-education effort" consists of packaged materials and instructions for different kinds of work. Over the past four years, Iowa has spent over $1 million developing 20 "career kits" that, according to promotional material, are designed to "permit students to experiment with many characteristics of work in the 'safe' environment of the school lab or classroom." These self-instructional packages are currently available for commercial art, hairstyling, advertising, auto-body repair, plumbing, greenhouse work, and medical patient care, among others. The masonry kit, for example, includes a mortar box, wire, a patio-block form, and a line level—along with instructions on how to use them. The school provides trowels, bricks, and concrete blocks—all that any mason needs. This is a far cry from students working side-by-side with a mason, but Ray Morley reports that career-kit sales are brisk, at $2,550 for a set of 20. The producers of Project Discovery plan to develop 60 additional career kits.

It is difficult to understand what students can learn about work this way. And it is harder still to understand how career-education curricula and films promote initiative, responsibility, and healthy work attitudes. According to one USOE official, job simulations and video tapes are a poor substitute for programs that take students into plants: "They miss the smells, the sounds, the whole ambience," he said. He doubted that students learned much about work in school, but thought it was better than nothing.

The response of teachers to career education thus parallels that of business and labor. School professionals still feel that education is the best preparation for life, but even if their ideas about the enlightening effect of schooling have been dulled by experience, professional self-interest dictates opposition to major structural changes. Just as business participates in career education by performing such familiar functions as plant visits, teachers also draw on the familar—inviting speakers to class, showing films about work, and managing the administrative details of placing youth in jobs.

A reform manqué

So an innovative movement designed to produce structural change seems to have been changed by the structure. The implementation of career education has mostly produced programmatic parodies of the original ideas. One wonders why this happened, and what it implies for efforts to reform the relationship between work and school.

One reason things turned out as they did is that the social division of labor simply overwhelmed the reform. The notion of using work as an alternative to formal schooling and as a stimulus to learning is appealing in many ways. But it seems to have had too little concrete appeal for too few. Teachers would like to get difficult children out of their classrooms, but it seems risky in a time of enrollment decline and job shortages. Some businessmen like the idea of exposing students to the world of work, and others like having students as employees or interns, but most business organizations are too concerned with productivity and profits to bother with more than a few visits or lectures. This belies the labor movement's fear that career education is a rate-busting, anti-union gimmick, but the fear has nonetheless helped to limit serious work opportunities for adolescents. And all these factors are given added force by a sluggish economy and high unemployment rates. "Letting teenagers out of school to work may be a great learning device, but it isn't viable today because it's really a full-employment idea," according to Walter Davis, education director of the AFL-CIO. Stagflation is not exactly a powerful stimulus for innovation.

Of course, this doesn't prove that the innovative ideas are wrong. Perhaps it only shows that the established order perverted a sound reform. And there is at least one very small program, still in its early development, which has met with more success.[4] But other forces besides the power of established institutions account for the sad fate of most career-education programs. One is that the movement is a professional phenomenon. The reform was not the brainchild of businessmen eager to reorganize the division of work and enrich their experience through teaching; nor was it the creation of workers bored with their tasks, seeking to improve their work and deepen their relationships with youth. Instead, it was conceived by university academics and public-school reformers, based on their pained vision of what was wrong with adolescents and school. As a result, like many other social programs, the career-education movement turned out to rest on a very narrow grouping of interests and to express a very narrow range of opinion about the relationship be-

---

[4] The National Institute of Education has supported one program—Experience-Based Career Education—which seems to have produced some real changes. At present, it operates in a few heavily subsidized demonstration schools.

tween education and work. As the programs were implemented, the reformers discovered just how diverse the competing views were. Far from winning converts, the reformers only seemed to have accentuated the divisions of opinion about work and school.

Indeed, the brief experience with this reform suggests that there are powerful competing fantasies about the relationship between school and work that are a serious impediment to change. The reformers see school as a pallid bore, and they think that real experience can teach many students more of the things they need to know. They think work is often a much more potent stimulus to learning than school. They think real experience should redeem the barren lives of students trapped in classrooms.

But vast segments of the society disagree. The spokesmen of organized labor think that much work is dull and intrinsically unsatisfying, and they see school as a redeeming force. As society becomes more modern, they think more work will become routine and mundane. As a result, they expect that people will need to find satisfaction in other things, and that school can help them. Thus they see career education as a move in the wrong direction, an effort to prepare students for adult lives narrowly defined by work. Career education, they fear, will make school parochial, and limit opportunities to find fulfillment in other parts of life. "Career educators give only passing attention to other purposes of school," one labor official said, "but there is a lot more to education than preparing kids to hold jobs. They need to learn to fulfill themselves, to understand and appreciate our culture, to become informed consumers. People don't necessarily fulfill themselves in a job."

Fantasies about modernity

These differences are important, for they reveal two important areas of ambivalence caught up in the career-education movement that help explain both its broad appeal and its weak implementation. One area concerns the sort of education that will be the best preparation for life. The old fantasy is familiar—the chief purpose of education is to expand opportunities and increase the potential of students to lead full and satisfying lives; education is an advantage that should be equally available and encouraged by delayed entry to work. By contrast, career education seems a newer fantasy—that schooling often impedes the preparation for life, and reduces the opportunity to find meaningful relationships with adults and to acquire economic and social skills.

But while the ideas seem novel, this recent reform movement evokes an old American conflict concerning modernization. School has seemed the best preparation for an industrial and highly technological society for more than a century now, but it also struck Americans as a necessity only because older institutions—family, apprenticeship, and community—seemed to have been severely weakened by modernization. Schools were needed because it seemed that socialization and career skills could no longer be provided on an informal basis in natural settings. For generations this diagnosis seemed to lead inexorably to the notion that formal schooling should replace informal learning on the path to adulthood. Now, because of spreading disillusionment with the effectiveness of schools, it seems that a return to informal learning is a better way of solving the problems of modernization. Of course, this ambivalence has never been far from the surface of American life. Many reformers of Horace Mann's generation sang the glories of informal learning in earlier, simpler communities—just as they organized madly to establish the formal schools that would meet the needs of the modern industrial age. And in a later version of the same story, John Dewey opposed his ideas about learning through experience to what struck him as the arid, empty formalism of the educational systems so recently established. Dewey's ideas later became parodied by the "Life Adjustment Education" movement, and career education promises to continue this tradition. Americans have long been torn by competing fantasies of modernity and competing ideas about the sort of education that will help, but whichever dream they choose, their expectations have been extravagant.

There is a related ambivalence concerning formal and informal institutions, and a similar pattern of high hopes. Modernization has long struck many as a destructive force, nearly sweeping society off its foundations, but from this dark diagnosis the ideologists of both formal schooling and informal learning have brought forth sunny and hopeful notions. Whether it is getting children into schools or out of them, reformers in both camps have thought that reshuffling institutions would overcome the threats of modernization. This is another familiar pattern of the history of social reform in America. When existing institutions seem inadequate to respond to changing social conditions, reformers frequently propose to loosen the boundaries between formal institutions and the larger society. They seek to shift responsibility from formal organizations to informal social arrangements. The recent call for penal reform, for example, centers on breaking down barriers between prisons and society by integrating inmates into the community through work-release programs, furloughs, and halfway houses. The notion is that community has a curative effect, that it offers more effective treatment than the institutions themselves. This notion has strong populist roots, and it evokes images of a simpler time in which people cared for each other through the bonds of family, community, and religion. The hope seems to be to recapture the past by creating it in the present.

This hope is easily nourished by the apparent ineffectiveness of formal institutions, for they regularly fail to live up to expectations. Formal schooling doesn't help train many who would prefer to be elsewhere, and it doesn't help those unfamiliar with the school culture, or those put off by it. Nor does schooling solve all the problems it has been supposed to, whether family decay, worker training, poverty, or auto accidents. This should be no surprise, since formal schooling is only a minor influence on students affected by much more powerful social arrangements—family, ethnicity, social-class or economic-class membership, and the like.

But the hopes for informal learning nourished by these failures are set on similarly frail foundations. In the division of labor produced by modernization, formerly private responsibilities—caring for the old, socializing the young, protecting and controlling deviants—have increasingly been committed to public experts. Now, when reformers call on the commuity to reconvene, the relevant people or institutions often have neither the time, nor the resources, nor the bonds of personal acquaintance, nor the motives to respond. The informal social arrangements supposed to assume the roles of failed formal institutions are not there in much strength. As a result, grand hopes such as those for career education fail to produce much in practice. The dreams of informal learning and community education regularly fall victim to the realities of a complex and formal social division of labor.

In a sense, these two areas of ambivalence frame the structure of social policy in education, and it would be foolish to think that there are simple ways to resolve them. But two points may be useful. First, these contrary fantasies about coping with modernity may themselves be part of the problem, for they often involve exaggerated ideas about both the damnations of modern life and the saving grace of either formal institutions or natural experience. Second, in seeking to deal with the inadequacies of formal institutions, it might make sense to recognize the limitations of informal alternatives in this post-industrial world. If the experience in penal reform, mental health, and juvenile justice is any example, it would probably pay to think in terms of inventing new community institutions—or offering strong inducements and supports to existing ones—rather than supposing that informal institutions will more or less naturally pick up the slack. Informal education and experiential learning may make sense, but they seem unlikely to find their way into practice without more institutional support and social inventiveness than current fantasies have mobilized. Lacking these things, innovative programs like career education seem likely to slip into the chasm between extravagant hopes for the natural and informal, and the realities of an increasingly formal and specialized social structure.

Moral education in the schools

WILLIAM J. BENNETT & EDWIN J. DELATTRE

THE belief that moral values should be taught to young Americans in the schools is at least as old as the nation itself. Thomas Jefferson's *Bill for the More General Diffusion of Knowledge* argued for an educational system that would fortify citizens with moral probity to resist the schemes of the enemies of liberty. In his *Proposals Relating to the Education of Youth in Pennsylvania,* Benjamin Franklin prescribed the study of ethics in an instructional program that would seek to instill "benignity of mind." Perhaps the most explicit embodiment of this drive to inculcate the young with moral lessons is to be found in *McGuffey's Readers.* On another level, John Dewey's forceful and highly influential writings concerning the interdependence of democracy, education, and moral character are a modern reformulation of the old belief that "virtue" can and should be taught in the schools. To be sure, an opposite belief—that the schools should teach *no* values, but should stick to imparting skills and basic knowledge—also has its adherents among educators and social theorists. But more and more in recent years, and especially now, in the aftermath of Watergate and accounts of corruption in government and business, there has been a call for reemphasizing moral education in the schools.

At the moment the entire discussion is dominated by two figures: Sidney Simon, of the School of Education at the University of Massachusetts, who advocates "values clarification," and Lawrence Kohlberg, of Harvard and the Center for Moral Education, who calls for "cognitive moral development." Although they differ in important ways, and although their respective followings are in different segments of the educational community, Simon and Kohlberg share an enormous popularity. Both are widely sought after for "workshops" in their methods, and their programs have gained broad support among the nation's teachers and are increasingly used in the classroom.

Simon and Kohlberg agree in rejecting what they regard as the fundamental error of traditional approaches to moral education in this country—what they call "indoctrination." In their shared opinion, moral education has amounted in the past to little more than an attempt by elders to "impose" values upon the young. They claim to offer something different, and better. In fact, what they offer is different, but certainly no better.

"Values clarification"

Sidney Simon's approach is the most widely used new method of moral education in elementary and secondary schools (though less well known in college circles). The theory behind it begins by criticizing traditional moral "indoctrination" as useless for making sense out of life: Traditional moral education is irrelevant today because the modern world is uniquely difficult and complex, and young people are confused as never before. "The children of today," Simon writes, "are confronted by many more choices than in previous generations":

> Areas of confusion and conflict abound: politics, religion, love and sex, family, friends, drugs, materialism, race, work, aging and death, leisure time, school, and health. Each area demands decisions that yesterday's children were rarely called upon to make.

Even more troubling than the ineffectiveness of "indoctrination" is the traditional principle that there are right and wrong ways of acting, right and wrong ways of thinking. In fact, Simon asserts, "none of us has the 'right' set of values to pass on to other people's children." Thus there is a need for a new approach—values clarification.

Values clarification is concerned not with "the *content* of people's values, but with the *process of valuing*." Its aims are to promote growth, freedom, and ethical maturity and to enable children to know "how to negotiate the lovely banquet of life ahead of them." These stated aims will be furthered if teachers, parents, and other adults commit themselves to the view that "there's no right or wrong answer" to any question of value. The process of values clarification is taught in classroom "simulations" in which students are offered various choices and taken through exercises (called "strategies") designed to encourage them to make a conscious effort to discover their "own" values. Simon describes the value of this process in these words:

> Each of you who is a parent could leave your own children no legacy more precious than for them to have years of experience in knowing what they want, having learned to set their priorities and rank order the marvelous items in life's cafeteria.

Much of Simon's writing consists of specific "strategies" designed for use in the school and home. In a typical exercise a student might be asked to answer the following:

1. Which do you think is the most religious thing to do on a Sunday morning?
    a. Go to church to hear a very good preacher
    b. Listen to some classical music on the radio
    c. Have a big breakfast with the family
2. Which do you like least?
    a. An uptight indoctrinator
    b. A cynical debunker
    c. A dull, boring fact giver
3. During a campus protest where would you be most likely to be found?
    a. In the midst of it
    b. Gaping at it from across the street
    c. In the library minding your own business

In making these and other similar choices, the student supposedly moves toward fulfillment of the Socratic ideal of self-knowledge. By answering and *knowing* his answer, according to Simon, he gains insight into himself, which in time brings clarity about his values. The student is then prepared to move freely and confidently in the world.

Other values-clarification exercises are more extensive. One "strategy" is called *Who are all those others? And what are they doing in my life?* A diagram dominates one page of the text: "ME" is at the center, with lines extending to blocks representing other people, e.g., "important teacher, a parent-guardian, best friend." The student is asked:

> Essentially, what do they count on you for? What demands do they place on you? What do they want you to be, to do, to think? What do they want you to value? . . . Consider the similarities and differences between what the various people in your life want from you. . . .

In another "strategy," called *Who Comes to My House,* the student is to consider "an inventory of the symbolic warehouse of your life." He is told to ask, "How many people are invited to your house only because you feel obligated to them?" Simon comments on this "strategy":

> When you come to think of it, there is something silly, certainly something nonessential, about paying off obligations, about spending too much precious leisure time with people who are millstones. . . .
>
> There are, of course, "Responsibility People," those toward whom we have an important personal obligation; perhaps an elderly relative or infirm "other." These are responsibilities that, for the most part, we bear graciously, keeping in mind the inevitability of the aging process. To be kind and to help those who need us demonstrates a personal value we respect.
>
> On the other hand, we can choose to spend our time with those who give as they take, who offer at least as much as they receive.

In *Priorities,* Simon "asks you and your family at the dinner table, or your friends across the lunch table, to rank choices and to defend those choices in friendly discussion." One example of Simon's "delightful possibilities" for mealtime discussion is this:

> Your husband or wife is a very attractive person. Your best friend is very attracted to him or her. How would you want them to behave?
> a. Maintain a clandestine relationship so you wouldn't know about it
> b. Be honest and accept the reality of the relationship
> c. Proceed with a divorce

Values-clarification strategies, says Simon, enable the student to achieve knowledge about values, free from the inhibitory inculcation of adults. Despite an admitted shortage of empirical evidence, Simon claims positive results: "Students have become less apathetic, less flighty, less conforming as well as less overdissenting."[1]

---

[1] In defense of his methods against what he regards as powerful dogmatic and political traditions of indoctrination, Simon sometimes disparages his opponents in authoritarian terms, thus avoiding the need to consider the merits or shortcomings of their arguments. For example, when the school district in Great Neck, New York, cut from its budget funds for training teachers in values clarification, Simon was quoted as saying, "An orthodox Jewish, right-wing group got hold of it and just raised hell."

"Simulations" or indoctrination?

Values-clarification "strategies" are supposed to give students the greatest possible freedom of choice and knowledge of themselves and the world. By accepting the idea that there are no right or wrong answers to questions of morality and conduct, students learn that being clear about what one wants is all that is required to live well. But do such "strategies" really provide knowledge about the world and freedom of choice? Do they actually make for self-knowledge and ethical maturity and autonomy? Or do they encourage something else? Simon's examples are instructive—in more ways than one.

The first exercise, about the most religious thing to do on a Sunday morning, asks the student to think about what he wants and likes to do on Sunday mornings. Yet it introduces no other considerations, and implies that whatever the student thinks is religious thereby is religious.

The second exercise asks the student to say which of three unattractive choices he likes least—an uptight indoctrinator, a cynical debunker, or a dull, boring fact-giver. Here again, the student is asked to consider only what he likes and dislikes. Moreover, it is assumed that these three are all meaningful choices to the students. No other possibilities or greater descriptions of these people are offered for consideration before a choice is made. The suggestion is clearly that factual information is necessarily boring, debunking necessarily cynical, indoctrination necessarily uptight.

In the exercise on campus protest, the student again answers on the basis of his immediate likes and dislikes, without any knowledge of the circumstances and other germane information about the protest. In this "strategy," it is not relevant whether the protest is a violent, illegal take-over of a university building, or a peaceful, legal demonstration against such an action.

The first of the longer exercises, *Who are all those others? And what are they doing in my life?* centers on the student and instructs him to consider other people only in terms of his and their wants and demands. Any larger aspects of their relationship to him—what they really are doing in his life—are not included in this "strategy."

In *Who Comes to My House,* the student is asked to think of people who are invited to his home only because he "feels obligated to them." The student is then told that "paying off obligations" is "silly" and "non-essential." He is also told that while he may graciously bear responsibilities toward elderly relatives, he can choose instead to spend time with people "who offer at least as much as they receive." The student's "precious leisure time" and what he wants to do with it are, again, the main considerations in the exercise. Elderly and infirm people are presented, *a priori,* as "millstones," and the exercise assumes that the student will not want to spend time with them. Further, in the options offered, the student is treated as if his wants always conflicted with his obligations. Note that it is never assumed that the student wants to be decent.

The last exercise asks the student how he would want his spouse and best friend to behave if they were attracted to each other. Typically, the spouse and best friend are presented as having desires they will eventually satisfy anyway: The student is offered only choices that presuppose their relationship. All possibilities for self-restraint, fidelity, regard for others, or respect for mutual relationships and commitments are ignored.

All these examples attest to the failure of Simon's approach to live up to his claims. They involve not "values" but only desires and self-gratification; they do little more than glorify a doctrine of the primacy of wants—the wants, likes, and dislikes of the student and of others. The "strategies" thus offer severely limited and misleading options for conduct. Moreover, the exercises are indifferent throughout to relevant facts—except those that Simon *wants* the student to consider. Absent in all the examples are many considerations—circumstances, context, history—to which moral judgment must be attentive. As a result, these exercises seem more likely to promote hasty, ill-informed, ignorant, and precipitous judgment than any kind of informed free choice. The student is hardly free to make creative choices, since he is closed in by the narrow options Simon gives him. Since the student is taught that clarity about one's desires is the only thing that matters, the importance of knowledgeable, informed, and conscientious judgment in life is entirely obscured.

The "strategies" thus reveal the moral content of Simon's approach. People are bundles of wants; the world is a battlefield of conflicting wants; and no one has room for goodness, decency, or the capacity for a positive exercise of will. Moral maturity is certainly not to be found in the clarification of values, which is cast solely in the language of narrow self-gratification and is devoid of any considerations of decency whatsoever. Finally and ironically, Simon's approach emphatically indoctrinates—by encouraging and even exhorting the student to narcissistic self-gratification.

"Cognitive moral development"

Kohlberg's work is also gaining in influence and popularity; but although its impact and following in the schools is increasing, Kohlberg's highest standing is among his colleagues in the university community—particularly in departments of psychology and philosophy, and in schools of education. Kohlberg regards values clarification as useful to some degree, but ultimately of limited value: Besides leaving unsolved problems, "a firm restriction to values clarification merges into an actual teaching that ethical relativity is true." Kohlberg believes that relativism is philosophically and scientifically false, and claims to offer instead a version of a long-standing account of objective moral truth: a "reassertion of the Platonic faith in the power of the rational good."

Kohlberg's position emerges from a much more extensive and complicated theoretical background than Simon's. Relying on a series of cultural and anthropological studies, Kohlberg contends that there is a universal and invariant series of six stages of cognitive moral development; that reaching any stage requires passing through the preceding sequence; and that each successive stage is morally superior to those preceding it. Although human beings may stop at any stage in the invariant sequence, they can be stimulated to ascend the scale.

Kohlberg agrees with Simon that moral education has, up to this time, been dominated by "indoctrination." He says that "traditional moral education . . . [is] undemocratic and unconstitutional." Kohlberg stresses the need for a new psychology and a new philosophy that recognizes "the child's right to freedom from indoctrination." Adults are to view the child not as a pupil but as a "moral philosopher" in his own right. Claiming to follow a tradition running from Socrates through Dewey and Piaget, Kohlberg argues that the sole justifiable end of moral education is cognitive moral development and that only exercises involving moral dilemmas and conflicts can promote such development. This strategy, Kohlberg says, reflects a "progressive ideology" with a "liberal, democratic, and non-indoctrinative" notion of education. Kohlberg sometimes even stresses the "revolutionary nature" of his program.

Kohlberg's six stages of cognitive moral development, in order of temporal sequence and moral value, are as follows. Stage One is *"The punishment and obedience orientation,"* in which the child defers to the superior position or power of the parent, teacher, or authority figure: "The physical consequences of action determine its goodness or badness regardless of the human meaning or value of these consequences." Stage Two is *"The instrumental relativist orientation,"* in which right action consists of instrumentally satisfying one's own needs and occasionally the needs of others. Stage Three is *"The inter-personal concordance or 'good boy-nice girl' orientation,"* in which the child seeks the approval of others and conforms to stereotypes concerning good behavior and the value of helping others. Stage Four, where Kohlberg claims most citizens peak and most civilized societies dwell, is *"The law and order orientation,"* involving obedience to authority, fixed rules, and the maintenance of the social order. Stage Five is *"The social contract-legalistic orientation,"* which recognizes the importance of an arbitrary element of, or starting point for, rules or expectations, for the utilitarian purpose of agreement. Stage Six is *"The universal ethical principle orientation,"* the apex of morality:

> Right is defined by the decision of conscience in accord with self-chosen *ethical principles* appealing to logical comprehensiveness, universality, and consistency. . . . At heart, these are universal principles of *justice,* of the *reciprocity* and *equality* of human *rights,* and of respect for the dignity of human beings as *individual persons* [italics in the original].

According to Kohlberg, "There is only one principled basis for resolving claims: justice or equality. Treat every man's claim impartially regardless of the man." With an approving nod toward John Rawls, whose philosophical position also fundamentally emphasizes equality, Kohlberg describes Stage Six in the following terms:

> To summarize, I have found a no more recent summary statement of the implications of our studies than that made by Socrates:
> First, virtue is ultimately one, not many, and it is always the same ideal form regardless of climate or culture.
> Second, the name of this ideal form is justice.
> Third, not only is the good one, but virtue is knowledge of the good. He who knows the good chooses the good.
> Fourth, the kind of knowledge of the good which is virtue is philosophical knowledge or intuition of the ideal form of the good, not correct opinion or acceptance of conventional beliefs.
> Most psychologists have never believed any of these ideas of Socrates. Is it so surprising that psychologists have never understood Socrates? It is hard to understand if you are not Stage Six.

In Kohlberg's view, "the basic referent of the term 'moral' is a type of *judgment* or a type of *decision-making process,* not a type of behavior, emotion, or social institution"; "Morality is a unique *sui generis* realm." His account of morality includes a disclaimer:

> We make no direct claims about the ultimate aims of men, about the good life. . . . These are problems beyond the scope of the sphere of morality or moral principles, which we define as principles of choice for resolving conflicts of obligation.

Moral education must therefore be non-indoctrinating, democratic, and directed toward justice and equality.

The effective teacher who employs the materials provided by Kohlberg and his followers is "something of a revolutionary, rather than an instiller of virtues." He is expected to be neutral, not imposing his own or other values on the students, but providing a stimulus for students to move through the stages of moral development on their own. Kohlberg says, with another authority (Israel Sheffler), that "to teach . . . is . . . to submit oneself to the understanding and independent judgment of the pupil, to his demand for reasons, to his sense of what constitutes an adequate explanation." The presentation of dilemmas creates internal cognitive conflict, inspiring the student "to see things previously invisible to him"; thus "the whole idea is to encourage students . . . to argue with each other." Students vote on dilemmas in class, to insure that there is sufficient disagreement to create conflict, but they must close their eyes so that none will be influenced by the others.

Examples of simple dilemmas are provided which, along with a standard scoring manual, set forth a series of "criterion judgments" that enable teachers to see where students are on the moral-development continuum. The teacher's responsibility is to use the dilemmas to show the child the insufficiency of his present stage of reasoning in comparison with the reasoning of the next stage. The teacher scores the child by matching student responses with the responses given in the manual for the different stages, by keeping track of the number of Stage One responses, Stage Two responses, and so on, and by noting progress from one level to the next. The teacher is instructed to establish a "non-judgmental atmosphere," and not to be "the enforcer of demands"; the teacher is advised "to relax and enjoy it," even to "swing with it."

Dealing with dilemmas

An example of a dilemma is presented in *Affiliative Roles and Relationships*. A mother promises her 12-year-old daughter, Judy, that she may go to a rock concert if she saves enough money. Judy saves $5 for the ticket and $3 more. But her mother then changes her mind and tells Judy she must spend the money for new school clothes. Judy goes to the rock concert anyway, after telling her mother that she saved only $3 and went to her friend's house for the day. Later, Judy confesses her lie to her older sister, Louise. In the *Standard Scoring Manual*, the main question about this dilemma is, "Should a daughter [Louise] help her mother exercise authority even if doing so means that her sister's contract or property rights will be violated?" Then for the teacher's use, subsidiary questions are offered:

1. In wondering whether to tell, Louise thinks of the fact that Judy is her sister. Should that make a difference in Louise's decision?
2. What do you think is the most important thing for a good daughter to be concerned about in her relationship to her mother in this or other situations?

At Stage One, or more precisely at Stage One-A, the "bottom level," the student responds that Louise should tell because "Louise *or* Judy will be punished when their mother finds out." A Stage One-B answer is that "Louise should tell *or* a daughter should obey her mother; since the mother is older, she knows more, is smarter, knows what's best, etc." An "Optimal Example" answer of reasoning at the bottom level comes in response to questions about what is most important in the relationship between mother and daughter. The dialogue supposedly goes like this: "[Student:] "Be honest. [Teacher:] Why? [Student:] Because it is her mother and she should keep promises to her because she is older. [Teacher:] Why? [Student:] She knows more and knows what's best."

From this "low" point the student should progress upward to Stage Two (Louise tells because of concern that Judy "might try to get away with lying or deceiving her mother all the time"); to Stage Three ("A good daughter should recognize that her mother loves her and has her best interests at heart"); to Stage Four ("Louise should tell her mother about Judy's lying out of respect for her mother's authority and in recognition of the fact that the mother is responsible for making decisions concerning her daughter's conduct and welfare.") This particular dilemma only goes as far as Stage Five, where the manual presents a fairly elaborate articulation of "Role Norm Obligations" and "Fairness and Equity." The answer at this level is, "The mother had no right to forbid Judy to go to the concert because Judy is an individual with rights equal to her mother's." At this stage, the answer to the second subsidiary question is this:

The most important thing the mother should recognize in the mother-daughter relationship is that her daughter is a free and unique individual who should be treated as such.

The manual describes this peak of moral reasoning:

This judgment focuses on the obligation to respect each person's individuality or right to autonomy without imposition upon that person of one's own expectations. . . .

The "Optimal Example" is characterized as follows:

A good mother should early respect her daughter as a person, as an individual with needs, and rights and emotions. If possible she should always deal directly and straightforwardly with her daughter; not condescendingly or authoritarianly.

The mother had no right to forbid Judy to go to the concert because Judy is an individual with rights equal to her mother's. [Students] may say that Judy's youth or ostensibly subordinate role as daughter should not be regarded as a morally relevant consideration. . . . The mother's authority is legitimate only insofar as it is based on mutual respect, is just, and could be freely accepted by all parties with informed consent.

And other examples of Stage-Five sophistication are offered:

What is a daughter but a person, and should be treated as such. Double standards should not exist for a subperson-children, over whom you have "power" and others over whom you don't. . . . A mother may guide or suggest the most advantageous use of property, but must not impose herself on her children, and accept their decisions and properties, as she must for other people as well, and may not use the excuse that they are too young to manage such things, to rule two lives and consciences. . . . When people are reacted to as people not as threats to one's self, or as an instrument for your power, but as people, is the only way harmony will ever begin to exist in the conscience and the world.

A full book of such dilemmas, *Hypothetical Dilemmas for Use in Moral Discussions*, has been prepared and distributed by the Moral Education and Research Foundation at Harvard. This is a typical dilemma found in the book:

Sex as a Need: The Johnson family (with four children) was a very happy and close one. Mr. and Mrs. Johnson were in their 30's. One day Mr. Johnson fell from a third-story building where he was working. He broke his back in this accident and was totally paralyzed from his waist down. The accident did not result in economic hardship because of workmen's compensation. Three months after the accident, when Mr. Johnson came home, the problem began. Ms. [*sic*] Johnson, who was a young person, realized that she would have to give up sexual intercourse with her husband. If she did not want to give up her sex life, she had the following choices: either get a divorce, or to have extramarital affairs.

1. Is it possible to separate sex from affection? What do you think she should do? Give reasons.

2. Do you think this woman should remain married to the husband? Why or why not?

3. What do you think would happen to the family if she had an affair?

4. If she decides to have an affair, should she tell her husband or keep it a secret? Why?

The remaining 50 dilemmas deal with similar crises. Twenty-one are related to sexual conflicts—homosexuality, swapping, extramarital sex. There are simple one- or two-page statements about the dilemmas of My Lai, Daniel Berrigan, Daniel Ellsberg, women's liberation, kidney transplants, Mayor Daley, draft evasion, abortion, and choosing one child over another.

A curious libertarianism

Kohlberg purports to have advanced far beyond the relativism and glorified idiosyncrasy of the Simon approach.[2] He claims to be returning to a rich philosophical tradition—that of Socrates, Plato, and Dewey—which has justifiably long been regarded as powerful and insightful. Moral education, in Kohlberg's account, does have an intellectual core: The exchange of ideas between teacher and student suggests a process that is an improvement over Simon's method. Kohlberg's belief that students can become more rational through education does indeed reaffirm, in principle, the faith of this tradition.

Kohlberg says his approach is designed to lead students through stages of moral development to greater and greater objectivity in their moral judgments. The ideal perspective, Stage Six, involves viewing the claims of others with "justice," that is, treating "every man's claim impartially regardless of the man." As the examples amply demonstrate, in Kohlberg's view, moral claims are to be decided by considering individual "rights." Presumably, the student progresses to an ever more impartial evaluation of respective claims to "rights." There is thus a distinct libertarian emphasis in

---

[2] This difference of opinion should not be exaggerated, however. In the Great Neck controversy, Kohlberg testified on behalf of Simon. Kohlberg commented that the "protestors" insisted that values should not be dealt with in the school, but should be left for the church and home.

Kohlberg, revealing his dislike of what he regards as the imposition of authority—by parents, rules, or traditional forms of indoctrination. Kohlberg's libertarianism is intended to remind the student that the rights of all must be respected equally: Moral judgment to a very large extent involves assessing competing claims of individuals about their rights.

The example of Judy and her mother, for example, is discussed in the language of the rights of each—Judy's right to go to the concert with "her" money (her contract and property rights) and her mother's alleged right to exercise authority. (The mother's "right" to have her daughter tell her the truth is never mentioned.) But in the progress up Kohlberg's scale, as the child supposedly gains in moral perspicuity, the mother's rights and her claims to rights get dimmer and dimmer, while Judy's rights seem to grow and to dominate the discussion. In the "enlightened" Stage Five, the mother has no right to forbid Judy to go to the concert, because Judy has "equal" rights. In fact, however, the mother's rights at this level have almost evaporated; Judy's "equal rights" appear to be more than equal to her mother's. The mother's rights are subordinated to her obligations, specifically the obligation to respect her daughter's rights. It is as if Judy is assumed to be disadvantaged; Kohlberg takes Judy, as a daughter, to be a victim of parental authority. In the progress upward through the stages, Judy increasingly gains support for her claims. The "optimal answers" stress that "a good mother should early respect her daughter as a person" and that "the mother had no right to forbid Judy." Reciprocity—real equality of claims to rights—seems to be absent.

According to Kohlberg's *theory*, students should impartially consider the rights of all the people involved in the example about the Johnson family. But in the narrative and the questions, the emphasis is entirely on Ms. Johnson's rights, desires, and rights to her desires. The student is invited to consider and focus on her choices, divorce or extramarital affairs, and whether she has the right to these things. Mr. Johnson's and the children's choices and rights are not discussed. With all the theoretical emphasis on the importance and value of impartiality, this example clearly seems sympathetic toward the "predicament" of Ms. Johnson and uncaring toward that of Mr. Johnson and the children. It is as if Mr. Johnson and the children lost their rights, including their right to consideration, when Mr. Johnson fell from the building. Again, paradoxically, only one person in a complex relationship seems to be entitled to "equal consideration in the matter": Ms. Johnson is taken to be *the* disadvantaged individual. The example ignores justice, reciprocity, and the equality and equal rights of all the persons involved.

The "hidden curriculum"

An additional and increasingly dominant thread in Kohlberg's thinking is that treating the child as a "moral philosopher" and stimulating moral development require a commitment by educators to create a "just community" in the school, because of what Kohlberg calls the "hidden curriculum" in most schools. This "hidden curriculum" embodies the values of the teachers and administrators, which are never made explicit to students but are ultimately used to evaluate them, and which express "the moral atmosphere of the school." The function of the "hidden curriculum," according to Kohlberg, is "moral education or perhaps miseducation." He gives an example of some of its dangers:

> To make the point I took a trivial episode. My son, then in the second grade, came home from school one day saying, "I don't want to be one of the bad boys at school." I asked, "Who are they," and he answered, "They are the boys who don't put their books away, and they get yelled at" . . . [The] guts of the hidden curriculum are the praise, the teacher's use of rewards or punishment; the crowd, or the life in a crowded group; and the teacher's power.

Kohlberg believes that his vision of moral education will do away with the "hidden curriculum." He concludes that the moral development of students depends upon a sense of working together for a just society in schools, "based on concepts of justice and participatory democracy."

Kohlberg offers an example of a real-life dilemma arising in an actual "just school": the experience of one of his disciples, Elsa Wasserman, at the Cluster School in Cambridge. There, according to Wasserman's description, "black and white students argue about a decision to correct racial injustice as they see it in their school community"; this suggests the benefits of a "just community" to Kohlberg—"that a school based on concepts of justice and participatory democracy can be a community which operates close to the level of its highest members and continues to progress upward." Wasserman offers the following example to show the "viable democracy," "moral growth," and "consideration for fairness" found at the school:

> This year a difficult issue of fairness focused on the admission of students for six remaining openings in the school. There were 47

white students in the school and 18 black students. The black students wanted more equal representation in the community. But there were already six students on the waiting list, only one of whom was black. The democracy class proposed that all six openings be filled by blacks.

Here is the student dialogue. A white student responded to the proposal:

Does that mean that there's only one black on it now, but you want to get five more blacks to jump in front of the rest of the waiting line?

A black student replied:

I'm one of the people that wants some black people to come in. . . . From what I see I feel I would be more comfortable with them here. I want them here. . . .

Another white countered:

If they were all black people [on the waiting list], it would be fair to let them in. I don't care if there were six black people on the waiting list, they could come in, but these five white people, they were first, right?

Still another white student asked:

But why can't everybody accept the fact that the blacks would feel more comfortable and get a better education with more blacks in school?

Another black student asked:

Can I ask all you white people something? I'm not prejudiced, but is it going to make that much difference if there's six more black people instead of white? Is it? There's 47 of you whites now. There's 18 blacks. Six more blacks isn't going to make one difference.

Still another black student concluded:

Never in my life have I seen as many of you who have outnumbered me and mine, anyway. O.K., then I get to know them. I say, these whites are all right. . . . And then I came back here and I try to get some of my brothers and sisters at this school so they can be helped like I'm being helped. And what do I hear? No. Because they don't want to hear it. Why can't they just give us 18 blacks a little personal satisfaction with ourselves to have some more of us so we can be together? All right. (Applause.)

Following this the community voted. A majority was in favor of the proposal. One student in opposition asked:

> The reason I voted against the proposal was that I wanted to hear more reasons from the black kids but I'm also feeling a little guilty because I want six black kids to come in, but I don't know what to say about the five white kids on the waiting list. What are we going to tell them?

Wasserman writes that the following justification for the decision was offered:

> All you have to do is explain to them that the community decided that it was the best idea to take all blacks this time for the community's sake and from now on, every June we're going to admit more kids, we'll admit half-black, half-white. By then eventually, it will be fairer and we can accept blacks and whites the same way.

The "viable democracy" then voted "almost unanimously" to adopt the proposal.

The reasoning of the students and the outcome of their vote are celebrated as an example of a community moving upward through stages of moral development to respect for justice. Yet the facts suggest something else. The one student concerned to treat the whites on the waiting list impartially—in Kohlberg's words, "to treat every man's claim impartially regardless of the man"—is never answered. His request for reasons that would show that something is wrong with the color-blind admissions policy and the rules of the school, and his clear willingness to listen to the arguments of other students despite their indifference to his, are answered with *a priori* assertions clearly favoring the other point of view without offering reasons. In fact, the entire discussion is weighted against reasons. "I want them here," says one student; "Blacks would feel more comfortable and get a better education," says another; "Give us blacks a little personal satisfaction," says a third. These responses—fairly characterized in Kohlberg's own terms as primarily the kind of instrumental relativism found in lower Stage Two—are not arguments; they are not reasons; and they clearly treat color and personal desires as overriding other factors, ignoring justice and impartiality and the questions of troubled students.

Kohlberg treats the discourse and the solution as exemplary of moral progress and objectivity, even though the teachers and the majority of the students do not consider claims, questions, or rights objectively. If this "just community" is to be praised, it cannot be in terms of justice and impartiality. At the end, the result is a pronunciamento of a "general will" of the "democracy class"—a tyranny of a particular majority over the students who ask questions (and over their rights), and over those on the waiting list who have a reasonable expectation to have themselves and their rights "treated equally." With chilling arrogance, the democracy class informs its opposition, "All you have to do is explain that the community decided that it was the best idea. . . ." This is very far from Kohlberg's libertarian celebration of Stage Six morality, and far from deciding questions on the basis of a "universal, ethical principle orientation."

The dismal science of pedagogy

As these and other examples suggest, practice does not square with theory in Kohlberg's universe. His theory appears to be transformed in practice into a particular ideology giving certain individuals and groups of individuals rights more than equal to those of others. The claims of those in authority and the claims of rules always yield to the claims of the "disadvantaged," or those whom Kohlberg takes to be disadvantaged. In this way, the examples belie the theory of impartial justice, suggesting progress less toward impartial justice—an appreciation of the power of the rational good—than toward sharing his sympathies and dispositions regarding the special claims of those victims of authority.

Whether or not this is a reasonable approach to moral education, it certainly conflicts with Kohlberg's theoretical edifice and its claims of impartiality. In this respect, Kohlberg himself conceals what can fairly be called a "hidden curriculum" of instruction in partial justice. This is not a program for justice as fairness to all parties regardless of the man, or for promoting principled, objective moral development.

In fact, it must be doubted whether what Kohlberg describes is really morality at all. Morality takes place among human beings and not among disembodied bearers of "rights," who are incessantly engaged in squabbling about them. Morality is concerned with doing good, with sacrifice, altruism, love, courage, honor, and compassion, and with fidelity and large-mindedness regarding one's station, commitments, family, friends, colleagues, and society in general. Morality among men is not merely legalistic and formalistic, it does not consist merely of so many non-negotiable demands.

Both Simon and Kohlberg also fail to avoid indoctrination. Both of their programs offer indoctrination in the "values" they take to be important—the celebration of wants and desires, the exhortation to self-gratification, and a particular ideology of rights and "special justice." Although they both claim to disavow traditional moral education because it indoctrinates, Simon and Kohlberg clearly do not oppose indoctrination per se, but the indoctrination of traditional values.

Yet Simon and Kohlberg's view of the world—the message they deliver, the values they recommend—is worth a good deal less than much of what they oppose. To them, goodness simply does not exist: People press for their wants or their rights and are continually at each other's throats. Although Simon and Kohlberg dislike authority, each offers a program that would impose on students an authority much more malevolent in its consequences than any traditional form of authority or "indoctrination." The tyranny of the passions and of minorities and majorities—the arbitrary exercise of power by special groups, be they advantaged or disadvantaged—offers not more freedom, but less, and a far less attractive world. Subjected only to one's wants or to the whims of special groups wielding arbitrary power, the individual and his life and moral relations are much bleaker than they actually are, or than they have traditionally been represented to be by the old to the young. In Simon and Kohlberg, responsibility and love are missing; life and man are oppressive; and the world is cold, ugly, brutish, and lonely. In this distorted view of life and morality, they fail to recognize the significance of what is possible among people across generations.

The barren world Simon and Kohlberg offer to students, teachers, and parents allows room for only an endless succession of conflicts and dilemmas. "Values clarification" and "cognitive moral development" neglect and deny precious and important features of morally mature life—friendship, love, fidelity, regard for work, care for home and family—which are, for the most part, not morally problematic. Finally, according to Simon and Kohlberg, there is no place for stories and lessons, no place for the passing on of knowledge and experience. Children are invited to a world where it is a travesty and an imposition for anyone to tell them the truth.

The "White Flight" Controversy

DIANE RAVITCH

IN the spring of 1975, James Coleman released the "preliminary results" of a new study concluding that school desegregation contributed to "white flight" from big cities and was fostering re-segregation of urban districts. On the basis of his findings, Coleman maintained that whites were leaving both large and middle-sized cities with high proportions of blacks, and specifically that whites in big cities were fleeing integration, while whites in middle-sized cities were "not moving any faster from rapidly integrating cities than from others." In short, according to Coleman, "the flight from integration appears to be principally a large-city phenomenon." In the most controversial passage of his study, Coleman argued:

> The extremely strong reactions of individual whites in moving their children out of large districts engaged in massive and rapid desegregation suggest that in the long run the policies that have been pursued will defeat the purpose of increasing overall contact among races in schools.... Thus a major policy implication of this analysis is that in an area such as school desegregation, which has important consequences for individuals and in which individuals retain control of some actions that can in the end defeat the policy, the courts are probably the worst instrument of social policy.

Coleman's study provoked bitter attacks from proponents of activist desegregation policies, such as Roy Wilkins and Kenneth Clark, not only because his findings were inimical to their cause, but because his "defection" seemed especially traitorous. After all, he had been the principal author of the Equal Educational Opportunity Survey (known as the Coleman Report), which had been authorized by Congress as part of the Civil Rights Act of 1964 and had served, since its publication in 1966, as the chief evidence of the beneficial effects of school desegregation. Coleman had also taken an outspoken public role as a leading scholarly advocate of school desegregation.

Coleman presented his paper (co-authored by Sara Kelly and John Moore of the Urban Institute) at a meeting of the American Educational Research Association on April 2, 1975, but it was not reported in *The New York Times* until June 7, 1975. (Some of Coleman's adversaries later attacked him for carrying his views to the press, but the delay in reporting the story indicates that he did not initiate the media attention.) Then, on July 11, 1975, Robert Reinhold of *The New York Times* reported that the 20 central-city districts in Coleman's study had not undergone court-ordered busing, and Coleman admitted that his views "went somewhat beyond the data." He acknowledged that he had not studied the effects of busing, since the cities under scrutiny had not been subject to court order, and he conceded that he had been "quite wrong" to have called the integration "massive" where it had occurred. But he nonetheless defended the overall implication of his work and continued to maintain that court-imposed desegregation exacerbated the rate of "white flight."

Mobilized by Coleman's well-publicized statements, scholars committed to desegregation lost no time in taking issue with his findings. On August 15, 1975, a "Symposium on School Desegregation and White Flight" was convened, funded by the National Institute of Education, co-sponsored by the Catholic University Center for National Policy Review and the Notre Dame Center for Civil Rights, and hosted by the Brookings Institution. Though Coleman was a participant, the papers that emerged from the symposium consisted entirely of rebuttals of his position. Later, Gregg Jackson, of the United States Commission on Civil Rights, criticized both Coleman's data and his methodology in two articles, a technical version in *Educational Researcher* (November 1975) and a popular version in *Phi Delta Kappan* (December 1975). Coleman's claim that desegregation accelerated "white flight" was vigorously denounced by Robert Green, of Michigan State University, and Thomas Pettigrew, of Harvard University, first at a press conference called by the NAACP, and then in jointly written articles in *Phi Delta Kappan* (February 1976) and in *Harvard Educational Review* (February 1976). Green and Pettigrew charged that Coleman had been selective in his choice of school districts and that their own reanalysis of districts with more than 75,000 pupils revealed no correlation between the degree of desegregation and the rate of "white flight."

There were three major criticisms of Coleman's study: that his conclusions were invalid because he did not look at enough districts and because the districts he did examine had not undergone court-ordered desegrégation; that "white flight" from central cities is a long-term phenomenon predating school desegregation; and that desegregation does not cause "white flight" since the same level of "white flight" can be observed in big cities whether or not they have enacted desegregation plans. The policy implication of these criticisms is that framers of desegregation plans need not be concerned about the impact of "white flight," because desegregation does not cause greater numbers of whites to leave than would have left anyway. Green and Pettigrew state this directly:

While extensive school desegregation may hasten the white flight phenomenon, particularly in the largest nonmetropolitan districts in the
South, the effect, if it obtains at all, may only be temporarily during
the first year of desegregation, and then only for those families which
have already made plans to move.

THE counterargument against Coleman was strengthened during
the summer of 1975 by another new study of the effects of
desegregation on "white flight," written by Christine Rossell, an
assistant professor of political science at Boston University. Her
paper, presented to the American Political Science Association in
September 1975 and published in *Political Science Quarterly*
(Winter 1975), sought to establish definitively that school desegregation causes "little or no significant white flight, even when it is
court ordered and implemented in large cities." Gary Orfield, editor
of the papers from the August symposium on "white flight" (and
also an author of one of the rebuttals to Coleman), called Rossell's
study "particularly impressive," and Robert Green described it as
"the most serious challenge to the Coleman position." And indeed,
Rossell sought not only to refute Coleman's arguments but to prove
that desegregation had little or no impact on "white flight," and that
"white flight" was, at most, a temporary and minimal occurrence.

Rossell collected data from 86 school districts and grouped them
by the degree to which students had been reassigned for purposes
of school integration. She came to the conclusion that of the 10 districts with the highest degree of desegregation, only two (Pasadena
and Pontiac) experienced any significant "white flight," but it was
"minimal (about a 3-percent increase over the previous trend) and
temporary." The whole group of cities with the highest amount of
desegregation showed "a negligible increase of about 1 percent from
the previous trend":

> The important phenomenon here is that any loss of whites occurs *be-*
> *fore* school opens in the first year of the plan. After that, white flight
> stabilizes to a rate slightly better than the pre-desegregation period.
> Therefore, white flight, if it occurs at all, occurs not from the problems
> experienced during the first year of desegregation, but from the fear
> of problems. In other words, if whites leave, it is typically not because
> they participated in the plan and did not like it, but because they
> refused to participate at all.

Busing did not cause "white flight," she held, since she found "no
significant increase in white flight in Northern school districts that
desegregated under court order." Where Coleman had asserted that
"white flight" was greatest in large districts undergoing rapid desegregation, Rossell disagreed:

> The two large school districts, San Francisco and Denver, that engaged
> in such massive and rapid desegregation show no significant white
> flight. Nor do most of the other large school districts that implemented

lesser degrees of school desegregation (Seattle; Milwaukee; Kansas City, Mo.; Indianapolis; Baltimore; Philadelphia; Los Angeles; and Chicago). Thus the data of the present study contradict almost every claim Coleman has made regarding school desegregation and white flight.

Indeed, according to Rossell, mandatory city-wide school desegregation may be the best means to insure racial stability:

> While almost all school districts (with the exception of Berkeley, California) are still experiencing white flight, it is quite encouraging that by the second and third year after desegregation, the school districts engaging in massive and rapid desegregation have a rate of white flight that is lower than their rate in the predesegregation period and lower than that of any other group [of cities in the study], including those that did not implement any desegregation at all. This is a heartening phenomenon and may mean that school desegregation and the educational innovation that typically accompanies it when it is city wide, could impede the increasing ghettoization of American cities.

Thus, in Rossell's view, not only is school desegregation *not* a cause of "white flight," it may actually be the *remedy* for whatever minimal "white flight" occurs.

But if Rossell is right, how could a distinguished scholar like James Coleman have become so concerned about a relatively insignificant problem? Why had the media accepted the idea that "white flight" was of large proportions, when it was no more than one or two percent of white pupils each year? Conversely, how did Rossell come to the conclusion that "white flight" was minimal and of little or no significance?

To understand Rossell's optimistic conclusions, it is necessary to follow her method of calculating the rate of "white flight." She measured the effect of desegregation on "white flight" by observing changes in the percentage of white pupils enrolled in public schools before and after the major desegregation plan in each city, for as many years as data were available, with 1972-73 the final year of the study. If a district was 58-percent white one year, then dropped to 56-percent white and then to 53-percent white, Rossell would say that the district lost 2 percent the first year, 3 percent the second, and so on. For example, Table I (on the following page) presents five of the cities she analyzed, all in her "high desegregation" group. Thus, Rossell represents the decline in percentage white in Pasadena before desegregation with the following figures: –2.7, –1.5, –1.9, –2.1, –2.0, –2.4. A desegregation plan was adopted in 1970, and in that year the figure representing white decline was –4.2; in the next two years, the figures were –4.5 and –2.5. In San Francisco, where a "massive and rapid" court-ordered busing plan was implemented in 1971, before desegregation the figures were –2.9, –1.2, 0, –4.1, –.2; after desegregation, they were –3.0 and –2.1. (Rossell ob-

TABLE I. *Change in Percentage of White Students in "High Desegregation" Cities (Rossell's Calculations)*[1]

	Percentage Of Pupils Reassigned	Years Before Plan Date								Plan Date		Years After Plan Date			
		7	6	5	4	3	2	1			1	2	3	4
Pasadena[2]	98.48%	71.6%	68.9%	67.4%	65.5%	63.4%	61.4%	59.0%	1970	54.8%	50.3%	47.8%	—	—
Pontiac[2]	83.47	74.7	73.4	72.4	69.4	66.3	64.6	62.2	1971	56.8	56.4	—	—	—
Berkeley	57.72	—	—	54.0	51.8	49.6	50.3	48.7	1968	46.5	45.9	45.1	45.2%	46.1%
San Francisco[2]	42.49	—	45.3	42.4	41.2	41.2	37.1	36.9	1971	33.9	31.8	—	—	—
Denver[2]	24.64	—	—	70.4	69.1	67.7	66.2	65.6	1969	64.1	61.7	60.3	58.3	—

[1] Source: Paper presented by Rossell before the American Political Science Association (September 1975).
[2] Court-ordered desegregation.

TABLE II. *Racial Change in Pasadena Public Schools**

Year	Total Number Of Pupils	Whites		Minorities		White Loss	
		Number Of Pupils	Percentage Of Total	Number Of Pupils	Percentage Of Total	Number Of Pupils	Percentage Of 1968 Number
1968	31,259	19,201	61.4%	12,058	38.6%	—	—
1972	26,225	12,523	47.8	13,702	52.2	6,678	34.8%

*Source: Author's calculations.

tained these figures by substracting the percentage white in any given year from the percentage white in the previous year.) As noted earlier, Rossell argued that none of the cities in her study except Pasadena and Pontiac experienced any significant "white flight," and even in those two cities it was minimal and temporary. Indeed, since her method of comparing percentages yields such small figures to represent the declining proportions of white pupils each year, "white flight" appears to be a sorely overdramatized issue.

Unhappily, this is not the case. Rossell has selected a statistical method that will show small declines even in the face of large absolute movements. Consider, for example, a school district with 250,000 pupils, 200,000 whites (80 percent of the total) and 50,000 blacks (20 percent of the total). If 40,000 white pupils were to leave the district in a single year, it would then have 160,000 whites (76.2 percent of the total) and 50,000 blacks (23.8 percent of the total). Rossell would say that the change in the percentage white was −3.8, that is, a drop of 3.8 *percentage points. But what has actually happened is that 20 percent of the white pupils have left the district* (since 40,000 is 20 percent of 200,000). It is precisely Rossell's method of calculating "white flight" by subtracting percentages that leads her to her conclusions. In Pasadena, for example, Rossell's tables show a decline in percentage white from 61.4 percent in 1968 to 47.8 percent in 1972, a drop of 13.6 points. But the absolute numbers of whites in the Pasadena school system declined by 34.8 percent, while the absolute number of minorities rose slightly (see Table II on the previous page).

Since Rossell maintains that "white flight" rarely occurs after desegregation, it is worth noting that the Pasadena school district continued to lose white pupils: By 1976-77, its total enrollment was 25,718, and its white population had declined to 9,839, a loss of 48.8 percent of the number of whites enrolled in 1968 and of 21.4 percent of whites enrolled in 1972.

Rossell explains why she preferred to compare percentages rather than absolute numbers:

> Coleman . . . measures loss in white enrollment in a way that may tend to exaggerate white flight in some cities. He compares the raw figures on white enrollment in the previous year and then claims white flight if the latter is lower than the former. Yet one can easily predict cases where due to job layoffs, factory closings, etc., both whites and blacks leave a city at a faster rate than before, but blacks leave at a higher rate. Although this would result in the percentage black decreasing and the percentage white increasing, Coleman would still call this white flight, even though it might more properly be called "black flight." In the final analysis, the most important variable for policy purposes is the percentage white, not the number white.

However, this criticism applies not to anyone using absolute numbers, which clearly reveal any joint fluctuation of racial groups, but to the researcher using only percentages, which can mask substan-

TABLE III. *Racial Change in "High Desegregation" Cities**

City	Year	Total Number Of Pupils	Whites		Minorities		White Loss	
			Number Of Pupils	Percentage Of Total	Number Of Pupils	Percentage Of Total	Number Of Pupils	Percentage Of 1968 Number
Pontiac	1968	23,832	15,789	66.3%	8,043	33.7%	——	——
	1972	21,141	11,929	56.4	9,212	43.6	3,860	24.4%
Berkeley	1968	16,204	7,535	46.5	8,669	53.5	——	——
	1972	15,213	7,017	46.1	8,196	53.9	518	6.9
San Francisco	1968	94,154	38,824	41.2	55,330	58.8	——	——
	1972	81,970	26,067	31.8	55,903	68.2	12,757	32.9
Denver	1968	96,577	63,398	65.6	33,179	34.4	——	——
	1972	91,616	53,412	58.3	38,204	41.7	9,986	15.8

*Source: Author's calculations.

TABLE IV. *"Percentage White in Boston Public Schools, 1964-1975" (Rossell's Calculations)**

1964	1965	1966	1967	1968	1969	1970	1971	1972	1973	1974	(Estimated) 1975
75.6	74.2	73.9	72.4	68.5	66.0	64.1	61.5	59.6	57.2	52.3	47.8

*Source: Press release by Rossell (December 1975).

tial changes in enrollments. In other words, Rossell is criticizing her own technique. For example, when black enrollment is growing while white enrollment is fairly stable, as it was in Boston during the 1960's, the method of comparing percentages gives an impression of "white flight" where none exists.

The best way to avoid the choice between percentages and absolute numbers is to supply both. When both are presented for the four other districts used by Rossell (in Table I), a very different picture emerges, as evident from Table III on the preceding page. Only in Berkeley, a small atypical university town that initiated its own desegregation plan, not under court order, was the white pupil loss truly insignificant. San Francisco, which Rossell maintains had "no significant white flight," lost one third of its white pupils during the period of her study. Furthermore, subsequent events in San Francisco and Denver (the two large urban districts with massive court-ordered desegregation) do not sustain her hypothesis that "white flight" rarely occurs after the implementation of major desegregation plans. A court order was enacted in San Francisco in 1971; the number of white pupils in public schools there declined from 26,067 in 1972 to 14,958 in 1976, a loss of 42.6 percent of white enrollment in only four years. Nor did Denver, where a city-wide plan was imposed in 1974, maintain its white enrollment: Its 53,412 white pupils in 1972 declined to 36,539 in 1976, a loss of nearly a third of the white pupils in four years. In September 1977, Denver's white pupils declined by another 3,000 to 47.0 percent of the Denver system, having dropped from a majority of 65.6 percent in 1968 and 58.3 percent in 1972. Any statistical method that declares these demographic shifts "insignificant" is, at the very least, not very useful.

The use of Rossell's statistical method in the case of Boston, that maelstrom of desegregation woes, is so at variance with common knowledge as to throw social science into disrepute. Rossell released the following statement to the press in December 1975:

> Much has been made of the claim that school desegregation in Boston (Phase I in the Fall of 1974 and Phase II in the Fall of 1975) has caused massive white flight. The accompanying graph and table indicate that the decline in the percentage white enrolled in the public schools is part of a trend that began at least as early as 1964 and probably earlier. While the implementation of school desegregation appears to have somewhat accelerated this trend, a projection of the former trend indicates that Boston would have been a majority non-white system, even if it had *not* desegregated, by the fall of 1976. Therefore, desegregation is only responsible for accelerating by one year, the trend toward a majority non-white school system.

This statement was accompanied by Table IV (shown on the preceding page).

But consider the absolute figures, which are shown in Table V (on page 143). The absolute figures reveal that white enrollment

TABLE V. *Enrollment in the Boston Public Schools, 1964-1976**

Year	Total Number Of Pupils	Whites		Minorities		White Loss	
		Number Of Pupils	Percentage Of Total	Number Of Pupils	Percentage Of Total	Number Of Pupils	Percentage Of Number In Previous Year
1964	91,800	69,400	75.6%	22,400	24.4%	——	——
1965	93,055	69,046	74.2	24,009	25.8	359	0.5%
1966	92,127	68,082	73.9	24,045	26.1	964	1.4
1967	92,441	66,927	72.4	25,512	27.6	1,155	1.7
1968	94,174	64,509	68.5	29,665	31.5	2,418	3.6
1969	94,885	62,624	66.0	32,261	34.0	1,885	2.9
1970	96,696	61,982	64.1	34,714	35.9	642	1.0
1971	96,400	59,286	61.5	37,114	38.5	2,696	4.3
1972	96,239	57,358	59.6	38,881	40.4	1,928	3.3
1973	93,647	53,593	57.2	40,054	42.8	3,765	6.6
1974	85,826	44,937	52.4	40,889	47.6	8,656	16.2
1975	76,461	36,243	47.4	40,218	52.6	8,694	19.3
1976	76,889	34,561	45.0	42,328	55.0	1,682	4.6

*Source: Author's calculations.

dropped by 7,418 (10.7 percent) from 1964 until 1970, an average loss of 1.8 percent annually. However, the loss in white pupils from 1970 through 1976 was 27,421 (44 percent), four times the rate of the previous six years. "White flight" was significantly higher during the implementation of the desegregation plan, and there is simply no way of knowing whether those who left had already been planning to go. It is possible to argue that the 1974-1975 desegregation of Boston's public schools was necessary and correct regardless of the number of whites who left the system. But it is indefensible to argue, against the evidence, that the desegregation plan caused only a one-year acceleration in the transition to a majority non-white school system.

W E have inspected Rossell's case against Coleman in detail because it illustrates some of the issues involved in the debate. But the argument concerns more than the proper presentation of the data on declining white enrollments. Coleman also used econometric models to attempt to determine the extent to which desegregation as such was leading to declining white enrollments. These models could take into account the effect of whether a city was Southern or not, whether it had nearby high-percentage-white suburbs, and whether a trend independent of desegregation was reducing white enrollment (suburban movement or other factors). On these matters, the debate is too technical to summarize easily.

One of the issues was the proper measure of desegregation. Coleman argued that, independent of the specific causes (e.g., a court order) leading to it, an increase in the degree to which whites are exposed to blacks seemed, under certain circumstances, to reduce the number of whites. Ultimately, Coleman's model required some important qualifications. The increase in the amount of "white flight" that occurred with an increase in desegregation was particularly marked in larger cities, in cities with a large black school population, and in cities with adjacent school districts with a high proportion of white students. Coleman's conclusions, supported by mathematical models, also seem to conform to common sense and experience. His models have been modified, attacked, and retested, but the general conclusions still hold. After reanalyzing the data and taking into account various criticisms made of Coleman, Charles Clotfelter has concluded:

> The estimates in the current paper of the effect of desegregation—measured by hypothetical changes in exposure rates—support the view that desegregation has a strong overall effect on white enrollments in the largest school districts. Within these large districts, however, desegregation is a significant stimulus of white losses only in districts where blacks make up more than 7 percent of students. . . . For smaller districts, response to desegregation appears to be less intense. . . .

By attempting to deny the long-term significance of "white flight" and by refusing to acknowledge the impact of court-ordered busing on white pupil losses, Coleman's critics have confused and confounded the analysis of desegregation policy. Worse yet, the issue has been unfairly politicized by the charge that those who worry about the relationship between desegregation and "white flight" are subverting the civil rights organizations. In view of the rate of white exodus from the public schools of Boston, Denver, and San Francisco, as well as the projected declines in Los Angeles after the implementation of busing, it is impossible to contend that court-ordered racial assignment does not accelerate "white flight" in large cities. It is not a contradiction to recognize that cities where there has been no court-ordered busing have also experienced significant "white flight" (though in no city has the rate of "white flight" been as great in a single year as it was in Boston in 1974 and again in 1975). No matter how many qualifications are attached to Coleman's methodology or research design, his central concern about the diminishing number of whites in urban schools remains valid.

This conclusion should not be misunderstood: Even if it were clearly proved that desegregation causes "white flight," it would still be imperative to eliminate unconstitutional racial discrimination. Certainly, no one—least of all, Coleman—would propose maintaining racially segregated schools as a way of inducing whites to remain in city schools. Coleman's question, raised not in defense of segregation but about the long-range utility of system-wide racial balance plans, was whether court-ordered busing makes desegregation harder to achieve by hastening the departure of whites from city schools. "White flight," in cities under court order and in cities not under court order, is a real problem; it will not be solved by denying its existence or seriousness.

The table on pages 146 and 147 demonstrates the extent of racial change in the 29 biggest cities in the United States from 1968 to 1976. (This list is of *big-city school districts,* not districts that have been made large by court order for purposes of integration.) All have had desegregation controversies, but only a few have court-ordered racial balance plans. *Of the 29 biggest city school districts in the nation, only eight still have a white majority:* Milwaukee, Jacksonville, Columbus, Indianapolis, San Diego, Seattle, Nashville, and Pittsburgh. And three of these eight are fast approaching the 50-percent mark (Milwaukee, Indianapolis, and Pittsburgh). During this eight-year period, the following districts made the transition from majority white to majority non-white: Los Angeles, Houston, Miami, Dallas, Denver, Boston, Cincinnati, and Kansas City.

It seems unlikely that we will ever know with any degree of certainty whether whites (and some middle-class blacks) are leaving the city because of concern about desegregation or crime or poor services or racial tensions or the quality of life or for some other reason or combination of reasons. But if it is impossible to measure the precise impact of school desegregation on "white flight," it is equally insupportable to claim that there is no effect whatever. Court-ordered busing may or may not be the primary stimulus of

TABLE VI. *Racial Change in Urban Public Schools, 1968-1976[1]*

CITY[2]	YEAR	TOTAL NUMBER OF PUPILS	WHITES NUMBER OF PUPILS	WHITES PERCENTAGE OF TOTAL	MINORITIES[3] NUMBER OF PUPILS	MINORITIES[3] PERCENTAGE OF TOTAL	WHITE LOSS NUMBER OF PUPILS	WHITE LOSS PERCENTAGE OF 1968 NUMBER	TOTAL LOSS NUMBER OF PUPILS	TOTAL LOSS PERCENTAGE OF 1968 NUMBER
New York City	1968	1,063,787	467,365	43.9%	596,422	56.1%				
	1976	1,077,190	328,065	30.5	749,125	69.5	139,300	29.8%	(+13,403)	(+1.3%)
Los Angeles	1968	653,549	350,909	53.7	302,640	46.3				
	1976	592,931	219,359	37.0	373,572	63.0	131,550	37.5	60,618	9.3
Chicago	1968	582,274	219,478	37.7	362,796	62.3				
	1976	524,221	130,785	25.0	393,436	75.0	88,693	40.4	58,053	10.0
Houston	1968	246,098	131,099	53.3	114,999	46.7				
	1976	210,025	71,794	34.2	138,231	65.8	59,305	45.2	36,073	14.7
Detroit	1968	296,097	116,250	39.3	179,847	60.7				
	1976	239,214	44,614	18.7	194,600	81.3	71,636	61.6	56,883	19.2
Philadelphia	1968	282,617	109,512	38.7	173,105	61.3				
	1976	257,942	82,010	31.8	175,932	68.2	27,502	25.1	24,675	8.7
Miami	1968	232,465	135,598	58.3	96,867	41.7				
	1976	239,994	98,362	41.0	141,632	59.0	37,236	27.5	(+7,529)	(+3.2)
Baltimore	1968	192,171	66,997	34.9	125,174	65.1				
	1976	160,121	38,992	24.4	121,129	75.6	28,005	41.8	32,050	16.7
Dallas	1968	159,924	97,888	61.2	62,036	38.8				
	1976	139,080	53,008	38.1	86,072	61.9	44,880	45.8	20,844	13.0
Cleveland	1968	156,054	66,324	42.5	89,730	57.5				
	1976	122,706	46,383	37.8	76,323	62.2	19,941	30.1	33,348	21.4
Washington, D.C.	1968	148,725	8,280	5.6	140,445	94.4				
	1976	126,587	4,484	3.5	122,103	96.5	3,796	45.8	22,138	14.9
Milwaukee	1968	130,445	95,161	73.0	35,284	27.0				
	1976	109,565	61,738	56.3	47,827	43.7	33,423	35.1	20,880	16.0
Memphis	1968	125,813	58,271	46.3	67,542	53.7				
	1976	117,496	33,848	28.8	83,648	71.2	24,423	41.9	8,317	6.6
Jacksonville	1968	122,637	87,999	71.8	34,638	28.2				
	1976	[illegible]	[illegible]	[illegible]	36,977	33.4	14,269	16.9	11,930	9.7

St. Louis	1968	115,582	42,174	36.5	73,408	63.5				
	1976	81,492	23,210	28.5	58,282	71.5	18,964	45.0	34,090	29.5
New Orleans	1968	110,783	34,673	31.3	76,110	68.7				
	1976	93,364	17,933	19.2	75,431	80.8	16,740	48.3	17,419	15.7
Columbus, Ohio	1968	110,699	81,655	73.8	29,044	26.2				
	1976	96,372	64,657	67.1	31,715	32.9	16,998	20.8	14,327	12.9
Indianapolis	1968	108,587	72,010	66.3	36,577	33.7				
	1976	82,002	45,187	55.1	36,815	44.9	26,823	37.2	26,585	24.5
Atlanta	1968	111,227	42,506	38.2	68,721	61.8				
	1976	82,480	9,231	11.2	73,199	88.8	33,275	78.3	28,747	25.8
San Diego	1968	128,414	98,163	76.1	30,751	23.9				
	1976	121,423	80,153	66.0	41,270	34.0	18,010	18.3	7,491	5.8
Denver	1968	96,577	63,398	65.6	33,179	34.4				
	1976	75,237	36,539	48.6	38,698	51.4	26,859	42.4	21,340	22.1
Boston	1968	94,174	64,500	68.5	29,674	31.5				
	1976	76,889	34,561	45.0	42,328	55.0	29,939	46.4	17,285	18.4
San Francisco	1968	94,154	38,824	41.2	55,330	58.8				
	1976	65,255	14,958	22.9	50,297	77.1	23,866	61.5	28,899	30.7
Seattle	1968	94,025	77,293	82.2	16,732	17.8				
	1976	61,819	41,623	67.3	20,196	32.7	35,670	46.1	32,206	34.3
Nashville	1968	93,720	71,039	75.8	22,681	24.2				
	1976	77,998	54,522	69.9	23,476	30.1	16,517	23.3	15,722	16.8
Cincinnati	1968	86,807	49,231	56.7	37,576	43.3				
	1976	65,635	30,697	46.8	34,938	53.2	18,534	37.6	21,172	24.4
San Antonio	1968	79,353	21,310	26.9	58,043	73.1				
	1976	65,712	9,962	15.1	55,750	84.9	11,348	53.3	13,641	17.2
Pittsburgh	1968	76,628	46,005	60.3	30,263	39.7				
	1976	59,022	31,954	54.1	27,068	45.9	14,051	30.5	17,606	23.0
Kansas City	1968	74,202	39,510	53.2	34,692	46.8				
	1976	51,047	17,560	34.4	33,487	65.6	21,950	44.4	23,155	31.2

[1] Source: Prepared by the author for a conference sponsored by the National Institute of Education and the Hudson Institute (September 15-16, 1977).

[2] Two big cities—Phoenix and San Jose—are not included because both have numerous districts not coextensive with the city's boundaries. Both are predominantly white.

[3] Includes blacks, Hispanics, Asians, and American Indians.

white withdrawal from city schools, but it is very likely a contributing factor—and, at least in Boston, an important contributing factor. Just as it is impossible to determine whether it is the direct cause, it is equally impossible to prove that it has no bearing at all on family decisions to remove children from urban schools.

BEHIND the controversy over Coleman's findings is a struggle over the future direction of policy. Coleman is urging a cautious and deliberate approach that takes into account the possibility of "white flight" and resegregation. His views, furthermore, support the idea that court remedies should be specific, rather than broad and system-wide.

Coleman's critics are committed to racial balancing of pupil populations as the best, most demonstrable assurance of full integration. The integration forces may not have won every court battle, but they have succeeded in popularizing the notion that every black school, regardless of the reason for its racial concentration, is a segregated school, the result of official discrimination rather than affinity or choice. In the aftermath of the Supreme Court's 1974 Detroit decision, which limited urban-suburban busing, integration advocates, in many instances, have had to confine their demands for busing to individual school districts. In our largest cities, this is not a solution likely to satisfy anyone for very long: "Success" in most big cities will mean a school system in which every school is predominantly non-white, and from which white pupils continue to leave every year. Unless "white flight" is stopped or reversed, racial balancing within cities will very likely produce the phenomenon of resegregation between city and suburb that Coleman has warned about.

The inadequacy of racial balancing within big-city school districts is likely to generate new pressures for metropolitan-area school integration. This is a proposal long favored by the United States Civil Rights Commission and civil rights groups, and it is already in effect in several smaller cities and counties. How such a proposal might be implemented in a city school district with a quarter-million, a half-million, or a million pupils is uncertain, as are the educational implications. What is predictable, however, is the political reaction: To date, no metropolitan region has voluntarily adopted a full city-suburban merger for school integration, and opposition can be anticipated from suburban districts (whose residents include many who fled the city schools), state legislatures (where urban interests are a minority), and Congress (which regularly passes ineffective busing curbs). Nothing less than a reversal of the Supreme Court's 1974 Detroit decision could produce the enforcement mechanism to impose metropolitan-area integration on a large scale. For now, at least, that is not in the offing.

But if racial balancing is of limited practicality because of the diminishing number of white pupils in most big cities, and if metropolitan cross-busing is of limited applicability because of the Supreme Court's 1974 ruling, what then? Few urban districts have had the capacity to look or plan beyond the latest political or fiscal crisis, but clearly some fresh synthesis is needed to restore a sense of direction to urban education. Atlanta is one city that offers hope of a new approach. Its schools are 90-percent black, and its professional leadership is predominantly black. At the instigation of the local NAACP (which defied the national NAACP), a deal was struck in court to forego busing in exchange for jobs and black control of the system. Now the system is intent on demonstrating that the schools can be made to work.

The Atlanta schools are stressing the kind of curriculum and values that will enable black children (and white children) to succeed in the mainstream of American life; this means an early emphasis on basic skills, taught in an orderly atmosphere in which achievement and hard work are rewarded. Atlanta has decided to build a new high school, and remarkably, it will be a selective, admission-by-academic-examination school, possibly the first new such school anywhere in the country for many years.

Meanwhile, the American Civil Liberties Union is pressing a court suit to compel the merger of the Atlanta school district and the surrounding white suburban districts, in order to make blacks a minority within a predominantly white metropolitan district; not surprisingly, the Atlanta district has shown no interest in surrendering its independence. The theory of Atlanta's educational leaders is that equal educational opportunity can be achieved through quality education. If they are right, and if they can create the kind of productive, effective schools that all parents want, their system could become a showplace for urban American schools and a magnet pulling back the children of those who fled the city during the past two decades. Andrew Young, while he was Atlanta's Congressman, predicted in a newspaper interview in 1975 that Atlanta's schools would ultimately prove to be better than the suburban schools, both because of their clear and purposeful educational approach and because of the city's considerable cultural resources, which no suburban shopping mall can match. Imagine that: "white flight" *to* the city, resulting not from coercion or condescension, but from an earnest search for good public schools.

A Response to "The 'White Flight' Controversy"

DIANE Ravitch's article, "The 'White Flight' Controversy," in the Spring issue of *The Public Interest* includes many misleading and inaccurate points which need to be corrected. It is also almost two years out of date. I would like to emphasize at the outset, however, that her central argument with regard to Coleman's work is correct. Despite all of the methodological critiques, competing analyses, and reanalyses, the major argument of the Coleman, Kelly, and Moore study, "Trends in School Segregation, 1968-73," has been substantiated empirically by the most recent works. My own updated and expanded study, "Assessing the Unintended Impacts of Public Policy: School Desegregation and Resegregation," (now including Southern school districts and data through Fall 1975), as well as recent works by Farley, Armor, Roberts, and Clotfelter, suggests that the implementation of a school desegregation plan, *if* it involves the busing of whites to black schools, significantly increases the decline in white public school enrollment in the year of implementation—averaging out to be a doubling of the "normal" white enrollment decline in the North and a tripling in the South. Although Ravitch scorns the suggestion in my first study that there appear to be less-than-normal white enrollment losses in post-implementation years, Coleman and his colleagues also found the same effect. Indeed, of the four most recent studies which have examined this phenomenon longitudinally, three have found strong "positive" effects after implementation. At the end of four years, the net effect of school desegregation on white public school enrollment is "non-negative" for most school districts and most plans. If she is going to criticize me for this finding, she should be fair enough to mention Coleman's similar finding.

In her criticisms of my first study, as well as in her own presentation of white enrollment data, Ravitch does not seem to understand social science research methods. In order to detect the impact of a policy on a phenomenon being studied (for example, the impact of a job-training program on unemployment rates or the impact of income redistribution schemes on the level of poverty), it is necessary to isolate the long-term trend from the impact of the public policy. The failure to do this is the most common mistake made by journalists, and it is precisely the error Ravitch has made both in her critique of my study and in her own "analysis." To use an analogy: No scientist of any merit would attempt to determine the effect of a daily vitamin pill on a normal child's growth by measuring his or her height at one point in time and then again several years later, attributing the observed growth to the daily vitamin pill. Yet that is exactly what Ravitch has done.

Although Ravitch refers to my statistical method throughout her article, she does not even discuss the actual statistical method I used —the interrupted time series with a non-equivalent control group— and falsely implies that I simply examined change in percentage white intuitively. Nobody trained in social science research methods would make such an egregious error. In reality, her only criticism of my study is of the way in which I measured white enrollment change, not of my statistical method. To measure white enrollment change I used change in percentage white, rather than proportional change in white enrollment, because I thought it might control for historical accidents, such as the closing of factories and subsequent unemployment which would cause both blacks and whites to move out of the city but would not change racial proportions. As it turns out, this was unnecessary and I now use proportional change in white enrollment as my dependent variable.

Nevertheless, my earlier study was not wrong because I used a measure of white enrollment change that has smaller units than the one Ravitch suggests I should have used. My conclusions were based on a test of significance (of the change in proportion white with desegregation, when compared to the pre-desegregation trend) and comparison with a control group. Since all cases and points in time are in the same units, changing the size of these units makes little or no difference in my findings because the *comparative* relationships remain the same.

Let me demonstrate with the six desegregated school districts Ravitch pulled out of my 86-city study (Table I). Column A shows the significance of the Mood test using the dependent variable I am

TABLE I. *Comparison of Significance of Mood Test Using Differing Dependent Variables*[1]

City	Column A SIGNIFICANCE OF CHANGE IN PROPORTION WHITE WITH DESEGREGATION FROM PRE-DESEGREGATION TREND	Column B SIGNIFICANCE OF PROPORTIONAL CHANGE IN WHITE ENROLLMENT WITH DESEGREGATION FROM PRE-DESEGREGATION TREND
Pontiac	Significant (.05 or better)	Significant
Berkeley	N.S.	Significant
San Francisco	N.S.	N.S.
Denver	N.S.	N.S.
Pasadena	Significant	Significant
Boston	Significant	Significant

[1] Source: Author's calculations.

accused of using to minimize the effect of desegregation. Column B shows the significance of the Mood test using the dependent variable Ravitch argues I should have used so that I would have seen the real effect of desegregation. These results indicate that the use of one dependent variable rather than the other has changed the results for only one case, Berkeley, a small, atypical, university town.

We can more clearly see the relative importance of these two variables by examining multiple-regression equations analyzing data from my updated and expanded study. These are shown below in a simple equation using variables implicitly controlled for in the interrupted time series.

TABLE II. *Effects of Differing Dependent Variables on Multiple-Regression Equations*[1]

INDEPENDENT VARIABLES	CHANGE IN PROPORTION WHITE WITH DESEGREGATION	PROPORTIONAL CHANGE IN WHITE ENROLLMENT WITH DESEGREGATION
	Beta	Beta
Percent Black	−.23[2]	−.57[2]
Southern City School District	−.10	−.15
Unemployment Rate	−.22[2]	−.15[2]
Crime Rate	−.04	−.10
Proportion Students Reassigned (Deseg.)	−.54[2]	−.39[2]
r^2	.36	.53
Observations	109	109

[1] Source: Derived from author's study "Assessing the Unintended Impacts of Public Policy: School Desegregation and Resegregation."
[2] F ratio—significant at .01 levels.

Thus even in the updated study using a different methodology the use of one dependent variable, rather than the other, makes no difference in a finding of a signficant relationship. Had a significant relationship between desegregation and white enrollment change existed in my sample (Northern districts only) and during the time period studied (through Fall 1972), I would have found it regardless of the dependent variable used. Thus when Ravitch states, "Rossell has selected a statistical method that will show small declines even in the face of large absolute movements," she would be correct only if I had intuitively examined the data as she did.

—Christine H. Rossell

Diane Ravitch replies:

In my article, I sought to show the nature of the response to James Coleman's finding that court-ordered desegregation, under certain circumstances, was accelerating "white flight" from large-city schools. Proponents of busing, instead of addressing the problem Coleman raised, attacked him and his work. I examined in detail Christine H. Rossell's "School Desegregation and White Flight," which appeared in *Political Science Quarterly* (Winter

1975-76), because it was widely cited as the definitive refutation of Coleman's thesis. Rossell's major conclusion was that "school desegregation causes little or no significant white flight, even when it is court ordered and implemented in large cities," and she held that her data "contradict almost every claim Coleman has made regarding school desegregation and white flight."

One beneficial consequence of Rossell's letter is that the central issue in my article is now settled: Rossell agrees that Coleman's controversial study "Trends in School Segregation, 1968-73" was substantially correct. This is a useful development, because I have found that there is a widespread belief, inside and outside the academic community, that Coleman's work on "white flight" had been thoroughly discredited. Now Rossell acknowledges that "the implementation of a school desegregation plan, *if* it involves the busing of whites to black schools, significantly increases the decline in white public school enrollment in the year of implementation. . . ." Thus, there no longer is disagreement between Rossell and Coleman on this key point, and that issue can be laid to rest.

But, having retracted the major conclusion of her 1975-76 article, she excoriates me because, first, I should have known that she had revised her views, and second, I criticized the way she arrived at her erroneous conclusion. I learned of Rossell's changed views from three unpublished manuscripts that she sent me after the appearance of my article; the one she mentions, "Assessing the Unintended Impacts of Public Policy: School Desegregation and Resegregation," did not become publicly available until August or September of 1978. Had I written my article in the Fall of 1978 instead of the Fall of 1977, I would have known and noted that Rossell had come to agree with Coleman that school desegregation, under certain conditions, increases "white flight." But even so, her original article would still have been an appropriate illustration of the response to Coleman.

As to methodology, my chief criticism was that Rossell measured white enrollment change by looking at change in *percentage* white on a yearly basis (she notes, correctly, that I made no reference to her *method*—the interrupted time series with a non-equivalent control group). As I argued, the change in percentage white can be misleading. When minority enrollment is growing while white enrollment is fairly stable, as it was in Boston in the 1960's, the percentage of white students drops even though no "white flight" exists; when "white flight" did occur in Boston during the implementation years, it appeared to be merely a continuation of a long-term trend, rather than a significant movement. Furthermore, the choice of this particular measure systematically understates the extent of "white flight" where it does exist, and this may be one reason why Rossell could find little or no significant "white flight" in her early work. The criticism must not be entirely irrelevant, because Rossell notes in her letter that she no longer uses change in percentage white as her dependent variable but has adopted proportional change in white enrollment.

My doubts about Rossell's assertion that "white flight" rarely occurs after the imposition of citywide desegregation are sustained by her latest study. According to Rossell, the greatest "white flight" occurs in the year of implementation. When those who object most to the desegregation plan have left, "white flight" diminishes. In districts that are less than 35 percent black, white enrollment losses return to the pre-desegregation rate or even lower, while in districts that are more than 35 percent black, "white flight" *continues* in the years after implementation (at a rate less than the peak of the implementation year). Where we differ is in the implications of this finding. Rossell sees the eventual slackening of "white flight" after desegregation as an indication that citywide racial balancing may be a good strategy for guaranteeing racial stability in American cities; additionally, she concludes in her latest study that "all school desegregation plans show a net benefit in interracial contact, and paradoxically this benefit is greatest in school districts at or above 35 percent black despite the fact that these are the school districts with the greatest white enrollment loss." But I am concerned that citywide racial balancing in a big-city district that is already predominantly non-white (and most big-city districts are at least 35 percent black) may leave few white students to integrate. Ultimately, then, the issue in the "white flight" controversy is not one of technique but of social policy, where reasonable people may disagree.

David J. Armor comments:

Diane Ravitch's review of the "white flight" controversy underscores the perils faced by researchers who question the efficacy of desegregation policy. The attack by certain social scientists and educators on Coleman's "white flight" report was of a ferocity unprecedented in the treatment of a scientist of Coleman's stature. What is especially noteworthy, as Ravitch brings out, is that none of these well-publicized critiques—which pounced on Coleman's alleged methodological mistakes—presented anywhere near as careful an analysis of the "white flight" phenomenon as did Coleman. For example, while Coleman's analysis shows that the "white flight" effect is substantial only when desegregation is accompanied by several conditions, such as large district size, a high percentage of black enrollment, and availability of white suburbs, none of the major counter-studies by Reynolds Farley, Christine Rossell, and Thomas Pettigrew and Robert Green attempted to control for these crucial factors.

What Ravitch does not mention, however, is that later and more detailed analyses by both Farley and Rossell yielded results quite consistent with Coleman's. (Farley's paper was presented at the American Sociological Association meetings in September 1976, and Rossell's first presentation was at a Boston University symposium in April 1976.) It is to their credit that both Farley and Rossell have admitted, publicly, that Coleman's original findings are essentially correct (Pettigrew and Green, whose critique relied heavily upon the original Farley and Rossell studies, have not been heard from.) On the other hand, neither of these two newer reanalyses has been circulated beyond specialist circles or published, so perhaps Ravitch cannot be faulted for failing to cite them. The important question is why none of the agencies who expedited publication of the early critiques—the National Institute for Education, the Brookings Institution, the *Harvard Educational Review*, the *Political Science Quarterly*—has been anxious to get the word out on these latest studies. The failure to do so prolongs confusion and ambiguity as to the actual state of social science on this issue. Worse, it raises the question of whether these agencies, entrusted with accumulating and promulgating objective scientific knowledge, are in fact bending to political pressures or ideological preferences.

A more important difficulty with the Ravitch review is her presentation of eight-year white-loss data in the 29 largest cities. A careful reading reveals that Ravitch does not claim all of these losses are due to busing; she acknowledges that some of the losses are due to other factors associated with declining white populations in urban centers. However, this type of data is frequently misunderstood, since many commentators have confused total white losses with the "white flight" due to busing. Coleman's report evaluated the effects of desegregation per se, above and beyond losses caused by other factors. In order to do so, it is crucial to separate losses due to desegregation from losses due to declining white births and outmigration arising from events unrelated to desegregation.

Since the Ravitch review may well raise many questions about the true magnitude of busing effects, it might be useful to summarize the results of a new study of "white flight." (See David J. Armor, *White Flight, Demographic Transition, and the Future of School Desegregation.* The Rand Corporation. P-5931. August 1978.) This study focuses specifically on court-ordered *mandatory* desegregation in larger school districts (over 20,000 students) with a significant minority enrollment (over 10 percent). It seems relatively well-documented that "white flight" is not accelerated in districts adopting voluntary desegregation plans, nor in districts with a very small proportion of minority students. The issue of district size is somewhat more complex, but certainly the larger districts raise the more important policy implications, since they encompass the vast majority of black students. The reason for singling out court-ordered cases is that they raise the most likely conditions for "white flight." Rossell's recent studies have shown that the number of white students reassigned (or bused) seems to be the crucial determinant of "white flight," but in fact this rarely happens to any significant degree without a court order. A court action also signifies considerable community opposition to certain types of desegregation, expressed through the elected school board.

The unique feature of this new study is that it attempts to pin down the total long-term effects of court-ordered mandatory busing by using a demographic projection technique to estimate what the white enrollment would have been in the absence of desegregation. While the original paper should be consulted for details about methodology, it suffices to say that the technique uses actual white births and pre-desegregation white outmigration rates (from census data) to project the school-age population. From this projection, the "natural" rate of white enrollment decline can be estimated. Like Coleman and the later Farley and Rossell studies, my study concludes that the "white flight" effect is strong in most court-ordered districts that have more than 20 percent minority students and available white suburbs.

The first important finding is that there is a substantial anticipatory effect the year *before* the start of desegregation, with the actual rate of white loss more than double the projected rate. This finding makes one of Rossell's methods, which predicts post-desegregation loss rates from pre-desegregation rates, very hazardous indeed, with a likely underestimation of "white flight." Second, the first-year effect is truly massive, with a loss rate four times higher than it would have been without desegregation. Finally, according to my findings the long-term effects are also substantial, with actual white losses still nearly twice the natural losses four years after the start of desegregation.

The effect of accelerated white losses on "resegregation" is substantial in most of these cases. In a majority of these school districts, more than half of the total white loss over periods of seven to eight years is attributable to desegregation events. Further, in many instances the effect of court-ordered desegregation is to speed up the "tipping" process, whereby a district becomes predominately minority; in a few cases, such as Boston and Denver, it is possible that the districts would not have tipped at all without the court orders.

There is no question that some experts will question these findings on the size and duration of "white flight" effects; all methods for determining desegregation effects must make assumptions, and while mine seem reasonable, they can be challenged. In fact, I agree with Ravitch that we will never know with certainty the precise impact of these court actions on white losses.

Nonetheless, debates over methodology must not be allowed to obscure the central policy issue. Most of the school districts I have studied are losing whites at a rapid rate. While part of the cause is demographic, the court action only increases the risk of "resegregation." For persons who sincerely desire to increase the total amount of integration, this risk has to be disturbing. At precisely a time when policies are needed to halt or reverse the normal white declines in urban areas, we have instead court actions which are exacerbating the condition. Although the effects may be relatively small in some cases, in other cases they are large. In either case they seem inappropriate during an era when most urban experts are urgently seeking ways to attract whites back into cities. Clearly, other school desegregation remedies must be considered.

What do you do when the Supreme Court is wrong?

DANIEL PATRICK MOYNIHAN

An institution charged with the role which the Supreme Court has successfully filled for so many years is entitled to our respect and understanding. If one criticizes the Court (as people have always done in the past, and should continue to do in the future), it should be essentially for the purpose of trying to contribute to that respect and to that understanding. The debt which we all owe to the Court is far greater than any individual can repay. Criticism of decisions of the Court or opinions of its members should be offered as an effort to repay that debt, and with the thought that conscientious criticism may be an aid to the Court in carrying out its difficult and essential task.

Erwin N. Griswold, 1963

Ｉɴ its Spring Term of 1979, the Supreme Court ruled in the case of *Gannett v. DePasquale* that the public does not have an independent constitutional right of access to a pretrial judicial proceeding. The case had been brought by the Gannett newspapers after one of their reporters was barred from a pretrial hearing in a murder case in upstate New York. Gannett argued that the guarantee of the Sixth Amendment to a "public trial" extended to the public at large, including, of course, the press. The Court held that this was not so. Mr. Justice Stewart's opinion for the majority of the Court declared: "The history upon which the petitioner and *amici* rely totally fails to demonstrate that the Framers of the Sixth Amendment intended to create a constitutional right in strangers to attend a pretrial proceeding. . . ."

Strangers? The press?

In a concurring opinion, Mr. Justice Rehnquist went further, and in such a manner as to highlight the fact that though, strictly speaking, *Gannett v. DePasquale* concerned pretrial proceedings, the decision is easily construed as applying to trials as well. The Court's recitation, he said,

> of the need to preserve the defendant's right to a fair trial . . . should not be interpreted to mean that under the Sixth Amendment a trial court can close a pretrial hearing or trial only when there is a danger that prejudicial publicity will harm the defendant. To the contrary, since the Court holds that the public does not have *any* Sixth Amendment right of access to such proceedings, it necessarily follows that if the parties agree on a closed proceeding, the trial court is not required by the Sixth Amendment to advance any reason whatsoever for declining to open a pretrial hearing or trial to the public.

The decision was the lead story of *The New York Times* the following day. It had, *The Times* reported, "aroused immediate strong criticism from both the press and the legal profession." The initiative of the Gannett newspapers in challenging the closing of a local court proceeding had been seen as a commendable effort to defend the rights both of the public and the press. The Edward Willis Scripps First Amendment Award for 1979 was presented to the Gannett Rochester Newspapers for pressing the suit and for their reporting and analysis of the issues involved. Allen Neuharth, Chairman of the Board of the Gannett newspapers and Chairman of the American Newspaper Publishers Association, called the ruling "another chilling demonstration that the majority of the Burger Court is determined to unmake the Constitution." The American Civil Liberties Union declared that the decision "erected an iron curtain between the criminal process and the inquiring press."

Editorial comment was not less severe. Much emphasis was placed on the asserted departure by the Court from historical, even ancient standards of justice. A forceful *Times* editorial began:

> For centuries the idea of open justice has been synonymous with justice itself. Before the Norman Conquest, before English judges spelled out the rudimentary rights of defendants, throughout the development of British and American jurisprudence, the tradition of open courts has been honored. Now a 5-4 Supreme Court majority has ordained an exception. . . .

In a commentary, Tom Wicker, Associate Editor of *The Times*, deplored the ruling. It would surely lead to miscarriage of justice, he wrote. Not just the press, but the general public could be barred from courts, discarding a standard "rooted in American history." For the Court "now to say that that tradition has no constitutional validity . . . shakes public confidence in institutions and rights long thought to be a citizen's birthright."

The most telling comment came from the Court itself. In a dissenting opinion, Mr. Justice Blackmun stated that in their constitutional argument the Gannett newspapers were right, and the majority of the Court was wrong:

> The Sixth Amendment, in establishing the public's right of access to a criminal trial and a pretrial proceeding, also fixes the rights of the press in this regard. Petitioner, as a newspaper publisher, enjoys the same right of access . . . as does the general public. And what petitioner sees and hears in the courtroom it may, like any other citizen, publish or report consistent with the First Amendment.

In "rare circumstances," Justice Blackmun allowed, exclusion could be justified. But, he concluded, "Those circumstances did not exist in this case."

II

It is difficult to avoid the judgment that Justice Blackmun was right and the majority of the Supreme Court was wrong. If so, the question arises: What to do?

This is a question for which we have no clear answer and little theory. The Court is not supposed to be wrong. Even *The Federalist*, much given to emphasizing the frailty of human judgment, does not adequately treat this possibility. To be sure, the doctrine of judicial supremacy—of the Supreme Court's power to void acts of Congress by declaring them unconstitutional—is not explicit in the Constitution and was not generally assumed to be implicit until Chief Justice John Marshall established it in *Marbury v. Madison*. But Hamilton, who believed in it, and in *Federalist* paper Number 78 made a strong argument for it, had to deal with the charge that "the errors and usurpations of the Supreme Court of the United States will be uncontrollable and remediless." In Number 81, he suggests several reasons why this charge, upon examination, is "made up altogether of false reasoning upon misconceived fact," but all but one of his points are actually further arguments for the necessity and rationality of judicial supremacy. The sole check upon supremacy suggested by Hamilton, other than that of appeals to superior courts, is the power of Congress to impeach individual judges:

> This is alone a complete security. There never can be a danger that the judges, by a series of deliberate usurpations of the authority of the legislature, would hazard the united resentment of the body intrusted with it, while this body was possessed of the means of punishing their presumption, by degrading them from their stations.

No other corrective is suggested. Rather, the argument is made with particular force that the judiciary is inherently and uniquely possessed of the necessary wisdom and disinterest to weigh the actions of the legislature and the executive on constitutional scales. But if the Court were wrong, what—short of impeaching its members—would be the remedy? *The Federalist* does not say.

It happens, however, that we have a considerable practical experience of just this situation. For long periods of American history the Supreme Court has been wrong about one or another of the principal constitutional issues of the day. It has been wrong in the specific sense that there later came a time when the Court reversed itself, and either directly or implicitly stated that it *had* been wrong.[1] Nor has this been without consequence. Charles Evans Hughes, in his 1928 volume, *The Supreme Court of the United States,* could refer to the Court's having suffered from a succession of "self-inflicted wounds."

Thus from the last decade of the nineteenth century into the fourth decade of the twentieth century the Supreme Court repeatedly declared that the due process clauses forbade labor legislation. Under the Fourteenth Amendment, it was held, for example, that the state of New York could not require that bakers work no more than 10 hours a day (*Lochner v. New York,* 1905). Under the Fifth Amendment, a District of Columbia Minimum Wage Act was held invalid (*Adkins v. Children's Hospital,* 1923).[2]

This was solemn nonsense, as Holmes pointed out in his acid

----

[1] Strictly speaking, the Court could have been right the first time and wrong the second. Walter Berns contends, properly, that the standard against which we measure a decision in order to say whether the Court was wrong must be the Constitution itself, not what the Court says about it. Still, experience is the life of constitutional law also, and I would hold that where the Court has reversed itself it has almost always done so to correct an observable error.

[2] In *Erie R.R. Co. v. Tompkins* (1937) the Court reversed *Swift v. Tyson,* acknowledging that they were abandoning a doctrine widely applied ". . . throughout nearly a century. But the unconstitutionality of the course pursued has now been made clear and compels us to do so."

comment in *Lochner* that "the 14th Amendment does not enact Mr. Herbert Spencer's *Social Statics*."[3] But the solemn nonsense persisted, thwarting for almost half a century the major social movement of the time. Then, as suddenly as it had begun, it stopped. Writing somewhat later, Mr. Justice Douglas declared in *Williamson v. Lee Optical Co.* (1955):

> The day is gone when this Court uses the Due Process Clause of the Fourteenth Amendment to strike down state laws, regulatory of business and industrial conditions, because they may be unwise, improvident, or out of harmony with a particular school of thought.

Or, as Mr. Justice Black put it in 1963 in *Ferguson v. Skrupa:*

> The doctrine that prevailed in *Lochner, Coppage, Adkins, Burns,* and like cases—that due process authorizes courts to hold laws unconstitutional when they believe the legislature has acted unwisely—has long since been discarded.

Of these episodes in American history, the most notorious was the *Dred Scott* decision of 1857 which held the Missouri Compromise to be unconstitutional, a matter in which the Court was, again, plainly wrong. The most pernicious was *Plessy v. Ferguson* (1896), which held that the Fourteenth Amendment permitted separate but equal public facilities segregated by race, a doctrine that persisted until *Brown v. Board of Education* (1954).

Apart from the *Dred Scott* decision which was, in effect, overturned by the Thirteenth Amendment, the essential fact in all these cases is, however, that the time came when the Court discovered its error and reversed itself.[4] This may appear much too optimistic,

---

[3] Holmes' suggestion appears to be misleading. The Court was not trying to enact anyone's social theories but its own. In James Q. Wilson's phrase, the Court had an idea as to what a "good economy" would be, and it was against this standard that statutes were measured. A considerable body of labor legislation and business regulation was in fact upheld by the "Laissez-Faire Court." My point is simply that there was precious little constitutional warrant for any of this.

[4] To be sure, the Sixteenth Amendment, permitting a progressive federal income tax, had the effect of reversing the Supreme Court's five-to-four decision in *Pollock v. Farmers' Loan and Trust Company* (1895), which had struck down such a tax. But many commentators feel that in this instance the Court was accurately interpreting Article I, Section 9 of the Constitution, and that changing circumstances in fact called for a constitutional amendment. The contrary view, expressed by some members of Congress during debate on the Sixteenth Amendment, is that the Court *was* wrong but had recognized this and was already diluting the effect of the *Pollock* decision and that the proposed amendment was therefore superfluous.

The Eleventh Amendment, ratified in 1795, which denied the Supreme Court original jurisdiction in law suits brought by citizens against individual states, responded to the Court's decision in *Chisholm v. Georgia* (1793) that it had such jurisdiction. But this could reasonably be described as part of the completing of the Federal structure embodied in the Constitution itself.

even pietistic a reading of American history, but there it is for those to refute who will. The question I would address is how these reversals have come about. It is a process not now described in political or juridical science. As a beginning contribution I would offer a simple hierarchy of response which in one or another combination has commonly led the Court to change its position in those instances in which it has been wrong. In ascending order: Debate, Litigate, Legislate.

(In theory the ultimate recourse of those who feel the Constitution has been misread is an amendment settling the issue. But this has *never* happened. It has never proved necessary. Apart from the evolving idea of Federalism that needed to correct *Chisholm,* the exceptional circumstances that followed *Dred Scott,* and the changed circumstances that caused a graduated income tax to appear more reasonable in 1913 than in 1787, sooner or later the Justices have rectified their mistakes. That is not the least ground for the loving fealty we owe the Court.)

As a "case history" I will first present in some detail the history of the issue of state aid to nonpublic schools. I will argue that the Supreme Court was wrong in its interpretation of the Establishment Clause in its decision *Everson v. Board of Education* (1947), but that after a generation the conditions are developing in which it may (will?) now reverse itself. That time is a considerable element in this process will be of small consolation to those now most distressed by the decision in *Gannett v. DePasquale,* but this also appears to be the general experience.

III

Some weeks before the lengthy *Gannett* decision was announced to the consternation of so many, the Supreme Court in 26 words announced its decision in *Byrne, Brendan T. et al. v. Public Funds for Public Schools*: "The judgment is affirmed. The Chief Justice, Mr. Justice White, and Mr. Justice Rehnquist would note probable jurisdiction and set the cases for oral argument." Thus yet another effort by a state government, in this case New Jersey, to provide a measure of assistance for nonpublic, mostly denominational schools was found to violate the Establishment Clause of the First Amendment, and hence to be unconstitutional.

This in itself was nothing noteworthy. Since 1947, when the Court in *Everson* ruled on a state school-aid statute (also of New Jersey) there have been altogether some 46 cases brought to the Court dealing with aspects of this subject. As the Circuit Court in the most recent New Jersey case stated in the opening sentence of the majority opinion, each of these presented "recurring and troublesome questions concerning the relationship between religion and government."

Withal, the 1979 action by the Supreme Court received some attention, for it involved tuition tax credits. New Jersey had enacted a state income tax to provide funds for public education. Included in the statute was a deduction for parents of children in nonpublic schools, it being reasoned that through tuition they contribute to the secular objective of education, and could receive some partial recompense. (For a parent earning $20,000, the total savings was to be $20.)

A more general, and national, measure, providing tuition tax credits at all levels of education—which is to say including college and university as well—had passed the House of Representatives in 1978. The post-secondary portion passed the Senate as well, while the elementary and secondary provisions failed by only 15 votes. This indicated considerable national support for such assistance, but in the New Jersey case the Circuit Court declared itself bound by a 1973 Supreme Court decision, *Committee for Public Education v. Nyquist,* which struck down a New York measure allowing a taxpayer with a dependent in a nonpublic elementary or secondary school to deduct an amount from his gross income, and thus pay less state income tax. The Supreme Court had held that this had the primary effect of advancing religion and that therefore—following the constitutional "tests'" established in prior decisions from *Everson* through *Lemon v. Kurtzman* (1971)—the state law and the deduction it established necessarily failed.

But the notable aspect of the New Jersey event went altogether unremarked. In a separate opinion of the Circuit Court, Judge Joseph F. Weis declared that while clearly the Supreme Court decision in *Nyquist* governed the case, just as clearly the *Nyquist* decision was wrong. It had been a split decision (as almost all these decisions have been) and in Judge Weis's view "the dissenters have far the better of it in the *Nyquist* opinion. . . ."

Those dissenters—Chief Justice Burger and Justices White and Rehnquist—had written a trio of powerful opinions, observing *inter alia* that:

> While there is no straight line running through our decisions interpreting the Establishment and Free Exercise Clauses of the First Amendment, our cases do, it seems to me [the Chief Justice], lay down

one solid, basic principle: that the Establishment Clause does not forbid governments, state or federal, to enact a program of general welfare under which benefits are distributed to private individuals, even though many of those individuals may elect to use those benefits in ways that "aid" religious instruction or worship. . . . The essence of all these decisions . . . is that government aid to individuals generally stands on an entirely different footing from direct aid to religious institutions. . . . However sincere our collective protestations of the debt owed by the public generally to the parochial school systems, the wholesome diversity they engender will not survive on expressions of good will.

Rather, as with the dog that Sherlock Holmes observed did *not* bark, the significant fact in the New Jersey tuition-deduction case is that the high court chose *not* to hear an appellate judge tell it that it was wrong.

Here close attention is required. There are two senses in which it may be argued that the Supreme Court has been wrong in this area. The first concerns the basic *Everson* decision itself, set forth by Justice Hugo Black, which announced a rule of law in the widest sense:

> The "establishment of religion" clause of the First Amendment means at least this: Neither a state nor the Federal Government can set up a church. Neither can pass laws which aid one religion, aid all religions, or prefer one religion over another.

The key elements of the rule, as Michael J. Malbin has written, are that Congress cannot give nondiscriminatory aid to religion and that neither can the states.

This is the basic ruling of the Court and it endures three decades later. It has not been challenged, albeit (in my view) wrong. Instead, the *Everson* doctrine has been the basis for numerous challenges to state efforts to channel modest amounts of aid into non-public education through one means or another, efforts which persist. (The actual holding in *Everson* itself was that New Jersey *could* provide bus transportation to parochial-school students.) The challenges have always been brought by persons opposed even to such small efforts and determined to maintain the *Everson* doctrine in as strict a form as possible.

This opposition has been organized (the list of plaintiffs in the recent New Jersey case begins: Public Funds for Public Schools of New Jersey, American Civil Liberties Union of New Jersey, Inc., Americans for Democratic Action . . .) and vigilant. As states have devised new forms of aid to accommodate each succeeding Court decision, the organizations have typically challenged the statute, leading in time to yet another decision by the Court. Thus there has followed from *Everson* a great number of interpretive, or exegetic rulings which not infrequently have been wrong, if you will, in their own right.

The result has been an intellectual shambles: one confused and convoluted decision requiring a yet more confused and convoluted explanation or modification. Professor Antonin Scalia of the University of Chicago Law School, former Assistant U.S. Attorney General, Office of Legal Counsel, and in that capacity the senior constitutional authority in the Executive Branch, testified before the Senate Finance Committee in 1978: "It is impossible, within the time allotted, to describe with any completeness the utter confusion of Supreme Court pronouncements in the church-state area." Professor Philip Kurland, also of the University of Chicago Law School, writes that "the Court is thoroughly unprincipled in the area," meaning, of course, that there is no coherent principle to be found in the ever-lengthening series of decisions.

Such incoherence has invited challenge from persons with no greater interest than intellectual rigor in the high court. Challenges to this secondary, exegetic body of decisions from Supreme Court Justices themselves have become increasingly frequent, even as challenges to the primary decisions have remained rare. The notable quality of the Weis opinion is that it challenges both.

Judge Weis's opinion treats first the exegetic decisions:

> An analysis of the cases touching upon state assistance to nonpublic schools could proceed at length, but would merely illustrate the lack of a principled and logical thread. The reality is that the Supreme Court has marked out a series of boundaries and points of departure on an ad hoc basis. Thus, school books may be loaned to pupils, *Board of Education v. Allen* . . . (1968), but weather charts may not, *Wolman v. Walter* . . . (1977). Buses may be provided to allow for transportation of pupils to school, *Everson v. Board of Education* . . . (1947), but not for field trips to courthouses or museums, *Wolman v. Walter, supra*. Financial aid for the construction of buildings may be given to colleges, *Tilton v. Richardson* . . . (1971), but grants to provide needed maintenance to parochial schools in slum neighborhoods are forbidden, *Committee for Public Education v. Nyquist, supra*.

The Weis opinion turns then to what is the fundamental constitutional issue:

> In many of the opinions in this area, I am struck by the frequent use of the metaphor that the first amendment was intended to erect a "wall" between church and state. E.g. *Committee for Public Education v. Nyquist, Everson v. Board of Education*. Insofar as this concept

expresses a guiding principle for constitutional adjudication, I find it unfortunate and historically inaccurate.

My first reservation is semantical. So often a wall implies fear and hostility, as the infamous structure separating East and West Berlin so dramatically demonstrates. No such emotions should dominate the relationship between government and religion and the use of a metaphor that encourages such concepts is not desirable.

A more fundamental objection, however, is grounded in the history of the Establishment Clause. Although an accurate description of the Framers' intent is beyond our grasp, it is dubious that the Madisonian-Jeffersonian concept of absolute separation was widely accepted by the draftsmen. . . .

Commenting upon the checkered constitutional history of the Establishment Clause, one scholar has noted: "[I]t remains at best ironic and at worst perverse to appeal to the history of the Establishment Clause to strike at practices only remotely resembling establishment in any core sense of the concept." (L. Tribe, *American Constitutional Law.*)

Yet that is what has been done in using the "wall" concept to justify a policy of judicial hostility towards state aid to nonpublic schools.

Perhaps a more accurate appraisal of the purpose of the first amendment is that the state is to be neutral in its relationship with religion. And so if a particular legislative enactment, particularly in the field of taxation, provides clearly observable secular benefits, then religious institutions should not be barred solely because of their status. See *Walz v. Tax Commission.*

Finally, constitutional adjudication requires that the courts read a particular clause with its historical context in mind, lest the fears and prejudices of an earlier age serve to distort the problems of today. As Justice Powell, who wrote the *Nyquist* opinion, noted some four years later:

> It is important to keep these issues in perspective. At this point in the 20th century we are quite far removed from the dangers that prompted the Framers to include the Establishment Clause in the Bill of Rights. See *Walz v. Tax Comm'n.* The risk of significant religious or denominational control over our democratic processes—or even of deep political division along religious lines—is remote, and when viewed against the positive contributions of sectarian schools, any such risk seems entirely tolerable in light of the continuing oversight of this Court. Our decisions have sought to establish principles that preserve the cherished safeguard of the Establishment Clause without resort to blind absolutism. *Wolman v. Walter.*

These cases require a realistic approach, not an exaggerated response to nonexistent threats. Simple justice would require that the court honor the decision of the New Jersey legislature where the *quid pro quo* weighs heavily in favor of the state. But as the majority correctly concludes, the narrow legal issue in this case is whether *Nyquist* or *Walz* governs. Although it seems to me that the dissenters have far the better of it in the *Nyquist* opinions, I cannot in all intellectual honesty say that case differs from the one *sub judice*. I am bound to follow the holding of the majority of the Supreme Court and I therefore concur, albeit reluctantly. . . .

". . . [J]udicial hostility towards state aid to nonpublic schools." It has now been stated from the federal bench.

Whence does this hostility derive? (Assuming, of course, that it exists, and this brief is clearly written from the partisan view that it does.) It does *not* derive from the Establishment Clause of the First Amendment. The Supreme Court is wrong. This is the heart of it. The matter must begin here.

The Establishment Clause is simplicity itself. It states that Congress may not set up a national church.

There are two ways to get at this meaning. The first is to acquire a moderate facility with the English language, and in particular with one word that has somewhat gone out of usage. The clause states: "Congress shall make no law respecting an establishment of religion. . . ." The term "establishment" referred to a state church, such as the Church of England, an altogether familiar concept at the time, and rather a familiar institution.

All 13 colonies had established churches or other official involvement with particular denominations at some point in their history. At the outbreak of the Revolution, the Church of England was officially established in five southern colonies (Virginia, Georgia, South Carolina, North Carolina, and Maryland); the Congregationalist Church enjoyed official status in Massachusetts, Connecticut, and New Hampshire; and the Anglican and Dutch Reformed Churches both had similar status in New York. This pattern remained in flux for some time. (Virginia, for example, took steps toward disestablishment in 1776 and 1786 but did not eliminate the vestiges of the previous arrangement until 1802). When the First Amendment was ratified, three states gave preference to particular denominations, Anglican, Congregationalist, and Dutch Reformed; four states gave special status to the Protestant religion; three required adherence to Christianity among public officeholders; and three granted full religious freedom.

The term "establishment" has become somewhat unfamiliar in the intervening two centuries simply because there are no longer any established churches around. (In much the same fashion the provisions of Article III that "no Attainder of Treason shall work Corruption of Blood" would puzzle many persons simply because we don't do that much anymore.) But the meaning of the term "establishment" as used in the First Amendment is altogether accessible and quite unchanged. The first definition given in Webster's Second Edition is: "The establishing by law of a church or religion, etc." It is not too much to ask that persons who profess to care about the Constitution take the trouble to learn the language in which it is written.

Neither, if Mr. Justice Powell is to be believed, is it too much to ask that such persons learn a little of American history. To be fair, this may be stated with perhaps more insistence today than three decades ago when the *Everson* doctrine came into being. For the longest while, the meaning of the First Amendment was clear to everyone concerned. Then a curious sequence took place. In the second half of the 19th century a movement arose to prohibit aid to Catholic schools. It was assumed that the Constitution would have to be amended to do this. But the "Blaine amendment," first proposed in 1876, was never adopted by Congress. (For what it may be worth, a clause in the amendment provided that "This article shall not be construed to prohibit the reading of the Bible in any school or institution. . . .") But somehow when the Court came to rule in 1947, it took the political attitudes of the late 19th century to be the constitutional purposes of the late 18th. In the Court's defense it may be said that in 1947, there wasn't much formal history to direct it otherwise.

This has now changed. In a predictable manner scholars have been drawn to the issue. In what may also have been predictable, it took them a good while to get the facts organized. In *Beyond the Melting Pot* (1963), Nathan Glazer and I may have helped reconstruct the early history of state aid to education. (In New York it went exclusively to church-related schools, as there were none other.) In *The Garden and the Wilderness* (1965), Mark DeWolfe Howe commenced a careful examination of the meaning of the First Amendment and the intentions of those who drafted and ratified it. Of the line of church-state decisions begun with *Everson*, he wrote:

> The Supreme Court, in my judgment, has gravely erred in its reading of two chapters of American history. An impulsive eagerness to find that the state and nation were subject to the same disabilities so far as religion was concerned, led the justices to make the historically quite misleading assumption that the same considerations which moved Jefferson and Madison to favor separation of church and state in Virginia led the nation to demand the religious clauses of the First Amendment. . . . Furthermore, it permitted the Court to fill the space from which it had removed the vivid complexities of the eighteenth century's political philosophy with a simple and false absolute—all aid to religion is unconstitutional.

Howe's analysis was followed, and powerfully reinforced, by Walter Berns in his splendid volume, *The First Amendment and the Future of American Democracy* (1976) and by Michael J. Malbin's extensive essay, *Religion and Politics: The Intentions of the Authors of the First Amendment* (1978). Although Berns and Malbin use different evidence, they reach similar conclusions, as summarized by Malbin:

> As the Court has espoused its doctrines, it has relied on an incredibly flawed reading of the intentions of the authors of the First Amendment. . . . Aid to religion was to be permitted as long as it furthered a purpose the federal government legitimately could pursue and as long as it did not discriminate in favor of some sects or against others.

The research continues, and we are gradually acquiring a solid understanding of the relationship between church and state that obtained in 1791, of the assumptions and intentions of the Founding Fathers, and of the practices that prevailed through much of the nineteenth century. Among the major works now in progress is a comprehensive history of the First Amendment by Professor Robert L. Cord of Northeastern University.

IV

In his dissent in the *Gannett* case, Justice Blackmun stated that the Sixth Amendment established "the public's right of access to a criminal trial and a pretrial proceeding" and that of the press also. Those who would persuade the majority of the Court of this view must begin by reconstructing the history of that Amendment and of the First Amendment. This is not as direct a matter as might be thought, but it is entirely doable. It has now been done with respect to the Establishment Clause.

The Bill of Rights was adopted in something of a hurry: Debate on the Establishment Clause took up about one day in each chamber. The standard, if somewhat shaky record for the House of Representatives is the *Annals of Congress,* first published in 1834, taken from contemporary newspaper accounts and from the shorthand notes of a reporter, Thomas Lloyd. It is not complete, but is the only serviceable record of the proceedings of the First Congress. An essential fact is that the texts of successive versions of the clause, in each body, are available and these make the intention of the Congress conclusively clear. James Madison introduced two amendments in the House on June 7, 1789. The first of the amendments read:

> The Civil Rights of none shall be abridged on account of religious belief or worship, nor shall any national religion be established, nor shall the full and equal rights of conscience be in any manner, nor on any pretext infringed.

And the second:

> No state shall violate the equal rights of conscience or the freedom of the press, or the trial by jury in criminal cases.

Malbin notes that Madison's language prohibited both states and the federal government from infringing on the rights of conscience. "In contrast, the Establishment Clause was to apply only to the federal government."

How so? Because, as noted earlier, various of the states still *had* established churches. This is the lesson Perry Miller has taught: that if there was no very great love of religious tolerance in eighteenth-century America, given the profusion of religious denominations there was a very great need of it.

Alas, it was this very fragility of the Union which led ultimately to the substitution of the present language for Madison's explicit prohibition against "any national religion." Malbin reminds us that "federalism was *the* overriding issue throughout the Congress." It was still a lively issue as to whether the Constitution had created a new nation, or merely a federation of states. The Federalists, insisting that the latter was the case, carefully left the word "nation" out of the Constitution. But they were suspected (correctly!) of having a nation in mind and of being determined to forge one. Accordingly, in the debate in the First Congress the Anti-Federalists seized on the word "national" in Madison's draft, declaring that the gigantic conspiracy, the massive subterfuge was at last revealed. Feelings were intense. Elbridge Gerry recalled that at the Philadelphia convention of 1787 the two factions were designated Federalists and Anti-Federalists. They should, he said, have been called "rats" and "anti-rats," i.e., ratification and anti-ratification. The phrase "national religion" promptly disappeared. Otherwise the theme of the debate, which took place August 15, was set rather by the opening address of Peter Sylvester of New York who apprehended that the clause "might be thought to have a tendency to abolish religion altogether."

Senate debate was secret at this time. (The doors of the Senate chamber remained closed until 1795, and no record of the debates is available until 1802 when journalists were admitted to the Senate floor. The official transcript embodied in *The Congressional Record* did not begin until 1873.) But the Senate Journal records the texts which were considered on September 3. The first substitute offered for the House language began: "Congress shall make no law establishing one religious sect or society in preference to others. . . ." The final language sent back to the House read: "Congress shall make no law establishing articles of faith or a mode of worship or prohibiting the free exercise of religion." A conference committee settled on the present language.[5]

A century and a half later, when the Supreme Court in *Everson* turned its attention to this subject the Justices did not accept the Establishment Clause at face value, as meaning what it said, nor yet did they inquire into this history. Rather, as much as we can judge, they inquired as to the views of Madison and Jefferson, and came up with the well known "wall of separation." This surely will not do. The question is not what Madison or Jefferson may have thought; the question is what the Congress did. It is perhaps not wholly irrelevant that Jefferson was not a member of the First Congress; he was Secretary of State at the time, and quite uninvolved. (He had spent most of the previous five years on diplomatic missions in Western Europe.) Madison was floor manager of a complex piece of legislation which required compromise. Compromise he did. What more evidence is needed than that his original draft in no way reflected his own, and for the time somewhat extreme views?

If it be the case, in Judge Weis's words, that "an accurate description of the Framers' intent is beyond our grasp," are we not then well advised simply to take the plain language for what it plainly says? No establishment of religion, period.

Does not the burden of proof rest with those who assert that it says more? The legislators of the early American Republic were entirely friendly to religion and religious purposes. The House passed the 10 amendments of the Bill of Rights on September 24, 1789. The *next* day the House passed a Joint Resolution calling upon President Washington to issue a Thanksgiving proclamation. The Senate passed the Bill of Rights on September 26, and on the 27th passed the Joint Resolution. It called for "a day of public Thanksgiving and prayer, to be observed, by acknowledging, with grateful hearts, the many and signal favors of Almighty God, especially by affording them an opportunity peaceably to establish a constitution of government. . . ." The first Congress wanted to encourage religion,

---

[5] Not at issue here is the "incorporation" doctrine, whereby the prohibitions imposed on Congress by the Bill of Rights have been expanded by the Supreme Court to cover the actions of States. The Supreme Court interprets the 14th Amendment to bind the States as well as Congress when they legislate "respecting an establishment of religion."

but in no circumstances to establish a church so as to prefer one to the other. Chaplains were appointed to the armed forces. Both House and Senate began—and still begin—each day with a prayer by a clergyman. The Northwest Ordinance of 1787, re-enacted by Congress in 1789, set aside federal lands in the territory for schools: "Religion, morality, and knowledge," the law read, "being necessary to good government and the happiness of mankind, schools and the means of learning shall forever be encouraged." If they were to aid education, how could they do otherwise? Who, in 1789 in the United States, could imagine a school that did not teach some religious belief or other?

Madison and Jefferson, say the Justices, and there the matter rests. The inferior courts follow, as they must. Early on, the majority opinion in the recent New Jersey case invokes the declaration of former Chief Justice Warren that the First Amendment "underwrote the admonition of Thomas Jefferson that there should be a wall of separation between church and state." This well-known phrase of Jefferson's first occurs in a letter to the Danbury Baptists in 1802.[6] How could it be said to underwrite an amendment to the Constitution which had been written 11 years earlier? But this has not infrequently been the level of argument used against aid to nonpublic schools.

The constitutional facts are obvious enough. The state, at any level, is allowed to cooperate with religious groups in a nondiscriminatory manner in the furtherance of acceptably secular purposes. Further, this is precisely what now happens, with the single exception of elementary and secondary schools. Thus city, state, and federal funds, in the usual baffling mix, provide most of the support for the Jewish Hospital in Brooklyn. Federal foreign-aid funds provide much of the resources for the relief work in developing nations of Church World Services, a Protestant agency. The federal government provides money to improve the curriculum and the teaching methods of Marist College, a Catholic institution in Poughkeepsie. And so it goes.

The exception, to repeat, is that of elementary and secondary schools with religious affiliations. (*Not* colleges and universities with such affiliations.) Slowly, however, this anomaly is emerging. Slowly, the hierarchy of responses that arise when the Court is wrong is beginning to appear.

---

[6] Although others—starting with Roger Williams in the seventeenth century—had employed this and similar constructions, a fairly systematic search of the literature indicates—and biographers of Jefferson concur—no prior appearance of this phrase in Jefferson's own writings and utterances.

<h2 style="text-align:center">V</h2>

1. *Debate.* This is the first and in every way crucial response. When the Court is wrong there must be those who will say so. Often as not this will be a dissenting member of the Court itself. But to be effective the question must become a political issue of the day. In his grand study, *The Least Dangerous Branch,* Alexander M. Bickel described Lincoln's response to *Dred Scott*:

> The principle that the Court proclaimed was that slavery was not only legal in states which had it but was constitutionally guaranteed in unorganized territories as well. In the debates with Stephen A. Douglas in 1858, Lincoln said that he was against this decision, that he thought it wrong, that he feared its consequences, that he deemed it altogether deplorable. Douglas, on the other hand, without admitting that he necessarily thought the decision right, dwelt heavily on the argument that "whoever resists the final decision of the highest judicial tribunal aims a deadly blow at our whole republican system of government." "I yield obedience," Douglas said, "to the decisions of that Court—to the final determination of the highest judicial tribunal known to our Constitution." To this Lincoln countered by deriding the notion that a decision of the Supreme Court is a "Thus saith the Lord." The Court, he said, can be wrong. There is nothing sacred about the Court's decisions. Men may properly differ with them.

As the initial decisions regarding state and church involved Catholic schools, the first arguments in opposition to *Everson* and its progeny came, generally, from Catholics. This made for difficulties (as the press, perhaps, will now find), it being easy for others to dismiss or ignore arguments that are necessarily self-interested. It may be Catholics were deficient in the skills and the access needed to mount a debate of this sort; it may also be that an element of prejudice worked against them. Surely there are episodes in this generation-long history that raise this latter question. Consider the instances in which Mr. Justice Douglas supported his opinions in *Tilton v. Richardson* (1971) and *Lemon v. Kurtzman* (1971) with references to a book, *Roman Catholicism* by Loraine Boettner, published in Philadelphia in 1962. This volume has been characterized by Douglas Laycock of the University of Chicago Law School as an "elaborate hate tract." Mr. Boettner's views on Catholicism generally may be summarized in the following brief quote:

> Our American Freedoms are being threatened today by two totalitarian systems, communism and Roman Catholicism. And of the two in our country Romanism is growing faster than is communism and is the more dangerous since it covers its real nature with a cloak of religion.

That particular passage is not cited by Mr. Justice Douglas, but here is one he quotes in footnote 20 of his concurring opinion in *Lemon v. Kurtzman:*

> In the parochial schools Roman Catholic indoctrination is included in every subject. History, literature, geography, civics, and science are given a Roman Catholic slant. The whole education of the child is filled with propaganda. That, of course, is the very purpose of such schools, the very reason for going to all of the work and expense of maintaining a dual school system. Their purpose is not so much to educate, but to indoctrinate and train, *not to teach scripture truths and Americanism,* but to make loyal Roman Catholics. The children are regimented, and are told what to wear, what to do, and what to think. (Emphasis added.)

Ponder Mr. Boettner's charge that Catholic schools do not teach "scripture truths."

As it happens, a number of Catholic laymen and clergy pondered just that and at the time tried to draw attention to the peculiarity of such a tract being cited as a reference work in an opinion of a Supreme Court Justice. Had Douglas in some similar connection cited the Protocols of the Elders of Zion, or a Kommunication from the Grand Kleagle of the Ku Klux Klan, there would have been some notice taken. But there was no response whatever to these citations. There is a climate of presumption, and it must be worked against. (Thus, on April 3, 1979, reporting that the Supreme Court would hear a challenge to yet another state statute providing bits of aid to parochial schools, a New York law providing expenses for state-required testing, *The New York Times* noted that "The Federal Constitution specifically forbids state aid to parochial schools. . . .") The dynamic of scholarship, which is both truth-seeking and competitive, at length responds to this kind of imbalance. Already the time is at hand when law clerks will have learned as law students that the *Everson* decision is disputed. In time there will be judges who learned it as students also. Just as importantly, Presidents may come to office committed to change. Roosevelt made no secret of his desire to appoint to the Court Justices who would not block New Deal legislation on the basis of a flawed reading of the Fourteenth Amendment. It would be unthinkable today for a Justice to be appointed who held to the *Plessy* doctrine.

The same may come to be true of *Everson.* This is a constitutional check on the Court: Justices are appointed by the President. Already both major parties have endorsed aid to nonpublic schools. It is becoming a familiar position for Presidential candidates since Senator George S. McGovern endorsed tuition tax credits in his 1972 campaign. It remains for a President to come to office either committed to the proposition as a matter of justice, or able, as a matter of politics, to balance the claims of the nonpublic schools with the fears of the public schools that they will lose whatever the other system gains.

Opinion polls indicate that the great majority of American people believe that educational pluralism is a principle deserving of active governmental support. And it is well to bear in mind Robert G. McCloskey's observation, in his magisterial study, *The American Supreme Court* (1960), that "the Supreme Court has seldom, if ever, flatly and for very long resisted a really unmistakable wave of public sentiment. It has worked with the premise that constitutional law, like politics itself, is a science of the possible."

Debate on the *Gannett* decision began immediately, and soon became almost formal. The Associated Press, for example, distributed to its news staff a prepared statement to be read aloud to a judge who has announced the closing of a courtroom. The statement, described by Louis D. Boccardi, executive editor and vice president of the Associated Press, as "concise and legalistic," objects to any closed proceedings, sets forth the reasons why, and asks for time for further argument before a decision is made. This would appear to be a model reaction, if the validity of the Debate, Litigate, Legislate model is assumed.

2. *Litigate.* The exemplar of litigation as a tactic for bringing the Court back to the Constitution is the prolonged but in the end triumphant effort of the National Association for the Advancement of Colored People to reverse the *Plessy* decision. This is more difficult with *Everson,* for the effect of that ruling is that things don't happen rather than do, and it is not easy to challenge a nonexistent regime. Still, experience argues that those who feel aggrieved need to take initiatives. A former United States Attorney, now teaching law, asks his class in constitutional law to explain why the United States government is *obligated* to provide financial aid to church- or synagogue-related schools. The answer, evidently, lies in the Free Exercise Clause of the First Amendment: an interesting thought, and worth a lawsuit. Harry J. Hogan, retired counsel to the House Subcommittee on Elementary, Secondary, and Vocational Education, has pointed to the potential inherent in the growing practice of teaching "values" in public schools. "The fascinating possibility is that as soon as public schools and universities are required to teach values, then church-related schools and universities will be able to demand equal access to state and federal tax funds."

The risk of litigation is that it divides. In the end *no* schools may receive support for ethics courses. But, as no other process, it educates the courts.

3. *Legislate.* Legislation is the most direct and open way for the Congress and President to advise the Court of their reading of the Constitution, views which have equal standing under the Constitution, albeit they do not have equal effect. This issue arose directly in the Lincoln-Douglas debates. Lincoln said: "If I were in Congress and a vote should come up on a question whether slavery should be prohibited in a new territory, in spite of that *Dred Scott* decision, I would vote that it should." Douglas was scornful, saying, "if you elect him to the Senate he will introduce a bill to re-enact the law which the Court pronounced unconstitutional. . . . I never heard before of an appeal being taken from the Supreme Court. . . ." Lincoln replied that Douglas "would have the citizen conform his vote to that decision; the member of Congress, his; the President, his use of the veto power. He would make it a rule of political action for the people and all the departments of the government. I would not." Commenting on this exchange, Bickel allows that while deference to the Court is surely in order from the other branches, this cannot be absolute:

> The functions cannot and need not be rigidly compartmentalized. The Court often provokes consideration of the most intricate issues of principle by the other branches, engaging them in dialogues and "responsive readings"; and there are times also when the conversation starts at the other end and is perhaps less polite. Our government consists of discrete institutions, but the effectiveness of the whole depends on their involvement with one another, on their intimacy, even if it often is the sweaty intimacy of creatures locked in combat.

That Congress can abuse its power, should cause no surprise. Indeed it has. Reacting to the Supreme Court decision in *Engel v. Vitale* (1962) which forbade school prayer, the Senate on April 5, 1979 and again on April 9 by margins of 47 to 37 and 51 to 40, respectively, voted to deny the Supreme Court appellate jurisdiction in such cases. This can be done under Article III, Section 2, at least with respect to cases in federal court. (It is contended that the power was intended as Congress's restraint on the Court, corresponding to the President's power of appointment.) But in this case the power was surely misused. Publicly prescribed prayer, voluntary or not, is precisely what "an establishment of religion" is all about and that is what the First Amendment forbids. (In the course of the debate, one Senator rose "to speak as a Christian" about what he called the "secular humanism that abounds in our children's schools today." He did not like this and thought "we Christians" should do something about it. One is reminded, from time to time, that this is a Protestant country.)

For all this, legislation is unequaled as a means to influence the Court. Labor legislation was finally accepted by the Court only because state legislatures kept passing bills. Even the venerable Charles Evans Hughes at last was converted. Writing for the Court in *West Coast Hotel Co. v. Parrish* (1937) he derided the "freedom of contract" argument: "What is this freedom? The Constitution does not speak of freedom of contract. It speaks of liberty and prohibits the deprivation of liberty without due process of law."

Similarly, the Congress through legislation has commenced the undoing of the *Everson* decision. First, in the Elementary and Secondary Education Act of 1965, provision was made for compensatory services in schools with high proportions of "deprived" children, of which denominational schools have a more than sufficient share. (In New York City, nuns initially had to teach the children to operate the television sets thus provided, as they themselves were forbidden to touch them. But even such silliness makes its impact.) Similarly, the Higher Education Act of 1965 provided federal funds for "strengthening developing institutions." These were understood to be, in the main, black colleges in the South. But federal administrators, in the manner of bureaucracies, found that denominational colleges in the North often met the criteria and they were given grants accordingly. Half the private colleges and universities in the nation have religious affiliations, and most seem to take part in the now considerably complex system of federal aid to higher education. Mild tensions persist. It was reported that at the First National Congress on Church-Related Colleges and Universities, held at Notre Dame in the summer of 1979, there were complaints of "federal officials who question whether theology should be taught in classrooms built with federally guaranteed loans." But this is the point. Federal officials are now merely nervous about support for activities which, if one were to read *Everson* and nothing more, it would be assumed are altogether forbidden. What is happening, of course, is that American practice is coming in line with that of the other English-speaking democracies where government support is provided to any *bona fide* educational activity, and the communal peace, on this score at least, is maintained.

Consider the Higher Education Facilities Act of 1963. In this law, Congress provided funds to build buildings on college campuses. In the course of events, Sacred Heart College (and several other church-affiliated campuses) in Connecticut received such funds. The familiar law suit followed. But the Court in *Tilton v. Richardson* (1971) held that this aid was constitutional on grounds that "There is substance to the contention that college students are less impressionable and less susceptible to religious indoctrination." Now there is, of course, no substance whatever to this. It can only be a matter of time, albeit this could be another generation, before five Justices agree that what is constitutional for 19-year-olds is constitutional for 18-year-olds, whereupon the legal issue will be behind us. The Weis dissent is surely a harbinger of this.

There will remain the issue of public policy. *Should* 18-year-olds receive assistance? That is a different question altogether. It has never been satisfactorily resolved, mostly because opponents have always succeeded in interposing the constitutional question. But it is not a constitutional question.

Legislation is not always to be advised. The press, for example, will want to be cautious indeed before deciding that it wishes Congress to make a law respecting its freedom. On the other hand, it may find it useful for Congress to make laws protecting the Sixth Amendment right of the public to be present at trials. To those who say the Court has decreed that no such right exists, there is Lincoln's retort that a Supreme Court decision is not a "Thus saith the Lord."

✦ ✦ ✦ ✦ ✦

Has this analysis any predictive power? The *Gannett* case will provide a test. As with most cases in which the Supreme Court would seem to be wrong, debate began promptly and it may be forecast that a good deal of litigation will follow. In the manner of *Everson*, one decision will lead to another: clarifying, adjusting, half-apologizing. Legislation will be contemplated: most likely dealing with the public's right to access to the courts, rather than that of the press as such. In the end the Court either will reverse itself, or set forth rules for the closure of courts so narrow and restricted in their application that the controversy will go away. It may be hoped that it does not require a generation for this to come about.

Addendum

In the closing paragraph of the preceding essay I asked: "Has this analysis any predictive power?" My main theme, familiar to Constitutional scholars, but perhaps less so to citizens at large, is that the Supreme Court is not infrequently wrong *by its own reckoning*. This is to say that it will hand down a ruling, and subsequently reverse that ruling as having been—wrong. This does not suggest a flawed institution, save as a measure of imperfection is the lot of all human arrangements. It reflects, rather, the simple fact that our reading of the Constitution changes as values change and, much to be emphasized, as aspects of our history either fade from memory, or are revived. I wrote principally of a revival of our understanding of what the Founders, or rather the members of the First Congress, intended by the proposition that "Congress shall make no law respecting an establishment of religion. . . ."

My main *purpose* in the essay was to argue that the Court had been wrong in the succession of cases beginning with *Everson* (1947) dealing with public aid to religious schools. It was initially held that such aid was, generally speaking, prohibited by the Establishment Clause of the First Amendment. In my view this was simply ahistorical. It seemed to me that the tortured quality of subsequent decisions suggested that this was beginning to dawn on the Justices. What was to be said of a decision such as *Wolman v. Walter,* (1977) which held:

In summary, we hold constitutional those portions of the Ohio statute authorizing the State to provide nonpublic school pupils with books . . . We hold unconstitutional those portions relating to instructional materials . . .

Backward reels the mind, I subsequently wrote. "Books are constitutional. Maps are unconstitutional. Atlases, which are books of maps, are constitutional. Or are they? We must await the next case."

I proposed that experience suggested a simple model of how the Court is brought around in situations where it has got things wrong. (Or where time has "made" them wrong.) Debate, I wrote, Litigate, Legislate. Note I did not write Amend. The specific with which I was concerned was the question of the constitutionality of tuition tax credits for the parents of students in nonpublic, mostly church related elementary and secondary schools.

In 1983, in *Mueller v. Allen* the Court held that income tax deduction for tuition provided in Minnesota does *not* violate the First Amendment. It should be noted that the tax deduction was available for both public and private schools, and that the Court felt constrained to base its ruling in terms of the earlier *Nyquist* (1973) decision which set out a three part test which legislation has to meet in order to pass muster. Even so I would claim a measure of confirmation with respect to the general theme of the essay and its specific purpose. There has been debate, litigation, legislation. A form of tuition tax credits has been upheld.

Thus emboldened, I will essay a forecast or two. First of all, the Court decisions with respect to school aid have become *so* tortured as to risk ridicule, something that great and prudent institution will very much wish to avoid. It is already well known that students cramming for the District of Columbia bar examination are rushed by the subject of school aid with the pneumonic "T". *T*ransportation is constitutional. *T*extbooks are constitutional. *T*una fish sandwiches provided as school lunch are constitutional. If in doubt declare everything else unconstitutional, although, as has been noted, *T*uition *T*ax Credits now raise problems for this simple memory device.

More important, however, we are retrieving our memory of certain essential past events. My essay argued the original intent of the Establishment clause. I believe I was right, but no matter. The *new* event is the appearance in 1983 of Diane Ravitch's brilliant study *The Troubled Crusade, American Education 1945-1980*. Here we begin at the beginning of the issue of Federal aid to education. And what do we find? (And how could we have forgotten?) We find Paul Blanshard's articles which began appearing in *The Nation* in 1947, later expanded into the *American Freedom and Catholic Power*. His simple thesis widely endorsed among progressive thinkers was that the former was threatened by the latter, and not least through the Catholic schools, "a system of segregated schools under costumed religious leaders." A year earlier in 1946 Senator Robert A. Taft of Ohio had introduced a bill providing Federal aid to education which as a matter of course included aid to Catholic schools as a state option. In 1948 Taft's legislation passed the Senate 58-22, only to run into bitter controversy in the House where aid to Catholic schools became *the* issue. In no time a vast and bitter public dispute was underway, featuring those most earnest if not most expert polemicists, Francis Cardinal Spellman and Eleanor Roosevelt. Diane Ravitch writes that any chance of moderating the rising level of religious animosity was lost in the process.

> The Spellman–Roosevelt exchange was one of those public events that serves as a symbolic vehicle for large political issues, in this instance dramatizing the depth of hostility and misunderstanding between Catholics and liberals.

Two events have since occurred. In the 1980s the pronouncements of the Catholic hierarchy on issues such as nuclear arms have emerged as among the most "liberal" of any significant group. While a *Republican* president, Ronald Reagan, has emerged as a firm advocate of tuition tax credits (a clumsy device, alas, but the product of the religious controversies of the 1940s and the Supreme Court decisions that accompanied and followed them). I write three days from the time the President's proposal came to a vote on the Senate floor. It lost: but would have passed had Democratic Senators had as much as evenly divided on the issue. As it happened, only nine Democratic votes were to be found in support of a measure designed to respond to the interests of what, at all events, was once a largely Democratic constituency. Out of such nice ironies and dilemmas, I perceive the makings of all manner of change.

Washington, D.C.
November 19, 1983

Crime
in
American
public schools

JACKSON TOBY

IN the early 1970's Senator Birch Bayh's Subcommittee to Investigate Juvenile Delinquency heard alarming reports of violence and vandalism in American public schools—not just occasionally or in the central cities but chronically and all over the United States. Partly in response to these hearings, partly because of increasing preoccupation with school crime by newspapers, magazines, and television, the 93rd Congress passed an amendment to an education bill in 1974 requiring the Secretary of the Department of Health, Education, and Welfare to conduct a survey to determine the extent and seriousness of school crime.

The study was an elaborate one. Principals in 4,014 schools in large cities, smaller cities, suburban areas, and rural areas filled out questionnaires and returned them to Washington. Then 31,373 students and 23,895 teachers in 642 junior and senior high schools throughout the country were questioned about their experiences with school crime—in particular whether they themselves were victimized and, if so, how. From among the 31,373 students who filled out anonymous questionnaires, 6,283 were selected randomly for individual interviews on the same subject. Discrepancies between questionnaire reports of victimization and interview reports of victimization were probed to find out exactly what respondents meant when they answered that they had been attacked, robbed, or had property stolen from their desks or lockers. Finally, intensive field studies were conducted in 10 schools, schools that had had especially serious crime problems in the past and had made some progress in overcoming them.

In January 1978, the 350-page report to Congress, *Violent Schools —Safe Schools,* was published by the National Institute of Education. Though a scientific report, inevitably it had political overtones. Public schools with reputations for crime and violence tended to be located in the inner cities and to enroll high proportions of minority students from low-income families; average reading and mathematical levels were usually one or more grades behind national norms. Was there a causal relationship among high crime rates, low academic achievement, and a high proportion of minority students? Were parents with middle-class values enrolling their children in private or parochial schools out of fear of crime as well as out of desire for better academic instruction for their children? And, if so, did the problem of school crime explain an appreciable amount of middle-class flight from inner-city schools?

Perhaps because of the sensitivity of these issues, the report handled the data cautiously, drawing attention to some differences in the incidence of school crime and skipping lightly over others. The report showed that the crime problem was worse in junior high schools than in senior high schools, but it required careful examination of a table in an appendix to find statistics demonstrating that students in urban schools were robbed and assaulted more frequently than students in suburban or rural schools. (These statistics are reproduced in Tables I and II, below and on the next page, respectively.) But the differences are not as great as some of us might have expected. Statistics on the victimization of teachers, presented in Table III on page 22, were reported in an early chapter and showed unequivocally that urban teachers were more likely to be victimized than suburban or rural teachers—especially teachers in

TABLE I. *Percent of Students Who Reported Being Robbed within the Past Month**

	URBAN SCHOOLS	SUBURBAN SCHOOLS	RURAL SCHOOLS
Junior High Schools	9.5%	7.5%	7.1%
Senior High Schools	3.9	2.4	3.5

* SOURCE: *Violent Schools — Safe Schools,* Appendix A, pp. A6–A7.

TABLE II. *Percent of Students Who Reported Being Assaulted within the Past Month**

	URBAN SCHOOLS	SUBURBAN SCHOOLS	RURAL SCHOOLS
Junior High Schools	8.2%	7.2%	6.2%
Senior High Schools	4.0	3.0	3.4

* SOURCE: *Violent Schools – Safe Schools,* Appendix A, pp. A6–A7.

the largest cities. But the report tells us more than that, and we will present its findings in the form of answers to key questions on school crime.

Answered and unanswered questions

1. *How much real crime is there in the schools? Does it consist mostly of juvenile mischief given the alarming labels, "crime" and "violence," by exaggerated newspaper accounts, or is school crime mostly acts that adult perpetrators would be arrested and prosecuted for?*

Schools are plagued with real crime, according to the study. *Violent Schools—Safe Schools* was not mainly concerned with mischief or with foul language—although it mentioned in passing that a majority of American junior-high-school teachers were sworn at by their students or were the target of obscene gestures within the month preceding the survey. The report was concerned mainly with illegal *acts* and with the fear those acts aroused, not with language or gestures. Both on the questionnaires and in personal interviews, students were asked questions designed to provide an estimate of the amount of theft and violence in public secondary schools:

> In [the previous month] did anyone steal things of yours from your desk, locker, or other place at school?
>
> Did anyone take money or things directly from you by force, weapons, or threats at school in [the previous month]?
>
> At school in [the previous month] did anyone physically attack and hurt you?

Eleven percent of secondary-school students reported in personal interviews having something worth more than a dollar stolen from them in the past month. A fifth of these thefts involved property worth $10 or more. One-half of one percent of secondary-school students reported being *robbed* in a month's time—that is, having property taken from them by force, weapons, or threats. One out of nine of these robberies resulted in physical injuries to the victims.

Students also told of being assaulted. One-and-a-third percent of secondary-school students reported being attacked over the course of a month, and two-fifths of these were physically injured. (However, only 14 percent of the assaults resulted in injuries serious enough to require medical attention.)

These percentages probably underestimated the true volume of student victimization. They were based on face-to-face *interviews* with students. The same questions asked of samples of students by means of anonymous *questionnaires* produced estimates of victimization about twice as high overall, and in the case of robbery four times as high. (Tables I and II are based on student questionnaires rather than on interviews.) Methodological studies conducted by the school-crime researchers convinced them that the interview results were more valid than the questionnaire results for estimating the extent of victimization; some students might have had difficulty reading and understanding the questionnaire. On the other hand, fear of crime kept some students from attending school. In reply to the question, "Did you stay at home any time in [the previous month] because someone might hurt you or bother you at school?" 8 percent of the students in big-city junior high schools said "yes," as compared with 4 percent in rural junior high schools and 5 percent in suburban and smaller-city junior high schools. Since the students who had an opportunity to reply to this question were those attending school on the day the questionnaire was administered (or on a subsequent make-up session), students in the sample who failed to fill out their questionnaires may have contained a higher proportion of victims of school crime and a higher percentage of those frightened into truancy.

The report also contained data on the victimization of teachers, data derived from questionnaires similar to those filled out by students. (There were no teacher interviews, perhaps because teachers were presumed more capable of understanding the questions and replying appropriately.) Table III on page 22 shows that an appreciable proportion of teachers reported property stolen, but that only a small proportion of teachers reported robberies and assaults. However, robberies were three times as common in inner-city schools as in rural schools, and assaults were nine times as common. Even in big-city secondary schools, less than 2 percent of the teachers surveyed cited assaults by students within the past month, but threats were more frequent. Thirty-six percent of inner-city junior-high-school teachers reported that students threatened to hurt them, as did 24 percent of inner-city high school teachers. Understandably,

TABLE III. *Percent of Teachers Who Reported Being Victimized within the Past Month: Thefts, Robberies, Assaults**

COMMUNITY SIZE	KIND OF VICTIMIZATION		
	THEFTS	ROBBERIES	PHYSICAL ATTACKS
Cities of 500,000 population or more	16.7%	1.3%	1.8%
Smaller Cities	15.8	0.6	0.7
Suburban Areas	12.0	0.5	0.4
Rural Areas	9.5	0.4	0.2

* SOURCE: *Violent Schools — Safe Schools*, p. 68.

many teachers said they were afraid of their students. Twenty-eight percent of big-city teachers reported hesitating to confront misbehaving students for fear of their own safety, as did 18 percent of smaller-city teachers, 11 percent of suburban teachers, and 7 percent of rural teachers.

Principals were questioned about a variety of crimes against the school as a community: trespassing, breaking and entering, theft of school property, vandalism, and the like. Based on these reports as well as on data collected by the National Center for Educational Statistics in a companion study, *Violent Schools—Safe Schools* estimated the monetary cost alone of replacing damaged or stolen property as $200 million per year.

2. *Are intruders from the outside community responsible for a major portion of school crime, or are the students themselves the main perpetrators of thefts, assaults, robberies, and vandalism? And, if the perpetrators are students, which students?*

According to the report, the notion that intruders are responsible for a great deal of school crime is a myth:

> Preventive strategies designed to keep "intruders" from entering the school assume that offenses in the school are usually committed by outsiders; relative safety is believed to require keeping students inside the school and others who do not belong there outside.
> Our data, however, suggest that rather than locking most offenders out, these strategies seem to lock the offenders in with their potential victims. Except for trespassing and break-ins, the great majority . . . of all reported offenses for which information about offenders is available were committed by current students at the school in question. . . . Even in the case of breaking and entering, slightly more than half (56 percent) of these offenses were committed by current students.

Another belief about perpetrators that the report called into question was that older students preyed on younger students. Although younger students were disproportionately victimized, three-quarters of those who attacked or robbed them were roughly the same age, according to estimates of the victims themselves.

Schools in which a majority of students were from minority backgrounds had rates of assault and robbery against both students and teachers twice as high as schools where white students predominated. But the data did not explain this finding. The issue is *what* characteristics of minorities make them more likely to engage in school crime. Here the report offered tantalizing hints that educational failure was causally implicated in school crime, but nothing conclusive. Teachers who said that they taught a majority of low-ability students were five times as likely to report being attacked and twice as likely to report being robbed as teachers who said that less than a third of their students were of low ability. Teachers who said that a majority of their students were "underachievers" were three times as likely to report being attacked and about 50 percent more likely to report being robbed than teachers who said that less than a third of their students were underachievers.

Staff members of the National Institute of Education had anticipated that students would prove to be the main perpetrators of school crime and had planned to include on the student questionnaire questions about crimes the students themselves had committed. This would have provided valuable information about the characteristics of student perpetrators and, inferentially, about perpetrators generally. But boards of education resisted; questioning students about their own crimes, even anonymously, was likely to arouse objections from parents, students, and perhaps from community groups. The plan was dropped.

The report did offer impressions about perpetrators based on its field studies in 10 schools—that is, on extensive observation over a period of at least two weeks in each school, and on intensive interviews with school counselors, school aides, security personnel, parents, and representatives of community organizations. Professor A. J. Ianni of Teachers College, Columbia University, the director of the field studies, had this impression of school-crime perpetrators:

> There was general agreement among respondents in many of the schools that a small percentage of students—the figure 10 percent was frequently cited—form a hard core of disruptive students who are responsible for most of the vandalism and violence in schools. While this troublesome group did not seem to be identifiable in terms of any specific racial, ethnic, or socioeconomic status background, school staff commonly described them as students who were also having difficulty

academically, were frequently in trouble in the community, and tended to come from troubled homes. These students were easily identifiable and generally seemed to be known both to staff and other students because of the frequency with which they were in trouble. These same respondents indicated that in their experience this group of troublesome students could find allies among the other students when specific issues, situations, or problems arose. Violence and disruptive behavior is thus described as interactive with a small group of students frequently causing problems and at times setting off a chain reaction among other student groups.

3. Do attacks on and robberies of students occur mainly during classes or mainly before, after, and between classes?

Not surprisingly, violence directed at other students was less likely to occur during classes than at other times. Thus, the presence of teachers seemed to protect students against violence. Apparently, hallways and stairs (where teacher supervision was weak) were the sites for about a third of the violent acts, and other poorly supervised places—toilets, cafeterias, and locker rooms—the sites for another third.

The report did not ask whether violence on the way to and from the school building was a special problem. If the trip to and from school were dangerous for students in the inner cities, such schools would continue to be perceived as dangerous even though violence might be adequately controlled inside the school building itself.

4. Who are the main victims of school crime?

Younger students and the youngest, least-experienced teachers were most likely to be attacked or robbed. However, *male* students were more than twice as likely to be victims of both forms of violence than *female* students. And male teachers were somewhat more likely to be attacked than female teachers, although less likely to be robbed. The most likely explanation for the fact that schools are more dangerous for males than for females is that since males are the main authors of violent crimes, their victims tend to be the other males with whom they associate. Propinquity, both physical and psychological, increases the likelihood of victimization.

Propinquity between perpetrators and victims also explains the higher rate of victimization of students and teachers from minority backgrounds than of white students and teachers. Minority students and teachers were more likely to be attacked and robbed because their schools tended to be urban schools with high crime rates.

5. What are the causes of school crime?

The word "cause" does not appear in the index of the report. This was not an oversight. The safe-schools study was designed to describe the crime problem in American public schools during a short period of time (1976 to 1977), not to probe causes. However, Congress expected that the study would show how school crime could be prevented. And this objective implied some knowledge of causes. The report waffled. It spoke of "potential contributions" to school crime and of "several factors that appear likely to have general explanatory value with respect to school crimes."

But more explicit concern with the causes of school crime would have made possible greater realism about what could be explained and what could be done. For example, even though the report suggested on the basis of other studies that levels of school crime had increased from the 1960's to the 1970's, the safe-schools study itself collected no data on trends in school crime; hence, it could not throw light on causes of the *increase* in school crime. Furthermore, it could not explain why some youngsters committed crimes and others in the same schools did not; it had not collected data from offenders, only from victims. All the study could do was to contrast the crime rates in some of the 642 schools of the sample with those of others and to attempt to identify characteristics of high-crime and low-crime schools. The report did this. Thus, high levels of violent crime occurred in schools with above-average proportions of children from families of low socioeconomic status and in schools located in high-crime neighborhoods. But its authors were extremely cautious in interpreting the associations in causal terms.

There are hints one can trace out. Among all the schools in the survey—urban, suburban, and rural—a strong relationship existed between laxness in enforcing school rules, as judged by teachers and students in the school, and rate of violent crime. But surrounding neighborhoods of low socioeconomic status and high crime resulted in lax rule enforcement only in urban schools, not in suburban or rural schools. Perhaps in high-crime communities of low socioeconomic status the enforcement of school rules was difficult for teachers and principals but not, as the rural and suburban data showed, impossible. Perhaps an urban school with sufficiently creative leadership could also enforce rules despite its adverse socioeconomic environment.

6. Did the report suggest anything that the federal government can do to reduce crime in the schools?

There *were* recommendations in the concluding chapter of the report, lots of them—but they were not recommendations for Congressional action nor indeed were they National Institute of Education recommendations. They were suggestions from school principals, teachers, and students, for controlling school crime. Principals and teachers were asked to write in their own words replies to the following question: "What measures would you recommend to schools having problems with vandalism, personal attacks, and theft?" Students were asked to make recommendations by means of a similar question: "If a school had a problem with personal attacks, theft, and property destruction, what could be done to make it safer?" The answers by principals, teachers, and students were grouped in the same eight categories: 1) security devices, 2) security personnel, 3) discipline and supervision, 4) curriculum and counseling, 5) training and organizational change, 6) physical-plant improvement, 7) parental involvement and community relations, and 8) improvement of school climate. Within each category, responses were carefully coded into subcategories to facilitate statistical tabulation. Although the victims and potential victims of school crime are not necessarily qualified to devise effective solutions, it may be worth noting that "discipline and supervision"[1] was the most popular recommendation of students and teachers as well as of principals.

The report also described—based on questionnaire responses from principals—efforts made by schools to cope with crime, and discussed the modest success (in the opinion of principals) of these different efforts to reduce "vandalism, personal attacks, and thefts." Big-city principals reported the highest proportion of successful practices, mostly in the areas of "security devices" and "discipline and supervision"; Table IV shows that, except for paddling—a measure more popular in rural and suburban schools and in smaller cities—schools in the big cities made the most serious disciplinary and control efforts. Aside from the impressionistic judgments of the principals, the report did not attempt to evaluate the effectiveness of these disciplinary efforts.

Social changes and school crime

The report described the current situation rather than attempting to explain how a less orderly school environment developed. The report did not consider social trends in American society that made it more difficult for public schools to control predatory, violent, or malicious student behavior.

---

[1] The responses classified under this heading included "enforcement of rules, suspensions, etc.," "restitution, payment," "special classes, expulsion," "monitoring, watching," "controlling student movement, I.D.," and others.

TABLE IV. *Percent of Schools Using Various Discipline and Control Procedures, by Location**

TYPE OF PROCEDURE	LARGE CITIES	SMALL CITIES	SUBURBAN AREAS	RURAL AREAS
Students must show I.D. card to authorized personnel when requested	6%	3%	3%	2%
Students must carry hall passes if out of class	41	23	20	18
Visitors must check in at the office	67	56	49	39
Suspension	47	36	33	27
Expulsion	6	3	4	4
Paddling	17	34	33	42
Assignment to special day-long class for disruptive students	10	7	7	5
Transfer to another regular school (social transfer)	35	19	7	3
Transfer to special school for disruptive students	10	7	4	2
Referral to community mental-health agency as disruptive student	40	29	20	17

* SOURCE: *Violent Schools — Safe Schools*, p. 147.

Historically, the development of American public education increasingly separated the school from the students' families and neighborhoods. Even the one-room schoolhouse of rural America represented separation of the educational process from the family. But the consolidated school districts in nonmetropolitan areas and the jumbo schools of the inner city carried separation much further. There were good reasons why large schools developed. The bigger the school, the lower the per-capita cost of education tended to be. The bigger the school, the more feasible it was to hire teachers with academic specialties like art, music, drama, and advanced mathematics. The bigger the school, the more likely that teachers and administrators could operate according to professional standards instead of in response to local sensitivities—for example, in teaching biological evolution or in designing a sex-education curriculum. But the unintended consequence of large schools that operated efficiently by bureaucratic and professional standards was to make them relatively independent of the local community. The advantages of autonomy were obvious. The disadvantages took longer to reveal themselves.

The main disadvantage was that students developed distinctive subcultures only tangentially related to education. Thus, in the 1950's Professor James S. Coleman showed in his book, *The Adolescent Society,* that American high school students seemed more pre-occupied with athletics and personal popularity than with intellectual achievement. Students were "doing their own thing," and their thing was not what teachers and principals were mainly concerned about. Presumably, if parents had been more closely involved in the educational process, they would have strengthened the academic impact of teachers. Even in the 1950's, student subcultures at school facilitated misbehavior; in New York and other large cities, fights between members of street gangs from different neighborhoods sometimes broke out in secondary schools. However, Soviet achievements in space during the 1950's drew more attention to academic performance than to school crime and misbehavior. Insofar as community adults were brought into schools as teacher aides, they were introduced not to facilitate control over student misbehavior but to improve academic performance.

Until the 1960's and 1970's school administrators did not realize that order is chronically problematical when many hundreds of young people come together for congregate education. Principals did not like to call the police, preferring to organize their own disciplinary procedures. They did not believe in security guards, preferring to use teachers to monitor behavior in the halls and lunchrooms. They did not tell school architects about the need for what has come to be called "defensible space," and as a result schools were built with too many ways to gain entrance from the outside and too many rooms and corridors where surveillance was difficult. Above all, they did not consider that they had lost control over potential student misbehavior when parents were kept far away, where they could not see or know how their children were behaving. The focus of PTA's was the curriculum, and it was the better-educated, middle-class parents who tended to join them. In short, isolation of the school from the local community always means that if a large enough proportion of students misbehave, teachers and principals cannot maintain order. It was not until the 1960's and 1970's, however, that this potentiality became a reality in many American schools, especially inner-city schools. The following paragraphs come from a case study of a particularly disorderly New York high school reported in *Violent Schools—Safe Schools:*

When the student turmoil in the late 1960's led to frequent fires started by students' dropping matches into other students' lockers, all the lockers, with the exception of those in the gyms, were closed and remain so. As a result, students must carry lunches and other belongings, and these are sometimes stolen when they are left out. Vandalism, while not nearly as dramatic or widespread as it was during the time of the disruptions, still presents problems. The cost to the school in 1976 for repainting or cleaning off graffiti was approximately $5,000. The principal explains that graffiti and the breaking of windows are a constant problem both because of the size of the school and the reduction in the custodial staff.

Another trend helping to explain how a less orderly school environment developed was the continuing pressure to keep children in school longer—on the assumption that children needed all the education they could get to cope with a complicated urban industrial society. The positive side of this development was rising educational levels. Greater proportions of the age cohort graduated from high school and went on to post-secondary education than ever before. The negative aspect of compulsory-school-attendance laws and of informal pressure to stay in school longer was that youngsters who didn't wish further education were compelled to remain in school. They were, in a sense, prisoners; understandably, some of them became troublemakers. When they became insolent, violent, or criminal, there was little the public schools could do about them. (The private schools simply expelled them—that is, sent them to public schools.) Since society now believes that public schools are ultimately responsible for primary and secondary education for all children—those with special physical, emotional, or behavior problems are diverted to special schools only as a last resort—public schools are less able to control their students than they used to be.

Discovering children's rights

A third trend indirectly affecting the school-crime problem was the increasing sensitivity of public schools to the rights of children. A generation ago, it was possible for principals to rule schools autocratically, to suspend or expel students without much regard for procedural niceties. Injustices occurred; children were "pushed out" of schools because they were disliked by school officials. But this arbitrariness enabled school administrators to control the situation when real misbehavior occurred. Assaults on teachers were punished so swiftly that they were almost unthinkable. Even disrespectful language was unusual. Today school officials are required to observe due process in handling student discipline. Hearings are necessary. Witnesses must confirm suspicions. Appeals are provided for. Greater democratization of schools means that unruly students get better protection against school officials, and most students get less protection from their classmates.

Related to this third trend is a fourth: the decreased ability of schools to get help with discipline problems from the juvenile courts. Like the schools themselves, the juvenile courts have become more attentive to children's rights and less willing to exile children to a correctional Siberia. More than a decade ago the Supreme Court ruled in the *Gault* case that children could not be sent to juvenile prisons for "rehabilitation" unless proof existed that they had committed some crime for which imprisonment was appropriate.

The *Gault* decision set off a revolution in juvenile-court procedures and fostered a growing reluctance on the part of juvenile-court judges to send youngsters "away." Furthermore, a number of state legislatures restricted the discretion of juvenile-court judges. In New York and New Jersey, for example, juvenile-court judges may not commit a youngster to correctional institutions for "status offenses"—that is, for behavior that would not be a crime if done by adults. Thus truancy or ungovernable behavior in school or at home are not grounds for incarceration in New York and New Jersey. Many experts believe that the differentiation of juvenile delinquents from "Persons in Need of Supervision" is a progressive reform. But one consequence of this reform is that the public schools cannot easily persuade juvenile courts to act in school-problem cases. Student abuse of teachers, for example, is more difficult to cope with.

These social changes provide background for understanding the most important change of all: the erosion of the authority of the classroom teacher. If run-of-the-mill teachers could control effectively the behavior of students in their classes, in hallways, and in lunchrooms, there would be considerably less school violence—though theft and vandalism still might be problems. Nowadays some individual teachers can control their classes through personal charisma. But what has changed is that the *role* of teacher no longer has the prestige it once did for students and their parents, and so less forceful, less experienced, or less effective teachers cannot rely on the prestige of the role to maintain control. They are on their own in a sense that the previous generation of teachers was not. The most visible symptom of loss of automatic respect is assaults on teachers, mainly from students—but occasionally from parents themselves!

According to the report, somewhat more than 1 percent of American seventh-, eighth-, and ninth-grade teachers were assaulted by their students *every month*. Male teachers reported being attacked more frequently than female teachers, younger teachers more often than older teachers, inexperienced teachers more than experienced teachers, minority teachers more than white teachers.

What happened to erode the almost sacred status of teachers? This question was not dealt with in the report. Doubtless, lessened respect for teachers is related to fundamental cultural changes by which many authority figures—parents, police, government officials, military leaders, employers—have been removed from psychological pedestals. In the case of teachers, however, the general demythologizing process was amplified by special criticism. Best-selling books of the 1960's like John Holt's *Why Children Fail,* James Herndon's *The Way It Spozed to Be,* Jonathan Kozol's *Death at an Early Age: The Destruction of the Minds and Hearts of Negro Children in the Boston Public Schools,* and Herbert Kohl's *36 Children,* portrayed teachers, especially white middle-class teachers, as the villains of education—insensitive, authoritarian, and even racist. The failure of large numbers of children in inner-city schools to learn as much as they ought to have learned by national standards was interpreted as a responsibility of the schools and of the teachers. These books did not pretend to be quantitative surveys. They made no estimates of the percentages of American teachers who resembled the anecdotal examples the authors provided. But the consistency of the illustrations created an image of American teachers as, at best, inept and unfeeling.

The authors probably intended to exonerate youngsters for lack of academic success by portraying them as victims of failings in the educational system. *The effect on readers was to blame teachers for the poor results.* To be sure, few inner-city residents read these books. Yet the anti-establishment ideas that they contained percolated through American society as the clichés of television interviews and college education courses. Because the 1960's witnessed an enormous growth of enrollments in higher education, especially of minority community-college students, the notion that teachers could not be trusted spread from these books to college classrooms to American families, including minority families. Striking a teacher might almost appear to be a deserved punishment. Of course, only a tiny percentage of students and their parents subscribed to this ideologically extreme position. Even among parents and students who assaulted teachers, momentary anger rather than ideological conviction was probably the predominant motivation. Nevertheless, ideologically motivated attacks had symbolic impact. They suggested to children who witnessed them or heard about them that distrust of teachers must have *some* basis. Why else were people so angry? Thus ideological extremism fed on itself, increasing the mutual suspicions of students and teachers in inner-city schools and motivating some teachers to retire early and others to leave the teaching profession for other occupations.

Another indication of the erosion of teacher authority has been the decline of homework in secondary schools. When teachers could depend on all but a handful of students to turn in required written homework, they could assign homework and mean it. The slackers could be disciplined. But when teachers can no longer count on a majority of students doing their homework, the assignment of homework becomes a meaningless ritual, and many teachers give up. Of course, when homework is negligible, classroom instruction is less effective. The decline of homework also suggests that teachers lack authority to induce students to do *anything* they don't want to do: to attend school regularly, to keep quiet so an orderly recitation can proceed, to refrain from annoying a disliked classmate. Indeed, there are American public schools where one-third of the enrolled students are absent on an average school day. In the classrooms of such schools, teachers cannot build on information communicated and presumably learned during the previous lesson, because so many members of the class missed it.

To sum up: I believe school crime can best be understood in the context of social changes that separated secondary schools from effective family and neighborhood influences, that have kept older adolescents enrolled in school whether they craved education or not, that made it extremely difficult for schools to expel students guilty of intractable and even violent behavior, and that reduced the authority of classroom teachers.

Why care about school crime?

School crime receives attention mainly because individual teachers and students are assaulted and their property stolen or because the school's property is stolen or damaged. A more pernicious aspect of school crime, however, is that it reduces the effectiveness of public education, particularly in large cities.

Crime and the anticipation of crime in the past decade reduced teacher and student commitment to the educational process. Teachers in high-crime schools became less ready to demand from students in-class and out-of-class effort: Learning is work, and many teachers grew afraid to insist on what students regarded as unpleasant. They also became afraid to intervene when students fought or attacked another teacher. Some teachers found their role so different from what they had expected that they abandoned the teaching profession entirely or transferred to safer ("better") schools. Some older teachers chose to retire early. Most teachers—having invested too much in a professional career to quit—continued to serve, but with low morale. Students began to reject the educational process. They cut classes more than previous generations of students, and they took unauthorized absences of days and sometimes weeks. They complained that they weren't learning much in school—and they were right.

Those parents aware of the inadequate progress of their children in reading and arithmetic sometimes tried to correct the situation. For families with the economic resources to do so, the easiest way was to transfer their children to private or parochial schools or to move to suburban communities with reputations for good schools. Parents without the means to transfer their children could only attempt to make the local schools better, possibly by joining the PTA. But, in truth, parents could not have much impact, given the organizational and geographic isolation of the school from the local community.

The effect of this process of deterioration was to alter the role of the public school in underprivileged neighborhoods of big cities. American public schools have traditionally taught basic skills that all persons need to know in order to participate effectively in a complex industrial society. But they also served to select for post-secondary education youngsters whose native abilities and personal motivation prepared them for responsible and prestigious occupations. "Opportunity" was an incentive legitimizing the school in the eyes of the parents as well as students, and thereby justifying teacher authority. However, as crime grew more serious in big-city schools, they became less and less functional as a channel of social ascent for able students from disadvantaged backgrounds; they became traps instead of springboards. (The relentless support of the NAACP for busing to promote racial integration in public education should be understood against a background of disorder in big-city secondary schools that increasingly serve a minority clientele. Whatever else busing accomplishes, it promises to enroll minority students in safer and educationally more effective schools than they would otherwise attend and thus to return public education to its mobility-promoting function.)

Controlling violence in urban schools is thus not only desirable for its own sake, but also for the possibility of ameliorating two of the intractable problems of American education: 1) the draining away of better students and the consequent increase of racial segregation in the public schools of the largest central cities, and 2) educational ineffectiveness in those schools so serious as to prevent even intellectually able students from learning enough. To put the matter more dramatically, failure to control the violence problem in big-city schools means that urban public schools cannot propel youngsters from disadvantaged families toward successful occupational careers.

One way to avoid this conclusion is to assert that the causal order is not from violence to educational ineffectiveness to the flight from high-crime schools by better students, but rather that schools that arouse frustration and resentment in their students erupt in school crime. This is essentially the thesis of the Children's Defense Fund. According to the Fund, American schools are excessively arbitrary, especially with minority students, and suspend and expel students from school for trivial reasons unrelated to the educational process.. The Children's Defense Fund refers to the "pushout problem" and argues that the disproportionate representation of black youngsters among those suspended or expelled is evidence at least of arbitrary standards and probably of racism on the part of school officials. The Fund's position is that schoolchildren need advocates to protect their legitimate interests against the oppressive authority of teachers and principals, and that more "due process" rather than less will reduce student frustration and therefore violence. Partisans of the youth-advocacy approach to crime reduction in the schools convinced the Senate Subcommittee to Investigate Juvenile Delinquency of the correctness of this approach. The Subcommittee's 1975 report, *Our Nation's Schools—A Report Card: "A" in School Violence and Vandalism,* put it this way:

> One common thread of particular interest to the Subcommittee running through many of the underlying causes of school violence and vandalism is what may be called the crisis of due process. Quite naturally schools, like other institutions, are compelled to issue rules and regulations concerning the conduct of persons within their jurisdiction. It is clear that without fair and meaningful control and discipline the schools would quickly lose their ability to educate students. Increasingly, though, educators and administrators are finding that the extent of stu-

dent conduct which is sought to be regulated, as well as the methods of regulation, are causing more problems than they are controlling. A 1975 NEA study interviewed a large number of students from different schools and found that "many students spoke of the need for consistent, fair discipline."

For example, the Subcommittee found that in numerous institutions across the country, students, administrators and teachers are embroiled in constant ongoing disputes over restrictions on hair style, smoking, hall passes, student newspapers and a myriad of other aspects of school life.

According to the Senate Subcommittee, the schools' failings in the area of due process incite students to violence, as do arbitrary expulsions and suspensions. The Subcommittee Report made the connections as follows:

> At first glance it might appear that the expulsion, suspension, pushout, force out and truancy phenomenon [sic], although certainly tragic for those involved, might at least create a somewhat more orderly atmosphere for those remaining in school as a result of the absence of youngsters evidently experiencing problems adjusting to the school environment. The opposite, however, appears to be the case. The Syracuse study, for instance, found that in schools where the average daily attendance was lower, the disruptions, violence and vandalism rates were higher. This may be explained by the fact that the vast majority of students who are voluntarily or compulsively [sic] excluded from schools do, in time, return to those schools. In many instances their frustrations and inadequacies which caused their absence in the first place have only been heightened by their exclusion and the school community will likely find itself a convenient and meaningful object of revenge.

It is not possible to dismiss the arguments of the Children's Defense Fund, the Subcommittee on Juvenile Delinquency, and the various proponents of youth advocacy out of hand. Nonetheless, it seems more plausible that school violence lowers the effectiveness of the educational process through the fears that it arouses than that arbitrary school rules so enrage students that they rob and steal from each other and teachers, and perpetrate assaults and vandalism. Conceivably though, some students seek revenge on teachers, on the school building, and on their fellow students for perceived unjust treatment.

Violent-Schools—Safe-Schools asked students and teachers questions about their perception of the fairness of school rules; a scale of perceived school fairness was constructed. Did schools where students and teachers felt the rules were unfair have higher levels of violence than schools in which students and teachers thought the rules were fairer? Apparently not in the urban junior and senior high schools where the violence problem is most acute. The tendency for "less fair" schools to have higher violence rates virtually disappeared when other co-varying causal factors were statistically removed. Thus, in addition to being implausible, the hypothesis that student resentment of unfair rules contributes substantially to school violence did not stand up under empirical test.

How to reduce school crime

Reducing school crime requires a long-run strategy rather than a search for panaceas. Informal influences, such as greater parental involvement, might prove useful in controlling school crime. Informal social controls are a factor in human behavior generally— and certainly in adolescent behavior in schools. To fail to utilize informal controls is to throw the entire burden of preventing school crime on *formal* agencies of control: security guards, teachers, principals. But channeling informal influences is more complicated than hiring security guards or buying stronger locks. Time and effort must be devoted to developing practical programs.

Parents and other neighborhood adults are already employed in urban *elementary* schools as teacher aides; they are supposed to increase the effectiveness of classroom teachers. They may also contribute to a more orderly classroom atmosphere. But in *secondary* schools teacher aides are rare. (Paraprofessionals seem less useful for helping the teacher of specialized subjects.) If it could be arranged, the routine presence of parents in junior and senior high schools might have appreciable effects on crime rates and on the fear of crime, whether or not parents make a direct contribution to academic achievement.

But how can the presence of neighborhood adults in school buildings be justified? One possibility is to hire them to perform useful services that justify their being in lunchrooms, halls, stairways, offices, and even classrooms. Hiring parents for their indirect impact on school crime is expensive. And, indeed, the informal control resulting from a parental presence in secondary schools might be achieved more cheaply. Schools are already used for adult-education courses in evening hours. Such courses could be scheduled for the school day. If crime reduction were attained at the price of increased congestion and of reduced autonomy for teachers and principals, most people would consider the tradeoff worth it.

Greater efforts could be made to involve another informal influence, the peer group, in the control of school crime. This has already been done, reportedly with success, in vandalism control. The cost of vandalism for a previous year is calculated, and the student body collectively is given the monetary equivalent of the reduction in property damage for the current year. There have also been efforts to heighten the consciousness of students about school crime through public discussions. Although these steps are in the right direction, they do not seem to mobilize strong peer sanctions against more serious crime. What is needed is sustained thought and experimentation to discover the most effective way to motivate students to disapprove of predatory behavior. Again, a long view is required.

But along with a long-term perspective for school-crime reduction there must be a set of priorities. For not even the federal government can deal with *all* school crime in *all* of the urban, suburban, and rural areas of 50 states and the District of Columbia. Some types of school crime, while undesirable, are not major threats to public education. Marijuana and alcohol use on school premises probably belong in this category; perhaps vandalism and after-hours burglaries are also bearable costs in an affluent society. On the other hand, violent crimes at school are serious threats to the viability of public education. Controlling them should be the first priority of a safe-schools strategy.

School violence is most serious in big-city junior high schools, where assaults and robberies are more than twice as frequent as in senior high schools. Furthermore, a major factor in junior-high-school crime is that junior highs are pressed to keep troublesome students because of compulsory-school-attendance laws. Expulsion is theoretically possible, but difficult in practice. A junior-high-school student who attacks a teacher may be given a five-day suspension, whereas a high school student committing the same offense would be expelled. High schools have greater proportions of voluntary students. True, some high school students are trapped by the school-attendance laws in the ninth or tenth grades, but they are outnumbered by students legally free to drop out—and therefore possible candidates for expulsion for misbehavior. These considerations explain why the problem of coping with school violence is more difficult in junior high schools than in other public secondary schools.

Can violence be controlled in big-city junior high schools? "Youth advocates" believe that designing more intriguing curricula and selecting more stimulating teachers will reduce violence. Yet no curriculum is universally intriguing, and no teacher can be stimulating all the time. Public schools may not be responsive enough to their clienteles, as proponents of youth advocacy allege, but responsiveness or lack of it is only marginally relevant to the problem of violence. Rural schools are the least responsive and the safest; some of them paddle students and conduct strip-searches for drugs. *What makes violence likely is weak control.* Big-city junior high schools have high rates of assault and robbery because they contain a handful of violent students whom they cannot control and cannot extrude, and because they have not devised credible rewards and punishments for the larger group of potentially violent youngsters who are susceptible to deterrence. Addressing these two weaknesses of control will enable big-city junior high schools to reduce violence. But coping with these weaknesses involves painful measures, not the cost-free "solutions" suggested by youth advocates.

First, to rid the junior high schools of the small percentage of violent students who have proved that they cannot be controlled by anyone, the public schools should be allowed to use expulsion more freely. This means recognizing that the limits to the right of students to remain in school for educational purposes are reached when their presence jeopardizes the education of classmates. Expulsion is a drastic remedy. Though home instruction and alternative schools will be available for expelled students, the likelihood is that expelled students will not make much further academic progress. That is sad. Nevertheless, society must be permitted to give up on students who are threatening the educational opportunities of their classmates.

Milder sanctions

The second remedy is linked to the first. It may be possible to devise innovative lesser punishments for misbehavior provided that more drastic punishments (such as expulsion) are available should the lesser sanctions fail. Suppose, for example, that a student subject to expulsion for slapping a teacher is offered the option of working 14 hours every weekend at the school—painting, scrubbing, polishing—for three months. Supervision is given by paid college students from the local community working alongside the offender. The offender receives no pay; he is being punished, not rewarded by participation in an employment program. Perhaps the assaultive student prefers expulsion to hard work on his "free" weekends. (Experience with coerced community service in New Zealand—called "periodic detention"—demonstrated that some offenders preferred jailing for a period of time to labor-punishment on the installment plan.) On the other hand, his parents may prefer that he remain in school; they press him to accept the weekend penalty and, reluctantly, he agrees. But what happens if he does not show up for his weekend drudgery? In New Zealand the failure to report for weekend work without a medical excuse results in a bench warrant being issued, and the youngster goes to jail. Were magistrates unwilling to issue bench warrants, periodic detention could not succeed; periodic detention is not a Quaker work project. In order for coerced community service to be effective as a sanction for controlling school crime, boards of education would have to expel youngsters who dropped out of the program.

The parallel is not exact. Expulsion from school may be perceived by offenders as not wholly undesirable. The New Zealand experience is with jail, not with expulsion from school. Only experimentation can show whether expulsion is a sufficient threat to motivate the majority of offenders to abide by a lesser penalty. If not, the cooperation of juvenile courts would be necessary. Since school violence is delinquency, and legally subject to the juvenile or criminal courts, judges can stand behind school-imposed disciplinary measures with the more drastic threat of incarceration. To be sure, mention of expulsion or incarceration in relation to school crime horrifies "youth advocates," and the hope, of course, would be that these fairly severe sanctions need rarely be used. Experimentation is necessary to find out whether the threat of such sanctions is sufficient to ensure compliance.

Experimentation is also necessary with more palatable forms of influencing student behavior: rewards for good behavior rather than punishment for bad. Psychologists say that "positive reinforcement" is more effective than punishment, and positive reinforcement does not involve denying some students educational opportunities in order to preserve educational opportunities for others. Unfortunately, it is difficult to hook all students on the rewards offered by principals, teachers, and conforming students. According to sociologists, the basic social reward is approval, but teachers cannot easily bestow approval upon students who are uninterested in the curriculum and flout the behavioral rules of the classroom. Furthermore, such students are likely to receive approval for their disruptive behavior from close friends and to weigh this approval against the disapproval of teachers, principals, and the majority of the student body. Consequently, as desirable as it is to search experimentally for rewards that will help control violent crime in big-city junior high schools, the likelihood is that punishments will also be necessary, and that to protect the educational process the penalties of expulsion and referral to the juvenile-justice system will have to be used for the foreseeable future.

Americans are not patient or fatalistic. Given a national problem as unpleasant as school violence, our tendency is to attempt to do something about it—fast. Unfortunately, a crash program may not ameliorate the situation; it may even make the problem worse. School violence has not triggered our usual activist response. There have been stories in the mass media, hearings in the Congress, studies by the Department of Health, Education, and Welfare, but surprisingly little in the way of systematic national effort to reduce school crime. Part of the reason that school violence has been handled gingerly is the American tradition of local control over education. The main role for the federal government has been to supply funds for school programs that the Congress and the President deem worthy. Another reason is the concentration of the problem in big cities—where it is entangled with other difficult problems. So far about all that has happened is that urban school districts have improved control over entry to and exit from school buildings and have stationed security guards in the schools. *Violent Schools—Safe Schools* summarized the situation:

> More than one-third of all big-city schools employ trained security personnel; more than half of the big-city junior high schools have them, as do two-thirds of all big-city senior high schools. In suburban areas the proportion is much lower (7 percent), and in rural schools their use is negligible (1 percent).

Meanwhile, other efforts at control illuminate ironic twists of "children's rights" in practice, as when big-city school systems attempt to move violent students from one school to another. The rationale for such transfers is that youngsters may start fresh in a new school where they do not have a bad reputation. But the case study of one inner-city junior high school, called "Rogers" in the report, shows how this system of musical chairs works in practice:

> Since it is not legally possible to expel students considered disruptive, it is customary at Rogers as in other schools, to transfer students to other schools. By board regulation, the school is not permitted to inform the receiving school of the reason for the transfer or to provide any disciplinary records. "This can present some real problems," the dean says of the confidentiality requirement: "We had a kid last year who slashed another kid's throat with a razor blade and we finally had to transfer him to one of the intermediate schools, but we couldn't tell them officially what he had done or even that they should keep an eye on him because he was potentially violent."

No one knows whether transferring violent students from school to school reduces the total amount of violence in big-city school systems. Yet in any case humane considerations suggest that after a student has committed violent acts against students or teachers in a school, they ought not to have to encounter him in the corridors day after day. (In point of fact, it is at least as common for victims—both teachers and students—to transfer out voluntarily as it is for perpetrators to be compelled to transfer.)

What is being done?

On August 30, 1978, the Office of Juvenile Justice and Delinquency Prevention of the Law Enforcement Assistance Administration announced in the *Federal Register* a national initiative to combat school crime. Proposals were invited for a National School Resource Network; one grant of as much as $2,500,000 would be made for an initial 15-month period to finance the successful proposal. The presumption was that further grants would be made to maintain the School Resource Network if it seemed promising. Here is how the solicitation justified the new initiative:

> At the present time, there is no overall or resource strategy to assist schools in meeting the challenge of serious school crime. Resources are minimal and fragmented with little capacity to develop new resources to meet this challenge. The development of a nationwide school resource network dedicated to systematic advocacy, reform, and a safer environment on behalf of students and teachers is needed to provide overall direction and coordination of existing and new school resources. The promotion of due process, fairness and consistency in school security, and disciplinary policies and practices is important in assisting schools to develop and operate crime prevention and control programs.

The words have a pleasant sound, but it was not obvious what the School Resource Network was supposed to do. Later in the solicitation, the strategy of John M. Rector, then Administrator of the Office of Juvenile Justice and Delinquency Prevention, became clearer. Rector's approach was to move information from schools that had learned to cope with crime to schools that had not. Rector explained in a paragraph included under the heading, "technical assistance":

> The grantee shall produce technical assistance packages containing a variety of information materials on serious school violence and vandalism prevention. Sufficient copies of each package shall be produced to allow dissemination to appropriate technical assistance specialists in the national school resource network system. The information materials

to be included in each package shall include, but not be limited to, the Office of Juvenile Justice and Delinquency Prevention publications and materials such as the national evaluation reports, model school crime prevention programs and research reports, abstracts, bibliographies, grant project summaries, brochures, directories, and pamphlets. Materials developed and compiled should take into account regional, local and ethnic minority differences.

The dissemination of information about school violence will be helpful. But in order for improved communication to serve as the cornerstone of a national strategy for the control of school violence, some schools must be markedly more successful at coping with school violence than others. All that would then be necessary is to package the secret and send it around the country. But if, as is true especially in the inner cities, all schools are groping more or less ineffectively, a national strategy for coping with school crime should stress the systematic search for new approaches.[2]

The National School Resource Network is currently the main effort of the federal government, and local school systems are planning no new initiatives of their own. Nevertheless, school violence may diminish somewhat. The decline of births that began in the 1960's is likely to help. Junior-high-school enrollments have begun to fall. With smaller numbers of students, teachers and security guards are better able to defuse potentially explosive situations. Furthermore, teachers and principals have learned from their difficult experiences of the past decade; they know what to expect. They are less likely to become demoralized than the missionary-teachers who streamed into big-city schools in the 1960's—and streamed out again when they discovered that the role required less a guru than a policeman. Waiting passively for school violence to go away means relying on the happenstance of demography and other natural forces to cope with the problem. There is another possibility: that parents will become indignant enough about violent schools to make safer schools a political issue. Let's hope so.

---

[2] The failure of Mr. Rector's solicitation to include a research-and-development component was partly personal idiosyncracy. A lawyer by training, Rector was doubtful that social-science research could demonstrate the usefulness of an approach that practitioners were not already using—*somewhere*. This prejudice forced the School Resource Network to rely on what little was known about the control of school violence; Rector's strategy was to get the pamphlets in the mail. Rector was dismissed as Administrator in June 1979. Whether his successor will try to extricate the National School Resource Network from its presently-designed role is not yet known.

The
mandate
millstone

EDWARD I. KOCH

OVER the past decade, a maze of complex statutory and administrative directives has come to threaten both the initiative and the financial health of local governments throughout the country. My concern is not with the broad policy objectives that such mandates are meant to serve, but rather with what I perceive as the lack of comprehension by those who write them as to the cumulative impact on a single city, and even the nation.

I want to emphasize that my criticism is directed at the shortcomings of a system that has evolved over the course of many years. This is not the fault of particular individuals nor of today's leadership; it is rather an inheritance from the work of several administrations and Congresses, including some in which I served.

The City of New York, as an example, is driven by 47 federal and state mandates. The total cost to the city of meeting these requirements over the next four years will be $711 million in capital expenditures, $6.25 billion in expense-budget dollars, and $1.66 billion in lost revenue.

On the federal level, the current crop of mandated programs is really the second stage in the evolutionary process of activist lawmaking exhibited by the Congress. First, in the 1960's came the

Great Society programs. The nation's cities could choose from a bountiful catalog of federal grants which offered to foot 80, 90, or even 100 percent of the cost of enormously ambitious programs. In a time of unprecedented prosperity, with only higher expectations ahead, local governments eagerly went after federal funds even, at times, at the expense of comprehensive planning.

Left unnoticed in the cities' rush to reallocate their budgets so as to draw down maximum categorical aid were the basic service-delivery programs taken for granted by the Great Society architects. New roads, bridges, and subway routes were an exciting commitment to the future, but they were launched at the expense of routine maintenance to the unglamorous, but essential, infrastructure of the existing systems. Further, the enticement of federal aid drew cities into new social service commitments that were soon to monopolize their budgets.

The 1960's left a bitter legacy for cities in two respects. As prosperity fell hostage to inflation, and then stagflation, the bright promises of programs so boldly launched with federal aid collapsed under exponential cost overruns. Projects under construction, such as New York's Second Avenue subway, had to be abandoned, and the now-concealed but still-remembered excavation serves to remind the public of how easily government can fall victim to monumental folly.

Perhaps more damaging was the shift in the 1970's in the legislative approach, particularly in Congress, to the grand commitments of the 1960's. Sweeping solutions to social ills were still in vogue, but this time the public purse had a bottom to it, and its guardians became adept at fending off the claims of local governments. The result has been an ever widening gulf separating the programmatic demands of an activist Congress from its concurrent fiscal conservatism. By the close of the 1970's, the cities found themselves under the guns of dozens of federal laws imposing increasingly draconian mandates. From the perspective of local government the mandate mandarins who write these laws appear to be guided by certain disturbing maxims, such as:

1. *Mandates solve problems, particularly those in which you are not involved.* The federal government, for example, has shown no reluctance in ordering sweeping changes, the impact of which it will never have to face since it does not hold the final service-delivery responsibilities in such areas as education, transportation, and sewage disposal.

2. *Mandates need not be tempered by the lessons of local ex-*

perience. Frequently a statutory directive will impose a single nationwide solution to a perceived problem, such as sewage treatment, that has been developed in the isolation of a consultant's office and rarely, if ever, exposed to real world conditions in the affected regions.

3. *Mandates will spontaneously generate the technology required to achieve them.* Congress has shown a disturbing penchant for prohibitions on existing approaches to problems such as ocean dumping, for which no practical replacement has been developed.

4. *The price tag of the lofty aspiration to be served by a mandate should never deter its imposition upon others.* Statutory commands are rarely accompanied by adequate financial assistance. Most extreme in this instance is the accessibility mandate for transit systems and the requirements relating to the education of the handicapped.

I do not for a moment claim immunity from the mandate fever of the 1970's. As a member of Congress I voted for many of the laws which I will discuss, and did so with every confidence that we were enacting sensible permanent solutions to critical problems. It took a plunge into the Mayor's job to drive home how misguided my congressional outlook had been. The bills I voted for in Washington came to the House floor in a form that compelled approval. After all, who can vote against clean air and water, or better access and education for the handicapped? But as I look back it is hard to believe I could have been taken in by the simplicity of what the Congress was doing and by the flimsy empirical support—often no more than a carefully orchestrated hearing record or a single consultant's report—offered to persuade the members that the proposed solution could work throughout the country. The proposals I offer address this problem by increasing the level of scrutiny applied to both the cost and feasibility of mandates directed at local governments.

Let me now turn to the case histories of some of the more onerous mandates faced by New York City. I use my city as an example because I know its problems best. The problems we face, of course, occur throughout the United States. The numbers may be larger in New York but these mandates have an equally significant impact on the budget and local autonomy of every city.

Transportation and education for the handicapped

An example of a mandate that may totally skew capital spending nationwide in the 1980's at all levels of government is the handicapped-access program required by regulations promulgated in response to Section 504 of the Rehabilitation Act of 1973.

No one would argue that we need not commit funds to make transit systems and buildings accessible to the handicapped. But one also has to deal with the limitations—both financial and physical—that exist in the real world beyond the printed page of the *Federal Register*.

The Departments of Transportation and Health and Human Services (the erstwhile Department of Health, Education, and Welfare), have issued regulations that set as a mandate total accessibility for the handicapped to transit *systems*, instead of dealing with the *function* of transportation: mobility. In rejecting numerous appeals for modest exemptions and waivers, these regulations impose a restrictive and inflexible interpretation of the basic mandate of Section 504. Ironically, in focusing on accessibility the regulations fail to benefit a significant portion of the severely disabled. Subways and buses may ultimately be made fully accessible, but a disabled person may not be able to get to the system to enjoy its accessibility.

In this instance, alternatives are available. New York City has a far more extensive and flexible bus system than subway system. Given the numbers of handicapped people affected—some 22,800 in wheelchairs and 110,000 semi-ambulatory for a system that carries about 5.3 million people on a weekday—a more reasonable approach can be formulated to meet the transportation needs of the disabled. The City of New York has proposed making its buses accessible and providing a paratransit system for the most severely disabled. Paratransit will provide door-to-door service and can make the difference between a handicapped person being a prisoner in his or her home or a mobile member of the community. Similar paratransit services are in planning or underway in other cities.

The DOT regulations presently proposed do not accept the alternative of a bus and paratransit mix. Beyond bus accessibility, the regulations appear to demand accessibility in 53 percent of our subway stations within 30 years, at a cost in today's dollars of some $1.3 billion. Added to this will be at least $50 million in recurring annual operating expenses. And the regulations make no affirmative provision for meeting the handicapped community's myriad difficulties in getting to buses and subways.

It would be cheaper for us to provide every severely disabled person with taxi service than make 255 of our subway stations accessible. Indeed, the Congressional Budget Office, in its report of

November 1979 on "Urban Transportation for Handicapped Persons: Alternative Federal Options," estimated that the cost of implementing the Section 504 regulations, when spread over the limited number of wheelchair users and severely disabled passengers, will be $38 per trip. In contrast, transit trips by the general public cost, on the average, about 85 cents.

Should we somehow achieve the prescribed level of systemwide rapid transit accessibility, I believe that even the most courageous will test it only once to satisfy themselves that they are able to ride the subways and that few will ride them on a regular basis.

The history of this mandate points up a basic fallacy in the process leading to its promulgation: unrealistic projections by federal agencies of the cost of realizing mandated goals. When the Department of Transportation issued its preliminary nationwide regulations for public review and comment in early 1978, it used a figure of $1.8 billion for the contemporary cost of making all transportation systems accessible. This was clearly an unrealistic estimate and implied an unwillingness by the Department to face up to the magnitude of the course they were proposing to require. The Congress acknowledged this credibility gap and in 1978 ordered the Department to submit by early 1980 a report on the costs of accessibility, based on a survey of all rail-transit operators.

Finally, the Section 504 regulations are crippled by the lack of available technology to achieve the mandated standard of accessibility. Bus lifts have yet to be developed that operate without frequent breakdowns; no American bus manufacturer would even bid to build the Transbus; and people are just starting to think about devices that can span the distance between a rapid-transit vehicle and the passenger-boarding platform.

The issue of transit accessibility is one that the Department of Transportation must deal with quickly. If an affirmative policy decision is not made to bring the demands of Section 504 in line with the practical limits on compliance efforts, transit subsidies in the 1980's will be severely distorted—making systems accessible to several thousand people, while forsaking improvements needed on the total system. The cost in operating reliability will very likely reduce the quality of service available to both current users and those who should benefit from improved accessibility. We may, in fact, build a system under the Section 504 mandate which most handicapped people won't be able to use because of the barriers still remaining, and which, if they do manage to board, breaks down far more frequently.

While the Congress may have been thoughtless or arbitrary in compelling universal access for the handicapped without sufficient consideration of the real world constraints on localities, it has been almost cynical in its implementation of the directive that all handicapped children be provided "a free and appropriate education." It is impossible to attack the virtues of this objective. Yet the structure of the program enacted to accomplish it not only dooms the compliance efforts of local school districts, but also jeopardizes the overall quality of education that can be offered to all children.

The federal law contains three fundamental defects. First, the formula by which accompanying federal assistance is measured looks to the national average cost of educating a non-handicapped child and thus completely overlooks the far broader scope of services that are needed to bring the promise of the mandate to the actual population it was designed to benefit. The formula contains a second fallacy in its use of a single nationwide average cost. It deprives school districts with high education costs and high concentrations of handicapped pupils of any recognition of the greater costs and special problems they face in designing compliance programs. In New York City we have had to budget $8,180 per handicapped pupil, nearly three times the cost of educating a nonhandicapped child. This compares to the national average figure of $1,400 per non-handicapped child employed by the federal government to determine the level of assistance for educational programs for the handicapped. Third, and most disturbing, has been the consistent failure by Congress even to appropriate the full measure of assistance authorized by an already restrictive formula. Here we have the Congress implicitly reneging on the delivery of an already meager federal share of the cost of meeting its own national mandates. The shortfall in appropriations has grown over the past two years to the point where less than half of the authorized amount has been distributed to affected school districts. The act authorized an appropriation in fiscal year 1980 of 20 percent of the understated federal calculation of national costs; the appropriation, however, was only 12 percent. In short, first they underestimate the costs and then they underfund the underestimate. New York City is receiving only $8.5 million in federal aid while spending an estimated $221 million in tax-levy dollars for special education in fiscal year 1980. Our commitment will grow to at least $278 million in fiscal year 1981 and we can only hope that the Congress will keep pace.

This mandate, combined with an inadequate level of federal

funds for its fulfillment, has compelled the diversion of increasingly scarce local resources from the education of the rest of the school population. And as in Section 504, the absolute terms of the mandate discourage any efforts at the local level to develop alternative approaches to the statutory objective—such as the use of special facilities providing intensive attention to the needs of handicapped children—which might ease the enormous financial burden imposed by the program.

Ocean dumping—a mandate gone haywire

Perhaps the most graphic example of a mandate gone haywire is the prohibition, effective on December 31, 1981, of current ocean-dumping programs, including New York's, for the disposition of sewage sludge. In the face of an absolute command to shut down ocean dumping we must look for alternate technology. It would seem elementary that the planet earth, reduced to its most basic elements, offers us only land and water and what cannot be dumped in the ocean must be deposited on land. Incredibly, the Congress and the Environmental Protection Agency have imposed the ban out of concern for water quality, in the absence of reliable land-disposal technology.

Every way the City turns with its sludge it encounters another federal regulation. Banned from the ocean, the alternative we must use—dewatering and composting—will create an end product ladened with heavy metals, the disposal of which may come into conflict with anticipated landfill regulations, permanently rob the landfill of future agricultural use and endanger the area's watertable. The dewatering and composting of sludge will require a $250 million capital investment and $35 million in annual operating costs. The federal government will provide 75 percent of the capital costs; but New York City must shoulder at least 75 percent of the operating costs with the State assuming the remaining 25 percent. This will be only an intermediate step toward an as-yet-undeveloped permanent replacement for the existing ocean-dumping program. It is anticipated that a permanent replacement will be available in ten years, at which time we will be forced to abandon $150 million of the capital investment in the interim solution because of the potential health and environmental hazards it poses. This is what you might call a classic example of planned obsolescence—all for an imperceptible alteration in water quality for a brief period of time.

While we are covering our land with sludge contaminated by toxic materials, full compliance with yet another EPA regulation, administered jointly with the U.S. Army Corps of Engineers, may result in the cessation of all commerce in the Port of New York. This commerce annually produces more than $32 billion in foreign cargo trade and generates $1.5 billion in personal and business income for New York City's economy. To accommodate the large container vessels that have become the standard vehicle for moving goods by water, the natural depths of New York Harbor must be continually dredged. We have secured a three year extension of the ban on ocean dumping of dredged material. The extension does not, however, relieve us from the obligation to perform the costly bioaccumulation tests required by EPA's ocean-dumping criteria, which are subject to evaluation by both EPA and the Corps of Engineers. The interpretation of these tests by the two agencies can be inconsistent, so that they may be judged to be within permissible parameters by the Corps of Engineers but not EPA.

The disposition of dredge spoil is plagued by yet another arbitrary standard: the requirement that localities assess seven alternatives for the disposal of the material. The review of seven "possibilities" is required even though only three practical options appear to be available: ocean disposal, contained upland disposal, and use of subaqueous burrow pits.

While the standard laid down by the ocean-dumping mandate is currently unrealistic, another federal standard compels the City of New York to operate its sewage-treatment plants at secondary-treatment capacity, even though area water quality does not require this level of treatment year round. It may be hard to argue against pure waters, but this standard will force the City of New York to spend $10 million in FY 1981 for superfluous secondary treatment. I might add that while the federal government contributes 75 percent of the cost of constructing sewage plants, it leaves to the locality the full cost of their operation. Furthermore, the federal government tells us how to operate and man the plants. New York State has used its interpretation of the federal regulations as an excuse to deny its 25-percent share of operating costs. We are now having to sue the State of New York over the denial of the City's application for reimbursement in the amount of $6 million withheld in FY 1977.

San Francisco, like New York City, plans to build new secondary-treatment facilities. It also contends that full secondary treatment is not necessary on a year-round basis. Consequently, San Francisco has asked EPA to allow it to operate the plant at the primary-treatment level during the winter months. Other localities such as Los Angeles and Boston have filed applications with EPA in an effort to obtain complete exemptions from the secondary-treatment requirements.

My concern is not simply with the needless expenditure of local dollars, but also with the federal dollars committed to these programs in amounts that, considered in the context of overall urban needs, are desperately required by other urban programs. We must respond to the fiscal and public-policy dilemma that is created by the *cumulative* impact of courses that individual mandates are blindly propelling us down. Mandates obscure priorities and encumber comprehensive planning.

Public assistance—strange thinking and skewed formulas

Another example of a federal statutory mandate that frustrates local efforts to administer vital programs is the ceiling placed on the use of restricted public-assistance payments. In New York State, the Aid to Families with Dependent Children program (AFDC) is structured to include a separate shelter allowance for welfare recipients. The total grant paid to each recipient is different depending on his or her rent expenses. The Congress mandates that these monies be included in the recipient's grant and not be paid directly to the landlord. The ostensible rationale for this measure is to preserve the tenant's basic freedom of choice in allocating his check to food, housing, and clothing in a manner consistent with his priorities. Exceptions to this policy are made only if a recipient is found to have mismanaged the federal funds. Historically, non-payment of rent for more than a month has satisfied the mismanagement test.

New York City is faced with an accelerating syndrome of insolvency and abandonment by landlords who provide many of the lower-income rental units to AFDC recipients, usually because monthly rent collections fall far behind costs. These building owners have repeatedly approached the City seeking relief in the form of "two-party" welfare rent checks which would be issued to tenants who receive public assistance but require co-signature by their landlord before cashing. The City has made a strong effort to implement a two-party check program in areas especially hard hit by urban blight.

Our efforts to improve the situation have been blocked by a

federal law that limits to 20 percent of the caseload the number of welfare clients who can be placed on restricted two-party payments. If we exceed this limit we are subject to federal and state disallowances that could result in the witholding of the 75 percent federal and state share of restricted rents exceeding the 20 percent ceiling. A flat 20 percent limit is unrealistic given the magnitude of the problem in New York City. In August 1979 restricted grants reached a level of 18.8 percent of total grant recipients. This required the launching of a crash effort last October to remove clients from two-party rent restrictions before we could recoup the funds advanced to prevent their eviction for non-payment of rent. We are now at a level of 17 percent of the overall caseload.

Our problems in this area could be compounded further. The Department of Health and Human Services (HHS) has aired a regulation that would prohibit placing a welfare recipient on the restricted-payment procedure solely for not paying rent on time.

HHS argues that failure to pay the rent may not be sufficient evidence of mismanagement. When pressed to provide an acceptable definition of mismanagement, HHS suggests that the City would, in every individual case, have to show a diversion of rental funds to such things as vacations, drugs, or liquor. Using rent money for items such as food and clothing would not be deemed evidence of mismanagement, despite the fact that the landlord will come up short in rent collections, and even though each recipient receives a special amount for rent, as well as food and clothing allowances.

The HHS answer to the loss of housing caused by non-payment of rent would appear to require the City to publicize counseling services to clients who have difficulty managing their budgets. HHS has even suggested that the City's social-service staff make home visits to clients to provide the counseling. This latter suggestion from Washington bureaucrats is particularly naive when it is made to a City saddled with an AFDC population of 736,000. The administrative cost of such a system would be enormous and its effectiveness a matter of speculation.

Fortunately, wiser heads appear to be prevailing. HHS officials are now discussing with State and City officials a more realistic approach to the problems associated with the definition of mismanagement. I am hopeful that this will yield an administratively practical way of protecting the interest of families, while not contributing to further deterioration of our housing stock.[1]

---

[1] In May 1980 officials of HHS agreed to revised procedures for the definition of mismanagement that are acceptable to the City.

The most severe impact of the restrictions imposed on the two-party check program is the loss of an important component of the City's housing-preservation efforts. Of far more immediate concern to our overall financial condition, however, is the statutory formula setting ceilings on the federal share of total AFDC and Medicaid programs. The underlying design of both programs directs that the City provide assistance to a potentially unlimited number of recipients, but allows little local control over the benefit levels or eligibility standards which determine their total cost. Having imposed these enormous expenditure commitments, the Congress then restricts its participation by a cost-sharing formula that has long been obsolete.

Enacted in the 1940's, the federal-share formula links the reimbursable percentage of program costs to the per capita income of each state. As much as 65 percent of AFDC and 70 percent of Medicaid benefits will be absorbed by the U.S. Treasury in states which rank lowest by this single measurement. New York, with one of the highest per capita incomes in the nation, is limited to the minimum 50 percent contribution for each program. The authors of the formula may have thought their index accurately measured the capacity of state and local government to generate the revenues needed to cover their share of the total costs of an open-ended program. But per capita income, in isolation, cannot reflect two other critical determinants: cost of living and the size of the overall tax burden that a state or city is asking its citizens to shoulder. Since New York ranks at or near the top in these criteria, the ability of its taxpayers to carry steadily-increasing public-assistance costs is, in fact, no greater than that of taxpayers from states enjoying the aid of the higher federal reimbursement rates.

Court and state mandates: not to be outdone!

In addition to the federal statutory and administrative mandates reviewed so far, the City must also cope with the staggering impact that decisions of the federal courts, interpreting and applying the sweeping mandates of federal law, can have on the fiscal stability of localities and on their ability to govern with some minimum degree of flexibility. In New York City, for example, a program was initiated in conjunction with a planned new hiring of entry-level officers aimed at increasing the total number of minorities on the police force. The Police Department spent $250,000 conducting an intensive recruiting campaign among minority groups, and arranged for test preparation classes at locations throughout the City that were readily accessible to candidates from minority communities. The City designed a civil service examination, with the aid of outside experts, that would produce the largest possible number of eligible candidates from all ethnic groups. Minority applicants represented 30 percent of those taking the test. When the Civil Service appointment list was prepared from the results of the test, 13,000 candidates—the number sought as the pool needed for hiring—had obtained a grade of 94 or better. When an ethnic survey disclosed that of the 13,000 placed on the list only approximately 15 percent were black or hispanic, a federal judge found not only statistical discrimination from the test results, but went further and held that the results were evidence that the City had practiced *intentional* discrimination. He then directed that a quota be used in hiring from the list, requiring 50 percent of new hires be black or hispanic candidates, until at least 30 percent of the total police force was black or hispanic. The net effect is that the courts are no longer examining the fairness of the test; they are examining the results. And if the test does not turn out the way the judge wants, he imposes the result that is consistent with his personal, political viewpoint.

I believe that the judge in the police case is simply wrong on the finding of intent, and the facts and the law.[2] But the real threat to the City from this decision is that under federal law, unless the City enters into a compliance agreement with the Office of Revenue Sharing in the Treasury Department imposing some kind of quota or affirmative action program—and, I might add, thereby violates our Civil Service obligations under the State Constitution—the City's unrestricted revenue-sharing funds, approximately $300 million per year, could be withheld by the federal government. That situation is simply intolerable and affects not only New York but every state and city in this country.

The problems posed by the self-styled altruism of the federal mandates reviewed thus far are compounded by equally and in some cases more arbitrary dictates of state government. The unique size and density of New York City usually precludes our legislature from using the shield of uniformity to cloak an inflexible directive.

---

[2] The United States Court of Appeals recently rejected the District Court's finding of intentional discrimination, and held that the test was job related. The Court of Appeals also ruled, however, that hiring from the list of successful candidates strictly by test-score-rank order violated Title VII, and that an affirmative hiring quota could be employed as a remedy. The City expects to appeal this ruling to the U.S. Supreme Court.

That has not, however, prevented Albany from imposing its own onerous requirements on the City.

The state, with local concurrence, has assumed since 1976 responsibility for the administration of the judiciary at all levels. The generosity of this arrangement has been tempered in large degree by legislation a year later which restored the local obligation to finance all maintenance, improvement, and expansion programs required to support an adequate level of caseload capacity. Thus reduced to the status of a silent partner, we face escalating annual local-tax-levy commitments to the state-run court system that will reach $23 million by fiscal year 1982.

The state public-housing program offers a second example of the serious fiscal implications of an imposed local partnership. Prior to 1961 New York State made separate payments to each state housing project. Then, the legislature consolidated its subsidy payments, and froze the state share at $44 million. This has left the City's budget as the bank of last resort for the chronic deficits experienced in metropolitan-area projects. With rents kept down to assure an adequate housing supply for lower-income tenants, and maintenance costs increased by inflation and the facilities of age, the City must increase its subsidy to this program by an average of 17 percent each year. We will be spending $13 million by Fiscal Year 1983 to comply with the state-mandated obligations.

An even more extreme example is the state mandate that the City provide legal services for indigent parties in the courts. This exposes our budget to still another significant and potentially unlimited expenditure requirement that will amount to at least $9 million annually in the next three fiscal years. The state's contribution to this program is zero.

Perhaps the most unfair type of state regulation is that which holds out the promise of fiscal relief but measures eligibility by an impossibly high standard. Public-assistance recipients in New York who are not eligible for the federal AFDC program are given Home Relief benefits financed jointly by the state and the client's locality. The state share of these costs is normally 50 percent, but increases from 50 percent to 60 percent for any social service district that can demonstrate an AFDC error rate of 4.5 percent or less. That has not proved to be an overly difficult task for upstate communities whose aggregate caseload permits intensive monitoring. In New York City, however, a marginal reduction-in-error rate is achieved only after enormous investments in detection and prevention programs which must survey a welfare population of 736,000—larger than most towns in New York State. We have made impressive progress in this area, and can point to an error-rate-reduction program that has brought the City from the 1973 level of 18 percent to the current 7 percent rate. But we are far from achieving the 4.5 percent rate specified as a condition for a 60 percent state share of program costs, and the $23.5 million saving that would bring. It is quite possible that a system as huge as New York City's can never reduce errors to 4.5 percent, or could do so only at a cost far beyond the proffered fiscal incentive.

No review of state-imposed mandates would be complete without reference to the Heart Law. This directive, first enacted in 1970, is the most frustrating example of how the legislature can tie the hands of local officials charged with the responsibility of administering a program in accordance with the best interests of their community. The law deprives public pension-fund trustees of the broad discretion traditionally given them, by erecting what the unions claim is an absolute presumption that every heart ailment reported by a retiring police or fire department employee was attributable to an "accident" in the course of his employment. Since the underlying retirement program authorizes a tax-free disability pension at three-quarters pay for such a condition, the Heart Law creates a huge potential loophole in the half-pay ceiling placed on standard pension benefits. The mandate reflects an overwhelming concern for the welfare of one group of City workers, who can develop a heart condition on the job but may also do so behind the lawn mower on a day off—a concern, I might add, which does not extend to the job title of Mayor, whose occupant routinely encounters stress throughout a far less predictable working day.

The City believes that fully half of the disability applications approved under the law's compulsion would not stand up under a thorough medical analysis of the ailment's actual cause. And while some may view the law as generous, it is a measure of generosity —amounting to $12 million to date—that the legislature did not choose to fund and that the City can ill afford.

Needed remedies

By cataloguing these arbitrary, restrictive, or counterproductive mandates I hope to have demonstrated both the complex demands confronting an urban chief executive today and the need for comprehensive revisions to the process by which such directives are formulated. A new mandate may appear to its authors to be a bold experiment in behavior modification for a worthy goal. But I do not think they view themselves as accountable for the hardship they may inflict on a particular locality. A superior level of government cannot, they would argue, be expected to anticipate every nuance in a far-reaching policy initiative. Indeed not—here lies the very reason why federal mandates must be flexible enough to accommodate local circumstances.

As the Mayor to whom those who must endure the hardship of irresponsible mandates look for relief, I can no longer accept the monotonous refrain that "it's up to Washington to correct its errors." It is long past time for the system to become responsive to the needs of those it purports to regulate, and for effective controls to be placed on the mandate machinery.

I do not claim to offer more than a rough outline for a modest measure of protection from the kinds of excesses now faced by a city like New York, but urge that prompt and careful consideration be given to the following proposals:

1. All mandates should include waiver provisions that afford an appropriate measure to recognition of a locality's efforts to address the objective through alternate means, or to integrate the required program with competing or complementary policies. New York, in several instances, commenced negotiations seeking administrative relief only to be met with an almost reflex hostility to allowing the slightest relaxation or modification of the mandate. This attitude may reflect a natural bureaucratic concern that the first variance breeds a collection of exceptions that will carve the underlying statute into an unworkable patchwork. But the administrators of these laws must be directed, by statute or Executive Order, to accommodate requests for waivers authorizing additional time or modified procedures from communities who offer reasonable evidence of an unfavorable impact.

2. Special consideration should be given to cities whose local revenue-raising and expenditure powers have come under the control of external authorities. It may be some years before we can measure the success of current efforts by all three levels of government to insulate the American metropolis from the twin cycles of declining revenues and spiraling costs. It makes absolutely no sense for the federal and state authorities to nullify their own ambitious urban assistance programs through the inflexible application of arbitrary mandates and the horrendous price tags they carry.

3. Action on any proposed mandate should be deferred until a report has been prepared on both the potential impact it would

have on local government expenditures and the state of existing or proposed technology available to achieve timely compliance. Agencies such as the Congressional Budget Office and the Office of Technology Assessment are already in a position to perform an objective analysis of this nature, which could be summarized in the reports that accompany legislative proposals brought to the floors of Congress. Such a procedure would assure that the mandate makers are fully informed of the potential shock waves their action may send throughout affected communities.

4. No mandate should be imposed unless alternative methods of compliance are offered, with the final selection left to local option. In the exceptional case, in which mandates' authors are convinced that a single standard and procedure must be imposed, they should authorize variations in the timing of and approach to compliance within appropriate parameters, proportional to the degree of hardship or potential program failure among affected communities.

5. Finally, it is of overriding importance that every mandate be accompanied by financial aid sufficient to achieve compliance. The aggregate tax-levy resources which must be committed to all of the federal and state mandates presently imposed on the City amount to $938 million at a time when we must identify $299 million in net-expense budget reductions for fiscal year 1981.

Throughout its history, this nation has encouraged local independence and diversity. We cannot allow the powerful diversity of spirit that is a basic characteristic of our federal system to be crushed under the grim conformity that will be the most enduring legacy of the mandate millstone.

The Mandate Millstone has been lightened—but not lifted—in the past two years. The Reagan Administration has enunciated a policy of easing the federal regulatory burden on localities, and some improvements have come, principally through favorable court actions in suits brought by municipalities.

Most significant has been the change in the transportation handicapped access regulations. In May 1981, the D.C. Court of Appeals struck down the regulations; interim regulations subsequently issued give greater local discretion.

The Administration has sought to simplify the regulations relating to the education of handicapped children. In the environmental field, it has softened its opposition to ocean dumping.

We now have a new wave of federally imposed hardships: budget cuts and economic policies that are compounding the mandate problem and further undercutting municipal budgets.

Christian schools
versus
the I.R.S.

PETER SKERRY

ECLINING public school enrollments have in recent years been accompanied by the sustained growth of non-public schools. Indeed, since 1975 the latter have registered enrollment gains of 1 percent or more each year. But among these the fastest growing—and least understood—are the schools sponsored by fundamentalist Protestants. Christian schools, as they are typically called, have been described by one official of the now-defunct Office of Education as "the fastest growing segment in private education today." At the same time, because these schools typically shun the inquiries of outside organizations, we have no hard evidence on how widespread they are. Nevertheless, data presented in a recent study sponsored by the National Institute of Education suggest that over the decade from 1965 to 1975 Christian school enrollments may have trebled. The same study goes on to estimate total national enrollments in fundamentalist-oriented schools at 900,000—or about one-fifth of all non-public school enrollments.

Though most prevalent in the South, where the traditions of fundamentalism are the strongest, Christian schools are to be found in all parts of the country. There are, for example, some 60 of them scattered across Wisconsin. In 1979 alone, 89 new schools opened in New York State. Christian schools are also found in rural Ohio and Vermont, as well as Southern California. Nevertheless, their prevalence in the South and their emergence around the time of public school desegregation have meant that Christian schools operate under a cloud of suspicion. They are labeled "segregation academies" by those who insist they were established to avoid desegregation. There is a marked tendency to dismiss the sincerity of the people involved. As Clarence Mitchell, former Washington lobbyist for the NAACP, puts it: "Every school that's been started to evade desegregation has called itself Christian. That's not my idea of being Christian." This view received its fullest expression in August 1978 when the Internal Revenue Service proposed affirmative-action guidelines intended to revoke the tax-exempt status of these schools. The furor in response to these proposals compelled the IRS to hold three days of stormy hearings in Washington in December 1978. The agency received over 120,000 letters of protest. And as one agency official put it: "The response is more than we've ever received on any other proposal." Eventually Congress was drawn into the fracas. It held its own hearings, and by the fall of 1979 had enacted legislation that blocked—at least temporarily—implementation of the guidelines. For the present, then, the threat of these proposals has been halted; but the misapprehensions informing public policy toward Christian schools persist and have yet to undergo dispassionate scrutiny.

During February 1979, I visited Christian schools scattered across the central Piedmont region of North Carolina for 17 days of observation and conversation with parents, students, and ministers on all sides of the issue. My experiences indicate that skepticism toward the religious orientation of these schools is altogether unwarranted, and furthermore, that the effort to reduce their emergence to a matter of racism is a gross oversimplification.

Christian schools in North Carolina

Some Christian schools operate independently of any specific congregation, but for most this does not seem to be the case. And certainly all that I visited in North Carolina were founded and operated by local churches. In most cases the congregations were in existence several years before the school was started, though in one or two instances the church and school began at the same time. Most of the schools I visited were started within the past ten years, although a couple are considerably older. In many ways the boundary is blurred between church and school. Even the most established schools share some facilities with the sponsoring churches, and frequently the school principal is the pastor, or a young ordained minister who serves as the pastor's assistant. On paper, the Christian school typically does not exist as a separate, incorporated entity, but rather is headed by the same board of deacons as the congregation as a whole.

Like the congregations that sponsor them, Christian schools are generally modest in size. The average in North Carolina is about 200 students, though some are as small as 30 or 40 and a couple as large as 800. These figures include all age groups, for the typical Christian school in North Carolina and elsewhere includes all grade levels. Moreover, all the schools I visited, and apparently most in North Carolina, provide day-long child care for preschoolers—in some cases infants as young as six months—as well as after-school care for school-age children. North Carolina has one of the highest rates of female labor-force participation, and the preachers who run these schools view child care as an important part of their ministry.

The facilities offered by the schools vary with the age and prosperity of the congregation. One or two are housed in million-dollar plants that rival most public school facilities. But the typical school is much more modest, housed in one or two buildings adjacent to the church, or sharing quarters with the church itself. In basketball-conscious North Carolina, a gym is a top priority and probably most expensive single undertaking of any school, and all the schools I visited have or anticipate building one. Some schools are housed in neat brick buildings complete with lawns and shrubs, but others are built on concrete slabs with corrugated metal walls and roofs, giving them a rough, unfinished appearance. Inside the typical school the furniture is adequate but second hand; the student's desks and bookshelves are constructed of plywood and obviously the work of some volunteer carpenter. There is generally no bell system, and the clocks on the walls come from someone's kitchen. Home-made curtains hang in the windows. Like classrooms everywhere, the walls are covered with the letters of the alphabet, exemplary work, drawings, and posters—as well as Bible quotations. The dominant impression that remains after visits to several such schools is that while they may lack the professional air of modern school buildings with designer-coordinated color schemes and expensive equipment, they do feel pleasantly homey and non-institutional.

Independent Baptist congregations

By far the most salient characteristic of the schools I visited is that they are operated by independent Baptist congregations. In this as in most other respects they are typical of Christian schools throughout North Carolina and, indeed, the nation. This is an important point frequently ignored in the debate over these schools. When critics have bothered to take the movement's religious orientation seriously, they have been content to describe it as "fundamentalist." This is of course true, but it neglects to explain the predominance of Baptists in the Christian schools movement.

Throughout their history Baptists have been fiercely protective of their right to practice their beliefs free of outside interference. Their origins can be traced to the social and political turmoil of sixteenth and seventeenth-century England when, along with the Puritans and Quakers, Baptists formed part of a generalized opposition to the state-established Church of England. At a time when temporal rulers across Europe were imposing their personal religious beliefs on their subjects, the Baptists demanded complete separation of church and state. As their name suggests, they vehemently opposed infant baptism, which they viewed as the device by which unwitting souls were conscripted into state churches, and they insisted upon adult baptism as the free acceptance of Christ by the fully-informed individual. Many Baptists came to America in search of the religious liberty they were denied in their homeland. But their struggle with state authority was to continue. Roger Williams battled with the elders of the Massachusetts Bay Colony and was finally forced to flee to Rhode Island, where in 1639 he formed what is generally regarded as the first Baptist church in America. In the South, Baptists gained an early foothold in North Carolina, which served as a refuge for dissenters fleeing the established Anglican Church of Virginia.

Unwilling to grant authority over their religious beliefs to political rulers, Baptists have been equally adamant about ceding their religious freedom to church officials. Throughout their history Baptists have been fervent congregationalists, insisting that the ultimate and sole authority over church theology and affairs rests not with any hierarchy but with the members of each congregation. This is perhaps the basic distinction between the Baptists and their longtime rival as the church of the common man, the Methodists, who are organized along more rigid, hierarchical lines and have not played an important role in the Christian schools movement.

In recent years, the Southern Baptist Convention, for decades little more than a consortium of autonomous congregations to raise funds for missionary work, has presented a challenge to such notions of Baptist congregationalism. As the Convention has edged ever so slightly toward the Protestant mainstream in its theology, and simultaneously begun to present itself as a denomination-wide organization representing all Baptists, some congregations have reasserted traditionalist values and split off from the Convention, declaring themselves "independent Baptists." The sentiments underlying this schism are suggested by the words of one mother reared in a "regular" Baptist church: "I read in the newspaper that the Southern Baptist Convention just endorsed the ERA. Now, no one in the Convention ever asked me how I feel about the ERA. Who told them they could speak for all Baptists?" This woman now belongs to a small independent Baptist church near Charlotte.

Implicit in this notion of congregationalism is the democratic ethos that pervades all church activities. Nearly every decision affecting an independent Baptist congregation, after approval by the church deacons, is brought up for a vote before the entire congregation. The decision to buy a new church piano or to start a school would be discussed and voted on by those present at Sunday morning services. And once a year the church's budget, including the pastor's salary and expenses, is brought up before the congregation for discussion and approval.

Sunday morning services are clearly the high point of the week, but there are several other well-attended activities. Sunday mornings begin with Bible study for adults and children. Later that day the congregation reassembles for evening services. During the week most members attend Wednesday night services. Thursday is visitation night, when members visit those who have been ill or unable to come to services. One evening a week is devoted to choir practice, and Friday to church-league athletic competition. In addition to enthusiastic participation in these organized activities, a spirit of eager voluntarism pervades these congregations. Generally too poor to hire outside help, they rely on member initiative to mow the lawn, paint the trim, sew the curtains, and in many instances construct the church itself. A good example of what I'm talking about occurred when, during my visit, a freak storm dumped a foot of snow over central North Carolina. The next morning—a Sunday—several families arrived unbidden to shovel out the church grounds.

Such voluntarism is not just a matter of sociability or community spirit; it springs from deeply held religious beliefs. Theologically, independent Baptists are similar to other fundamentalist denominations in that they believe in the Bible as literally the word of God, accepting the biblical account of creation and vehemently rejecting any hint of the theory of evolution. Most believe we are now in the reign of the anti-Christ, described in the Book of Daniel as preceding the imminent return of Christ. In preparation for that day of judgment these Baptists observe a "principal of separation" that requires them to reject such "wordly" habits as tobacco, alcohol, drugs, card playing, gambling, dancing, coed swimming, listening to rock music, going to movies, and in some cases watching television. In some ways they resemble the Amish and Mennonites, with whom they share a literal interpretation of the Bible and extremely conservative social views. But unlike these other groups, the independent Baptists have chosen to live and proselytize in the secular world. As they frequently put it, they live in this world— but are not of it. All the congregations I visited enthusiastically contribute to the support of missionaries scattered all over the world, many of whose pictures are proudly displayed on the walls of the church.

Thus, for a good many of the families I met, the congregation is the focus of their social as well as spiritual lives. Because they have a say in its direction and perhaps because the congregations are rather small, members feel their contributions—or lack thereof —really make a difference. As one young mother explained to me, "If we didn't tithe, there'd be a hole in the budget." This sense of efficacy and responsibility is not easily found in many institutions today. The Lamar Society, a group of Southern liberals frankly critical of Christian schools, makes the same observation in its study, *The Schools That Fear Built*:

> A local fundamentalist church... is both homogeneous and highly stable. It is the only organization which its members control at a time when they feel government institutions are out of control. It is often the only structure they trust and certainly the one in which they feel most comfortable, since much of their social as well as their spiritual life revolves around it.

A typical Christian school

As an integral part of this kind of community of faith, it is not surprising that fundamentalist religious and social values pervade these schools. The day begins with prayer, and pledges to both the American and the blue-and-white Christian flag. Each class begins with prayer, and meals with grace. School-wide chapel meets once or twice a week; and although Bible study is only one part of the curriculum, all subjects are taught from a "Christian perspective." In contrast to what is continually referred to as the "secular humanism" pervading the public schools, these schools emphasize the essential depravity of man and the absolute necessity of accepting Christ for salvation. No effort is spared in rooting out all traces of the secular humanist inclination to place man rather than Christ at the center of all human endeavor. Textbooks are scrutinized for objectionable material—for example, the new "nonsexist" reading materials are as offensive to these fundamentalists as science texts containing evolutionary theory. For a while these schools used older editions of public school texts, but as these grow increasingly scarce, they are turning to Christian publishing houses.

One of the most distinctive features of these schools is the strict discipline code. Each school I visited had a written list of rules and regulations backed up by threat of corporal punishment or expulsion. Insubordination or disruptive behavior of any sort is simply not tolerated. Even in the elementary grades, youngsters must stand when addressing teachers and use "sir" or "ma'am." It goes without saying that students are forbidden to smoke, use drugs, listen to rock music, go to the movies, or dance. Instead of a prom there is a senior banquet. And as for boy-girl relations, even hand-holding is prohibited.

Each school also has a detailed dress code, calling over and over for "modesty" and "good taste." Girls must not wear makeup or pants; other strictures prohibit long hair, sideburns, moustaches, beards, tank tops, blue jeans, bell bottoms, tie-dyed clothing, male jewelry, sandals, or stenciled T-shirts.

It is hard to read such a list and not feel that these schools must be full of rebellious youngsters and obsessive adults. But this is not at all the case. After all, these rules are merely the reflections of everyone's values, teachers and parents alike. Willingness to abide by them is the primary admission criterion, much more important than the academic one. As a result the interaction between teachers and students is marked not by fear and intimidation but by mutual respect and friendliness. Students of all ages are well behaved without anything like the constant surveillance so necessary in the public schools. Even the largest schools have no need of that infamous administrator, the assistant principal, who serves as the de facto disciplinarian in public schools. Little or no time and energy are spent in ritualized negotiations over the rules. Everyone knows what they are, and if a student consistently refuses to abide by them (which does occur now and then), he or she is simply asked to leave.

Christian teachers and Christian parents

The teachers too must accept strict rules. Of paramount concern to the pastors, who take ultimate responsibility for these schools, are the religious beliefs of their teachers. Nearly all the teachers in the schools I visited had been certified by state authorities; indeed, many of them were former public school teachers who for one reason or another had left the public sector. But as the pastors readily admit, academic qualifications are really of secondary importance. The first question they ask prospective teachers is the nature of their religious belief. All the pastors I talked with require their teachers to be born-again Christians, sign the congregation's doctrinal statement, and abstain from the same list of worldly practices that the students do.

In addition, Christian-school teachers must be willing to settle for extremely modest pay. The typical salary in the schools I visited is around $6000 for the academic year; a few schools pay even less. On occasion an unmarried woman who must support herself is paid slightly more. More frequently, male teachers who must support families are paid more than their female colleagues—an arrangement everyone I spoke to readily supported. But even these male teachers barely reach $7500 per year. In general, Christian-school salaries are a good deal less than those in elite private schools in the South, and easily half of public school salaries. Not only that, but they include no benefits such as medical or life insurance or retirement plans.

Teachers are crucial to any school, but especially to Christian schools. Without their sacrifices the Christian schools could not remain financially viable. This contributes to the clear sense of purpose displayed by the teachers I talked to. Moreover, they see themselves, and are viewed by the congregation, as pursuing a religious mission. Their sacrifices earn them a special place in these communities of faith. Certainly these are the factors that explain the dedication and openness of the Christian-school teacher. But if we are to believe the critics of these schools, this is a dedication grown out of the race prejudice believed to be the real force behind these schools. And perhaps racist sentiment could be perceived as sufficient to elicit the financial and other sacrifices made by parents who send their children to these schools. But it strains credulity to suggest that so many people, over so long a period, would be willing to accept such cuts in salary and such restrictions on their behavior just for the privilege of teaching someone else's white children.

By any standard, the involvement of parents in Christian schools would have to be described as intense, in most cases flowing directly from their commitment to the congregation. In addition to working as volunteers, families make considerable financial sacrifices on behalf of the schools. Beyond their weekly tithe to the congregation, parents with children in the schools pay tuition ranging from about $500 to $800 per year for each child. Though relatively modest—about half the tuition at traditional college-preparatory schools in North Carolina—this is frequently a strain on these predominantly working and lower-middle class families. Nevertheless, many sacrifice further by making pledges to capital fund drives launched at one time or another by all the schools, in most cases taking out personal bank loans to do so.

To bear these burdens, many mothers must work—a necessity that conflicts with their firm conviction that women belong in the home. A common compromise is to work in the schools as teacher aides, secretaries, cafeteria workers, and very often bus drivers. In schools I visited, virtually all the helpers are parents of children attending the schools. Thus it is not surprising that parents feel these schools belong to them; after all, their sacrifices help keep them going. And the parents I met seemed to enjoy feeling needed. One couple explained that they had had a choice between sending their son to a small, struggling Christian school or a large, well-established one. They chose the former, because they felt a commitment to the school was a commitment to their son's future. As they put it: "We are really in on the ground floor of something good."

When asked specifically why they reject the public schools, parents make it clear they need the Christian schools as much as the schools need them. Most frequently cited is the Supreme Court's 1963 school-prayer ban. A few parents mention a recent controversy over the singing of Christmas carols in public school assemblies. Many complain of the virtual disappearance of the pledge of allegiance from the public schools. A few are troubled by sex education. Such changes are seen by fundamentalist parents as direct assaults on God and country, the pillars of their universe.

On another level, parents are displeased with what they've seen or experienced as the declining academic standards of the public schools. They recite the familiar litany of open classrooms, curriculum fads, wide-spread social promotion, declining test scores, and illiterate high school graduates. Neither products of higher education themselves nor especially concerned that their children be, the salesmen, millworkers, and auto mechanics who send their children to Christian schools are particularly incensed that the public system does such a poor job of teaching the basics, and they point with pride to the impressive record of the Christian schools in teaching reading and math skills. In every school I visited, four-year-olds were prepared so that by the first grade most were reading above grade level.

Furthermore, as is suggested by the dress codes mentioned, these parents are rejecting the youth culture they feel now dominates the public school scene. One young mother in Charlotte explained why, after two and a half years in the public schools, she had decided to change to a Christian school. She had been quite pleased with the desegregated public school her son had gone to for first and second grade, but the following year the family moved, and he had to attend a different school—which she felt was academically inferior and rife with petty thievery and vandalism. But the last straw, she told me, was when she discovered that each day the children were allowed to play records for an hour, and her 9-year-old son had become infatuated with a rock group specializing in ghoulish costumes, demonic lyrics, and vomiting blood on its fans. Over the Christmas holidays she and her husband placed the child in a Christian school.

Like working and lower-middle class parents elsewhere, these people tend to be rather protective of their children—inclinations which are of course reinforced by their religious beliefs. As one father of five children, all of whom attend the same Christian school, said to me: "My son doesn't know ten people I don't know, and if he does, I want to meet them." For such parents, to send their children to the public schools would be to yield them up to institutions that will expose them to violence, drug and alcohol abuse, disrespect for authority, and sexual experimentation. These are parents who, it should be remembered, reject smoking and dancing as wordly sins. They see the public schools as institutions over which they can exert little control and which in turn seem unwilling to control their children.

The social problems of the public schools are also paramount to parents who are less devout. Indeed, a number of families who send their children to Christian schools are not actually members of the congregation, though they come from similar Protestant denominations. Many turn in desperation to the Christian schools as strongholds of values and standards of behavior long since gone by the boards in the public schools. One mother told me that in junior high school her son had been intent upon "drinking up all the liquor and smoking all the marijuana in town." When it came time for high school, she persuaded him to go to a Christian school —which succeeded, somewhat beyond her expectations, in turning him into a born-again Christian headed for the local Bible college. She was grateful to the school for turning him around, but unwilling to follow him into the fold—as of course the congregation hopes will happen when they accept such students.

Desegregation and Christian schools

It would be misleading to say that concerns over desegregation do not figure into the shift to Christian schools. Some of these parents were scared away or simply fed up with the turmoil surrounding desegregation in cities such as Charlotte, where for months police were required to quell disturbances between white and black youths. Other parents complain of petty thefts, vandalism, and physical intimidation of their children in integrated schools. It is always difficult to assess the extent of such problems and their relation to desegregation efforts. Less problematic, however, are the concerns expressed by numerous parents about safety on public school buses. With widespread busing to achieve desegregation of county school systems, North Carolina has had to rely on a high proportion of teenage bus drivers, who work cheaply but also have higher accident rates. By contrast Christian schools across the state boast that they rely on adult drivers, many of whom are mothers. Another problem parents have had is with paired-school schemes that arose from desegregation. When it came time for one third-grader to leave the desegregated neighborhood school he had attended for four years, his misgivings, along with the inconvenience of the crosstown bus ride and his parents' other doubts about the public schools, convinced this family and others like it to make the change. If their son had to go to a different school, they reasoned, it might as well be one over which they would have some influence.

Of course, as the pastors will readily admit, some parents send their kids to Christian schools because they just don't like blacks.

But for most, desegregation is only the proximite cause of their abandonment of the public schools. Perhaps desegregation symbolizes the social turmoil they see pervading the public schools and the alien values they see dominating the culture; but for these "ordinary working people," as they describe themselves, not accustomed to voicing discontent to public officials, it is more like the last in a long series of affronts they have endured for years. And for these independent Baptists who refuse to take orders from other Baptists, let alone federal judges and bureaucrats, it is only natural that their accumulated grievances would find expression in the one institution they feel is theirs, the church.

Those who reject this interpretation of the Christian schools movement and reduce them to segregation academies must explain, among other things, why none of the schools I visited displayed the least evidence that racist doctrines are taught. In fact, they all espouse open admissions policies and in several schools black children are enrolled. Those who see nothing but racism lurking behind Christian schools would do well to ponder the development of one school described in a recent *Washington Post* article. The Riverdale Baptist High School in Prince George's County, Maryland was founded in 1971. In 1972 court-ordered busing was implemented in the county, and that year the population of the school jumped from 50 to 500. By 1977, when desegregation was in full swing, the school's popularity had grown to the point where it moved into impressive new quarters with an enrollment of 1300 students—*20 percent of whom were black.*

Those who routinely dismiss Christian schools as segregation academies must also explain why these schools are so radically different from public schools in terms of curriculum and religious orientation. Or, for that matter, why they are so fundamentally different from elite prep schools—which Christian parents dismiss as glorified public schools. Finally, skeptics need to be reminded that these are not the so-called "private" schools that miraculously appeared in the wake of public school closings in states such as Virginia, Louisiana, and Mississippi in response to the first Southern desegregation orders. The latter were supported by tuition grants, textbooks, and transportation supplied by the states, and were in fact the same segregated public schools that had always existed, hiding behind a "private school" label. Christian schools, by contrast, exist solely through the voluntary efforts of the congregations that support them, who as staunch supporters of the separation between church and state, take not a dime of public funds.

Perhaps the social forces behind the Christian schools can be seen more clearly by examining the events in Kanawha County, West Virginia a few years back. In the fall of 1974 a sometimes violent controversy erupted over the county school board's adoption of innovative "language-arts" textbooks featuring unexpurgated excerpts from modern literature—complete with the usual profanities and challenges to traditional values. The protest was spearheaded by a school board member, Mrs. Alice Moore, the wife of a local fundamentalist Baptist minister, who had been elected as an opponent of a proposed sex-education program. From the hills surrounding Charleston there emerged three fundamentalist preachers to share the spotlight with Mrs. Moore—one of whom "vowed before God and man to kick out those filthy books that's in our schools." Just as in North Carolina today, the public schools were denounced as "anti-Christian" and "havens of creeping humanism." And in the wake of bombings, a miners' strike, and school boycotts, several Christian schools were set up. But through all this, the issue of race was nowhere in evidence. Indeed, Charleston's small black community had several years before been peacefully and uneventfully integrated.

Kanawha County is only the most dramatic episode in a virtual fundamentalist counter-revolution evident in schools across the nation. In Nassau County, New York a school board was recently persuaded to remove from library shelves eleven books denounced as "anti-American" and "anti-Christian." The *New York Times* reports that in Indiana, Iowa, California, and New York, fundamentalists have begun to challenge the teaching of Darwinian evolution. And in the early 1970's, born-again Christians had a lot to do with blocking implementation of "Man, A Course of Study"—the multimillion-dollar social studies curriculum developed by the National Science Foundation. All these are part of a more general resurgence of conservative and fundamentalist churches throughout the country. As Dean Kelley points out in his provocative book, *Why Conservative Churches Are Growing*, Seventh-Day Adventists, the Church of the Nazarene, Jehovah's Witnesses, and other fundamentalist groups have been growing at rates of up to 9 percent a year, at a time when mainstream denominations such as Methodists, Presbyterians, and Congregationalists have experienced unprecedented declines. Nor is the phenomenon limited to whites; some of the groups mentioned here have a strong following among blacks as well. On all these fronts, at least since the late 1960's, social and religious conservatism has been on the march. To reduce this conservatism—and the Christian schools that have emerged from it—to racism is simply to ignore two decades of social and cultural upheaval.

The IRS proposals

In contrast to the view we have been developing, the Internal Revenue Service has offered its own interpretation of the Christian schools movement. After years of prompting by civil rights activists and public-interest law groups such as the Lawyers Committee for Civil Rights Under Law, the IRS in August 1978 issued proposed guidelines to determine "whether certain private schools have racially discriminatory policies as to students and therefore are not qualified for tax exemption under the Internal Revenue Code." The guidelines stated:

> A prima facie case of racial discrimination by a school arises from evidence that the school (1) was formed or substantially expanded at or about the time of desegregation of the public schools, and (2) has an insignificant number of minority students. In such a case, the school has the burden of clearly and convincingly rebutting this prima facie case of racial discrimination by showing that it has undertaken affirmative steps to secure minority students. Mere denial of a discriminatory purpose is insufficient.

The IRS went on to define "an insignificant number of minority students" as "less than twenty per cent of the percentage of the minority school age population in the community served by the school." Schools against which such a prima facie case had been established—the so-called "reviewable schools"—would lose not only their exemption from Federal taxes (including social security and unemployment contributions), but of more crucial importance, the right of individual donors to deduct charitable contributions to the schools from their federal income taxes. And in its specific refusal to exempt church-sponsored schools, the IRS directly challenged the sincerity of the religious sentiments I have identified as central to the Christian-schools movement. While any government agency is entitled to determine the sincerity of religious beliefs to which it accords special benefits, in this instance the IRS proposed to do so *not*—as wisdom and prudence would seem to require— after detailed inquiry and formal proceedings, but through summary administrative action triggered by an arbitrarily established quota. Thus the IRS reduced a multifaceted social phenomenon to a simple case of race prejudice. Moreover, as it makes plain in these proposals, the agency would place the full burden of proof directly on the schools. Assuming in advance the guilt of reviewable schools, it would act first and ask questions later. Thus the small and struggling schools, like those I visited in North Carolina, would be forced not only to undergo the expense of litigation, but to do so while deprived of the special tax status on which their existence substantially depends. In brief, these proposals posed a mortal threat to Christian schools.

In response to the furor created by their proposals, the IRS in February 1979 issued "revised proposed guidelines." These softened the more abrasive aspects of the original, but the fundamental thrust remained—the agency still assumed the guilt of schools not meeting its affirmative action quotas. The revised guidelines offered six examples of the kind of "affirmative steps" reviewable schools would need to take to regain their special tax status:

—active and vigorous minority recruitment programs;
—tuition waivers, scholarships, or other financial assistance to minority students;
—recruitment and employment of minority teachers and other professional staff;
—minority members on the board or other governing body of the school;
—special minority-oriented curricula;
—participation with integrated schools in sports, music, and other events and activities.

The most striking thing about these proposals is their inapplicability to Christian schools such as those I visited—all of which would lose their tax privileges if the IRS had its way. Each of these proposals would impose unreasonable burdens on these schools. Perhaps most egregious is financial assistance to minority students. As should be evident by now, the families who send their children to Christian schools are of modest means. The schools themselves live a hand-to-mouth existence, relying on tuition payments to cover operating expenses. Very little, if any, financial assistance is available to presently enrolled students. And whatever is available is certainly not enough to meet the IRS demands. By contrast the nation's traditional college preparatory schools—the "independent schools" as they like to be called—have with relatively substantial amounts of financial aid been able to attract enough black students to account for just over *4 percent* of their total enrollment. Viewed in this light, the IRS quotas on Christian schools seem neither reasonable nor equitable.

The proposal that Christian schools recruit minority teachers is also misguided. Relevant again is the experience of the nation's independent schools, which report great difficulty in attracting minority teachers away from relatively high-salaried public sector jobs. Certainly, Christian schools would be at an even greater disadvantage. And aside from financial considerations it seems doubtful that many educated minority teachers would be willing to abide by the strictures Christian schools place on staff.

Finally, the notion that Christian schools must place minorities on their boards seems wrongheaded. The boards of these schools consist of members of the congregations—usually the pastor and his deacons. To require that minorities be included means that individuals who have not participated in and contributed to the activities of the congregation must now be granted the status and prerogatives of its most respected members. It also means the IRS does not respect the right of blacks and whites in the South to go to separate churches. The fact that they do, and have for many generations, is scarcely the simple result of white racist machinations the IRS seems to imply.

Black churches and public schools

Separate black and white churches date from the post-Civil War era, prior to which slaves were seldom allowed to establish their own religious institutions, and were compelled instead to worship under the watchful eyes of their masters. As religious historian Sydney Ahlstrom demonstrates, the typical ante-bellum arrangement was integrated but paternalistic churches where blacks, frequently outnumbering whites, were confined nevertheless to separate areas of the church. There they were required to sing the songs and pray the prayers of their masters. To be sure, slaves worshipped in their own way whenever they could—the so-called "invisible institution"—but only the free blacks in the cities were allowed to establish their own churches, such as Richard Allen's African Episcopal Methodist Church, founded in Philadelphia in 1816.

Upon emancipation, the freedmen eagerly and immediately set up their own churches, which served in the difficult years that followed as important refuges from a hostile society. But by the 1960's the black church had, in the view of some, begun to outlive its usefulness. In 1963 E. Franklin Frazier could characterize the black church as "the most important institutional barrier to integration and the assimilation of Negroes." Today, of course, such pronouncements appear curious and dated, as black leaders reassert the strengths and uniqueness of the black religious experience. Rev. Joseph Roberts, successor to Rev. Martin Luther King, Sr. at Atlanta's Ebenezer Baptist Church, describes his own changes:

> I graduated from seminary in 1960 when integration was still big. I was the pastor of two integrated churches—trying to help the people live together as Christians—and almost denigrating the black experience in so doing, compromising by allowing the church service to be what I had learned in seminary: a modern version of the English Puritan worship of the 17th and 18th century. And then sort of disavowing who I was as a black person.

As the saying goes, the most segregated hour of the week is 11 o'clock Sunday morning. It would be wrong to ignore the influence of racism in the development of racially separate churches—especially in the South. But it would be foolish to ignore the fact that the continuing separateness of black and white churches reflects the needs and desires of blacks as well as whites.

Such factors may contribute to the difficulty Christian schools have in drawing sufficient numbers of black students to satisfy the IRS. Critics seldom consider the possibility that many black parents may not be interested in what these schools have to offer. They typically assume that black people are being denied something they desperately need and want—rather as if these were elite prep schools, the key to success. In fact, although Christian schools are successful at teaching basic skills in the lower grades, beyond this their accomplishments are minimal. The working and lower-middle class parents who rely on these schools have rather modest ambitions for their children—either Bible college, which may or may not be accredited, or no college at all.

By contrast, the educational aspirations of blacks are intense. As sociologist Sara Lawrence Lightfoot puts it, among blacks "education is not only valued, but formalized schooling is often seen as the panacea." This eagerness for education has translated in recent years into unprecedented increases in the educational attainments of young blacks. Black college enrollment from 1965 to 1976 grew by almost 400 percent, while white enrollment during the same period increased only 62 percent. Today the percentage of working and lower-middle class blacks attending college is actually higher than their white or Hispanic counterparts. Thus it seems doubtful that black parents would flock to the meager educational offerings of the Christian schools.

This is borne out by the fact that Christian schools which have responded to the IRS pressure by actively recruiting black students have in many cases been unable to do so. For example, the headmaster of a Baptist school in Memphis with an enrollment of 3800 testified before Congress that six years of active recruitment had succeeded in enrolling only 46 black students in the summer program and two in the regular school program. In his opinion, black leaders contributed to his lack of success by discouraging parents from sending their children to Christian schools. Indeed, the head of the Memphis chapter of the NAACP testified at the IRS hearings, "No right thinking black Baptist minister would counsel his parishioners to participate in such a racial undertaking when, after two decades of constant struggle, a desegrated public school system is on the horizon."

Similar counter-pressures from within the black community are reported in a study of a rural Georgia county by the Center for Research and Social Change at Emory University. In this instance the county's one private school, under pressure from the IRS's proposed guidelines, sought to enroll minority students but met with a campaign of radio and newspaper ads urging black parents to keep their children in the public schools: "Don't be used up in the private schools" and "Don't be a backlash on your roots." The fact of the matter is, despite the recruitment efforts of some Christian schools, blacks see them as segregation academies, pure and simple. Black people I spoke with in North Carolina certainly felt this way. Black mistrust of these schools is sufficiently great that no amount of regulation by the IRS will persuade black parents to send their children there. Indeed, one gets the impression that nothing short of closing the Christian schools down will satisfy many black leaders.

Of course, the black parents not only distrust Christian schools, they are understandably reluctant to abandon the public schools after investing years of effort in them. And for blacks who have gained positions of leadership and responsibility in teaching and administration, public education is obviously where the action is. Moreover it is clear that black people tend to feel more comfortable with public rather than private programs. While private institutions are tainted with particularistic impulses frequently harmful to blacks, public institutions embody universalistic principles of free access and equal treatment. And while private programs frequently carry connotations of charity by a few individuals, public ones appeal to the black community because they represent a commitment by the entire society. As the one immigrant group that did not arrive here willingly, blacks tend to feel that American society still owes them a debt; that reparations, as they were called in the 1960's, are still due. The commitment of significant public resources to free and equal education is just such a reparation.

Invidious distinctions

As we have already noted, the guidelines originally proposed by the IRS refused to distinguish between religious and nonreligious schools. But even those sympathetic to the agency's approach quickly saw problems with this approach. As a *New Republic* article outspokenly entitled "Subsidizing Segregation" pointed out:

> It's possible to imagine a situation where genuine religious schools could be trapped unfairly by the proposed IRS guidelines. ... A Jewish or Amish school, for example, might have a hard time meeting the alternative tests for continued exemption, because of the rarity of Jewish or Amish blacks.

In response to such concerns the IRS proposed two exemptions from its racial quotas. The first applied to any school that was "part of a system of commonly supervised schools"—provided the entire system satisfied the guidelines. The other applied to schools with "special programs or special curricula which by their nature are of interest only to identifiable groups which are not composed of a significant number of minority students." What became evident during the Congressional hearings was that the first exemption was directed primarily at Catholic schools operating as part of a diocesan system and the second at Jewish day schools.

Unfortunately, this understandable effort to reconcile the logic of integration with the reality of exclusive religious groups creates more problems than it solves. The obvious question arises: Are Jewish day schools or Catholic parochial schools more "genuinely religious" than the Christian schools I have been describing? This is, of course, precisely the kind of invidious distinction between religious groups that the First Amendment is meant to obviate. And perhaps not surprisingly, ill feelings toward Catholics and Jews were at times evident among many who testified against the IRS proposals. For some the solution to this problem is to grant religious groups absolute freedom from all government regulation. I cannot adequately deal with this difficult issue here, but attention certainly can be drawn to the dangerous path taken by the IRS.

By now it must be evident that the forces involved in the Christian school movement are sufficiently complex that the issue of racial motives requires detailed investigation into the specifics of each case. Of course, this would normally be triggered by a complaint by, for example, parents who felt they had been discriminated against by a particular school. The ensuing litigation would then allow for judicial scrutiny of the policies of the school and of the motives of those involved with the school. It is precisely this careful, time-consuming examination of intent that the IRS seeks to avoid with its single-minded reliance on numerical quotas.

And in this regard it is important to note that the proposed guidelines represent a drastic and questionable departure from previous IRS policy. Since 1970 that policy has been to require private schools seeking tax exempt status to make various public declarations of nondiscriminatory admission policies. Curiously, the basis of that policy is a federal district court decision which the IRS now cites as the basis of its affirmative-action guidelines. In *Green v. Connolly*, a class of black parents successfully challenged the tax exemptions of several Mississippi private schools. But unlike the Christian schools we have been discussing, these were self-declared segregation academies. As a result the court enjoined the IRS from granting exempt status to any Mississippi schools that failed to declare publicly a "racially nondiscriminatory policy as to students." And as to what the court meant here, there can be no doubt. To monitor compliance with its decision the court required affected schools to submit relevant data to the IRS, including enrollment figures. But here the court explicitly avoided any hint of racial quotas and emphasized:

> Our requirements do not establish substantive criteria but are information requirements, to assure that the Service will have salient information at hand before it makes a certification or gives an assurance of exemption or deductibility.

Similar questions arise with another case to which the IRS frequently refers as a basis for its affirmative-action proposals. In *Norwood v. Harrison* another federal district court ruled that private schools against which a prima facie case of discrimination had been established were ineligible to use textbooks purchased by the State of Mississippi. The court went on to specify that the absence of black students and teachers in a school was at least partial basis for such a prima facie case. Aside from the fact that the Christian schools discussed here receive no state subsidy such as textbooks, it is crucial to note that here again racial quotas were explicitly rejected:

At this point, it is important to emphasize that the ultimate issue in administering Mississippi's textbook program to private schools is not whether black students are actually enrolled at the school, but whether their absence is because the school has restrictively denied their access; simply, does the school have a racially discriminatory admissions policy?

The nature of a tax exemption

Perhaps the most fundamental—and least examined—aspect of the IRS proposals is the assumption that tax exemption is a government subsidy that, like a federal grant to a university, triggers affirmative action requirements. IRS Commissioner Jerome Kurz cites Title VI of the Civil Rights Act of 1964 as requiring the proposed guidelines. It reads in part:

> No person in the United States shall, on the ground of race, color, or national origin, be excluded from participation in, be denied the benefits of, or be subjected to discrimination under any program or activity receiving Federal financial assistance.

Without stopping to question here the disputable notion that this section requires the enforcement of racial quotas, we move on to ask whether tax exemption constitutes "federal financial assistance." The IRS clearly thinks so and cites *Norwood v. Harrison* to justify its proposals. But this case, which involves direct state aid in the form of textbooks to private schools in Mississippi, clearly has no bearing on Christian schools that refuse all state aid on religious grounds.

Nevertheless, the primary basis for the IRS's argument that tax exemption constitutes a government subsidy is the *Green v. Connally* decision in which the court, in addition to its other findings, concluded that tax exemption was unquestionably a form of governmental support to which schools practicing racial discrimination were not entitled. As the IRS emphasizes, this decision was later affirmed by the Supreme Court. At the same time the IRS neglects to mention that the Supreme Court has also explained that the *Green* decision, for technical reasons, lacks the weight of precedent and that as far as the Court is concerned it has not reviewed the question whether discriminatory private schools are entitled to tax-exempt status.

Beyond these legal arguments the proponents of the IRS's position stand on less technical grounds. Harvard Law Professor Stanley Surrey, for example, argues persuasively that tax exemptions

represent a "cost" to the federal government in the form of fore-
gone revenues. And since 1975 Congress has required the federal
budget to include an accounting of such "tax expenditures." Nevertheless, this apparently common-sense accounting device raises
some difficult issues. As Professor Richard Wagner has pointed out,
the theory of tax expenditures assumes that everything not taxed
by the government represents a government expenditure; or at least
it does not offer a reasonable rule for what is and what is not to be
considered an expenditure. For example, should husbands be taxed
for the imputed value of their wives' services as homemakers? The
tax expenditures notion seems to suggest this is feasible, and that
government's failure to tax this represents an expenditure and, in
effect, a subsidy to husbands.

Others argue that tax exemption represents a reimbursement to
institutions providing services that the state would otherwise have
to provide. This notion of a *quid pro quo* makes a good deal of sense
in the case of charitable institutions such as hospitals, orphanages,
and even private schools. But in the case of churches and religious
schools this argument makes little sense. After all, these offer services that the state is constitutionally prohibited from providing or
subsidizing! In addition, this argument would not apply to a range
of philanthropic activities such as museums that the state might
very well not feel the need to finance. In sum, the *quid pro quo*
argument is only a partial justification for tax exemption.

Beyond these considerations, we must clarify some important differences between government subsidies and tax exemptions. Government grants, by their very nature, are rooted in the statutory
process. Legislative bodies debate the merits and appropriate
funding level of a particular grant; administrative agencies make
the appropriations and are empowered to ensure that they are spent
in accordance with legislative intent; and the grant is subject to
periodic review which may expand, contract, or discontinue it.
Upholding the constitutionality of property tax exemptions to
churches, the Supreme Court states in its *Waltz v. Tax Commissioner* decision:

> Obviously a direct money subsidy would be a relationship pregnant
> with involvement and, as with most governmental grant programs,
> could encompass sustained and detailed administrative standards, but
> that is not this case. The grant of a tax exemption is not sponsorship
> since the government does not transfer part of its revenue to churches
> but simply abstains from demanding that the church support the state.
> No one has ever suggested that tax exemption has converted libraries,

art galleries, or hospitals into arms of the state or put employees on the public payroll.

With a subsidy, the initiative is always with the government. The system of tax exemption, on the other hand, puts the initiative elsewhere. By means of a grant the government can create or sustain an organization or program; it can do no such thing by means of a tax exemption, for the survival of the tax-exempt organization depends wholly upon the generosity and commitment of individual citizens. The amount of help such an entity receives is similarly dependent, not on state action, but on the decisions of citizens. Finally, no one is compelled to contribute to tax-exempt organizations, but a subsidy in effect forces contributions from all citizens.

Most important, the tax exemption system has deep roots in uniquely American notions of pluralism and individual initiative. This emerges most clearly when we consider the tax exemption of religious institutions. From the beginning, the American colonies exempted churches from local property and other taxes—in accord with well-established English custom. But in America, exemption was to take on a new and different meaning. To be sure, only a few colonies like Pennsylvania had anything like today's religious freedom. There were established churches, such as in Massachusetts Bay, from which dissenters, such as Roger Williams, had to flee. But even in these, the incredible diversity of the colonial peoples led to considerable accomodation and freedom. The emerging American solution to the religious turmoil of the sixteenth and seventeenth centuries was, in a word, tolerance.

The nineteenth century reinforced these tendencies, although the emphasis shifted somewhat from religious tolerance to the classical liberal concerns of limiting government and fostering private initiative. As President Eliot of Harvard made the case in 1864:

> It has been often asserted, that to exempt an institution from taxation is the same thing as to grant it money directly from the public treasury. This statement is sophistical and fallacious. . . . The exemption method is emphatically an encouragement to public benefactions. On the contrary, the grant method extinguishes public spirit. No private person thinks of contributing to the support of an institution which has once got firmly saddled on the public treasury. The exemption method fosters the public virtues of self-respect and reliance; the grant method leads straight to an abject dependence upon the superior power—Government.

By the time Congress got around to enacting a federal income tax at the beginning of this century, the exemption habit was so deeply ingrained it was simply taken for granted that religious and charitable institutions would be exempt. There was virtually no discussion of the matter, and the burden of proof is definitely upon those who argue that tax exemption is a subsidy, since there is no evidence Congress ever intended it as such.

The genius of tax exemption is as a mechanism by which government encourages individual initiative and freedom of association without fostering entanglements and dependencies. Yet these IRS proposals would use the same mechanism to extend, not limit, the reach of government. The assumption that tax exemption is a government subsidy obliterates the distinction between public and private basic to our political traditions. It would be a dangerous precedent, established by the IRS to accomplish what?

To eliminate what is still, in spite of recent growth, a small number of schools—the IRS Commissioner himself admits he does not know how many would be affected. To attack a culturally marginal phenomenon that subsists not on large financial contributions but on the zeal of a few fundamentalists whose extreme disaffection with the direction of American society is not likely to be widely imitated. To extend government control over institutions that are private in the fullest sense, refusing on religious grounds to accept a penny of state funds.

Certainly not all private schools established in recent years are free from suspicion as to their origins. Yet the schools I visited form part of a class of schools that has been grossly misundertood. And beyond this, the IRS proposals raise the larger question: How far can government reach into realms long held inviolable? This is not to argue, as do the proponents of Christian schools, that as religious organizations they should be exempt from government scrutiny. After all, schools perform a function in which the public has a vital interest. But as the Supreme Court put it fifty years ago in *Pierce v. Society of Sisters*, "the child is not the mere creature of the state." Nor, we might add, are institutions that exist solely through the free initiative and voluntary commitment of their members.

The conflict in moral education: An informal case study

MARTIN EGER

Some years ago, the State of New York released a publication setting forth ten "educational goals" to guide designers of programs and courses. The fifth goal on this list reads as follows:

> Competence in the processes of developing values—particularly the formation of spiritual, ethical, religious, and moral values. . . . [The resposibility of the] school: a. knowledge of the diversity of values, b. skill in making value-based choices. . . .[1]

Three words are remarkable in the above formulation: "competence," "skill," and "process." To elucidate, even in a small way, what these terms may mean within today's culture requires a long story—and we have one; but the words are significant also in a more direct sense.

"Skill" and "competence" are associated with such matters as carpentry, language, and mathematics. They hint at a science or craft, suggesting authority, implicitly relating themselves to proven methods or facts. When social support for moral values seems to be crumbling, new sources of authority are naturally welcomed, especially science.

For the uninitiated, however, there is a serious problem here, because science deals with what *is* or *is possible,* and from this no logical operation can derive what *ought to be*. To claim scientific backing in morals is therefore suspect, and could do more harm than good if the claim proves erroneous or misleading. Apparently, then, we face a classic dilemma of secular education: That schools omit values from their concern is highly undesirable, and possibly an instance of social negligence, but the appeal to science is fraught with other dangers. Moral judgment does require authority, a ground of legitimation, but where is the *science of value* fit for such a role?

For those who *are* initiated in the teaching movements that have recently commenced, there is no problem whatsoever. "Sciences" of "value formation" have long been sought and are now available; the "is"/"ought" disjunction is no longer an obstacle. The state's booklet takes this for granted, obviously, and the key to it all is the third word we have noted—"process." If values themselves are not derivable from facts, some theorists believe, the *process* of valuing may well be.

The studies that underlie this view—genetic and humanistic psychologies, associated with such names as Jean Piaget, Lawrence Kohlberg, Carl Rogers, and Abraham Maslow—are widely discussed today. But in addition to psychology, there is another field—increasingly important—that also contributes: the group of "decision sciences" based on computers, initially developed for military and managerial use. What such diverse theories have in common is a concern with the "how" of valuing, with the structure of decisions rather than their outcome. One uses "is" to derive not the "ought" of morals themselves, but another "ought": the manner of thinking about morals, and the way of evaluating that manner.

Those who avail themselves of these achievements see the educational dilemma as essentially bypassed: If we teach value science as political science is taught (without telling the student which party to belong to) then *all* values are within our purview. Logic is not violated, and the student becomes morally responsible in the highest degree, for he gains the "competence" to "develop" his own values, and to justify them in the light of reason. There is little doubt that the apparent advantages of this approach contribute heavily to the proliferation of "values programs" in the schools.

Yet in spite of the new outlook, and in spite of initial public receptivity, there has emerged during the past few years a widespread resistance to the project, including stunned and disillusioned parents, as well as reasoned doubts in scholarly quarters.

The clash points again to the dilemma described, and raises an important question: Is harm already being done? If so, is it related to the "sciences" guiding such policies as adopted by the State of New York? Or are the protests we hear of incidental phenomena, reflecting undue fear, to be expected when anything new is tried?

This is the question we examine here—by probing the connection between one type of values program, in one school district, and the social conflict to which it gave rise. A controversy over *curriculum* that shakes a town is bound to reveal something contemporary about the relation of theory to practice. Recently, such a conflict took place, distinguished by the clear and extensive record it leaves us. Looking at what actually occurred, what was said and done by different sorts of people—teachers, parents, school board members and professors—we immediately find two striking features: on the one hand, a living enactment of what some analysts are trying to tell us; on the other, odd happenings and strange inversions, as thought-provoking as they are unpredictable.

The case of Spencer-Van Etten

In the hilly region south of Ithaca, New York, only 20 miles from Cornell University, lie the small towns of Spencer and Van Etten. All around are silos, Holstein herds, barns of every style and condition—yet farming is not the only occupation familiar here. From village homes and those adjoining the cornfields, people drive away each morning to work for Cornell, or for sophisticated industries in Ithaca, or commute south toward the IBM plants along the Susquehanna. Quite a number of families are relative newcomers, having left city and suburb to seek something else still: nature, a less treacherous environment for children, peace, and perhaps a chance for the spiritual side of existence.

For such a purpose the place seems well chosen. But in the Spring of 1979, as the local district prepared for its school board election, an uncommon battle raged through these valleys, and the village of Spencer was a center of intrigue. Neighbors met in each other's homes to make policy; professors were visiting to lecture; reporters from Ithaca, Elmira, and towns unknown were dropping by—even CBS's "60 Minutes" was there, cameras shooting a classroom scene.

The reason for all this was the school system's use of a "technique" known as Values Clarification (V.C.)—to many parents, the antithesis of wholesome moral guidance.[2] The election marked the climax of a protest movement already in its second year, and involving other issues also. But gradually the values program became the main target of criticism.

To picture the mode of these protests, how logic and bewilderment roused each other, let us go back still further in time. If months earlier you happened to be nearby and stopped to pick up the local weekly, you might have read an item like this:

> The following are 8th Grade Decision Making questions given to the children of our school.
>
> Q. Which would you prefer to give up if you had to? A. Economic freedom? B. Religious freedom? C. Political freedom?
>
> Q. Are you in love right now?
>
> Q. Do you think there are times when cheating is justified?
>
> Q. Do you think people should limit the size of their families to two children?
>
> These are my questions to those questions: Who says one "has to" give up any of these freedoms? . . . Does an 8th grader really know if people should limit their families to two children? . . . What are they talking about? Cheating in school? Cheating in society? I feel these questions are "picking at a child's brain."

Under attack is a course of broad scope called "Decision Making" (D.M.), designed to help youngsters choose not only an occupation, but their lifestyles too. However, before people can make such choices, so it is explained, they must first determine what their true values are; and for this purpose the school had adopted the approach of Sidney Simon and his collaborators. Exercises, questionnaires, and "strategies" brought together by Simon's group in a teachers' handbook are used extensively in this course, as is their basic metatheory of values.[3]

Since parents had not yet discovered professional criticism of this new trend, the complaint quoted deserves notice. Its *style* reveals a level of emotion typical of many letters appearing at that time; but its *content*, just as typical, expresses in terse language several objections to which pages of scholarly prose had been devoted—questionable use of forced choice, violation of privacy, and superficiality.[4]

In Spencer, however, this was only the beginning, a kind of introduction, while really tough arguments turned on the philosophical concept of "choosing freely." And rightly so. For if the values-teaching movement makes any idea crucial it is this: A value must be "chosen" by the individual himself, "free," as much as possible, from authority, "conditioning," and "social pressures." Only in this way does it become one's "own," and therefore something positive rather than oppressive, something to be "prized," "cherished," and to "be proud of."

To many parents this naturally comes as a shock—and, incidentally, to not a few children also. (Some parents became opponents when their children complained.) These people, old and young alike, had thought until now that whether to become an engineer or a farmer was certainly their own choice—truly a "free" and personal decision—but they never believed that whether or not to cheat, for example, was quite in the same category. And this, it seemed, is what the school was saying: "If I teach my child that cheating is wrong" wrote one mother, "and V. C. teaches a child that there are no right answers, no wrong answers but rather to choose freely, it most certainly upsets the house."

Have these parents misunderstood? Have they missed the point in regard to *process*? If so, they are not alone. The charge of ethical relativism is made by scholars as well—in the philosophically grounded disciplines especially. In this case, an average group of parents sees what the academic community sees. The mechanic and farmer agree with the professor of philosophy. "Ethical relativism"—the technical term—had to be defined in Spencer, yet its significance was known long before.

But "relativism" is not taught here, the school retorts in frustration, and "philosophical generalities" are not relevant to what we actually do. The technique is *professional,* and scientifically tested; it raises to consciousness the cause of our ideals. "We understand ourselves as not teaching values," explains the Director of Guidance, *"but* teaching students to identify the values their parents, friends, churches, and society have already imparted to them." This is the local version of the oft-mentioned claim that V.C. "accepts all viewpoints," does not "promote particular values," and should therefore be offensive to no one. Moreover, the advocates insist, to avoid inculcation is not to say all values are equally good. Simon and his associates write: "If we urge critical thinking then we value *rationality.* If we promote divergent thinking, then we value *creativity. . . .* If we uphold free choice, then we value autonomy or *freedom.*"

This is the theory. And many parents have shown good will toward it, even in the face of disturbing practice. When the professional speaks, citing surveys and statistics, most people listen respectfully—especially those less versed in the conceptual apparatus of recent trends. But naturally they also listen to their children.

Take for example the afternoon of May 12, 1979. At the Spencer Grange, the seats and benches around the hall are filled. A photographer walks about popping his flashbulb at whoever seems newsworthy, a television camera bobs up and down on someone's shoulder, and in back, near the door, a young woman stands up to speak:

> My little girl came home and told me how she said lying was *wrong*—because Jesus said so—and the teacher told her, "but many people do lie." Well, I don't know . . . maybe I'm wrong, maybe I shouldn't believe what she told me—but I *do* . . . I *beeeelieeeeeve* her!

The mother repeated the key word, drawing it out and raising her voice, and one could not tell whether all its meanings were intentional.

Various people were gathered in this audience—farmers, executives, housewives, engineers, and also teachers from the local school system, their administrators, and members of the Board of Education. They had come to listen to a lecture on Values Clarification and to discuss its problems. The speaker, a philosopher at Cornell, was finished.[5] Now people from the floor were telling their stories, and when the mother of the girl who thought lying was "wrong" sat down, there was a momentary silence in the place. Then a young defender of the new methods answered from the front of the large hall, "Would you like it better if the teacher said nobody lies?"

A man turned to his neighbor with a wry expression. Scholarly debates surrounding the is/ought problem have not reached most parents of the Spencer area, but this they did sense: Not the fact of lying but another kind of "is" was making itself felt at this meeting as it does in the school—the "is" of language, the reality of *style*. What is new and noteworthy is not that "people lie," but what educators now *say* about people who lie—or cheat or steal.

A short distance to the south at Elmira College, an assistant professor hears of the controversy; indeed, it touches his town too. A trainer of teachers in the V.C. technique, he gives a talk to clear up the confusion. Suppose you tell a shoplifter that stealing is wrong—what do you accomplish? "It places the other person on the defensive, and the person making the judgment on a plane above the shoplifter." Some people may clarify their values in accordance with the best methodology, and still decide to shoplift. In that case, explains the educator, "you have to respect that decision if they have reached it intelligently . . . at least in this approach, you are respecting the person as a decision-maker."

Soon afterwards a newspaper version of the professor's views is placed in front of every chair at a meeting of the Board of Education in Spencer-Van Etten. Some parents are puzzled, others shrug; but months earlier, an answer had been given to this now familiar stance:

> If the child "chooses" freely to steal, who do I send the officer to? The
> school? I tell my children *stealing is wrong*. D.M. states "choose freely"
> —does that mean D.M. will be responsible for the child they have
> taught? No, hardly, the parents will be responsible. . . .

And in a formal letter to the Board of Education, the same concern
from another viewpoint:

> If the school assumes the responsibility of dealing in areas of personal
> values, morals . . . does the Board feel it is up to assuming the respon-
> sibility to these children that involves seeing them through the hurts and
> consequences of the decisions about morality? We as parents are suf-
> fering with them. . . .

One fear is that the non-judgmental aspect of the program is
formal only, that indirectly a type of value system is indeed being
promoted—not just creativity, justice, and the like. In such a "receptive" atmosphere, parents suspect, the "is" of fashionable attitudes, professionally systematized and synchronized with an as-
similated youth-culture, acquires artificially enhanced power; so that
thought-structures deemed "advanced" are substituted for the
"ought," usurping the normative function of the latter.

Here, for example, is a key general definition used in the controversial course dealing with moral values: What is a "good decision"? The answer given by the D.M. Teacher's Manual: "the result of a decision is only good or bad in terms of the decision
maker's own personal preferences."

And so, from the newspaper, a voice asks about the victims of
such personal preference.

> If one chooses to steal, destroy, cheat—the list goes on—what about the
> victims? . . . *Thou Shalt Not Kill* . . . On the other hand there is val-
> ues clarification which teaches to "choose freely." I would say that
> Hitler fit into this category. As he chose freely to kill. . . . Bineum
> Heller, in reaction to the big lie of Hitler and its horrible consequences
> wrote this:
>
> > Perhaps part of the blame falls on me
> > Because I kept silent, uttered no cry
> > Fear froze my heart and confused my mind
> > And I did not resist the lie.

So I have spoken up.

Thus a writer in the *Spencer Needle*.[6] The point must have been
made elsewhere too, for in the Adirondack foothills, in a center of
V.C. work, a reply for trainers and teachers has already been composed, and appears in a recent book:

> *Could a Person Use the Valuing Process and Become a Hitler?* This

question represents a classical test for the morality inherent in the valuing process. . . . *Short Answer:* No. A psychologically disturbed person is severely hampered in his or her ability to make free choices and to rationally examine a wide range of alternatives and consequences. Hitler was clearly paranoid and could not effectively use the choosing process of valuing.

At Cornell, speaking on moral education, a professor recalls those charges of old leveled at "corrupters of youth"—and smiles. The audience, knowingly, returns the smile. But vague resemblances, hurriedly glimpsed, may conjure a distorted image. The quotations above, with their awesome subject, suggests perhaps a truer resemblance—in the emphatic juxtaposition of a "scientific" perspective to the concepts of "good and evil."

The protesting parents did not do particularly well in the school board elections of June 1979—for reasons which will be touched upon. Though they received a respectable portion of the vote, none of their three candidates was elected. (One, however, elected the previous year, remained on the Board.) In September of that year, a new private Christian school opened in North Spencer with a starting class of 23 pupils, and this year there are 50.

It would be misleading to suggest that the values controversy alone was responsible for the fact that children are now being withdrawn from this public school system, though many pupils in the new school are children of the protesters. Scholastic achievement had been a major concern before the values issue arose. Strangely enough, "Decision Making" was in part developed to meet that concern—to combat apathy, and demonstrate how valuable *thinking* could be in making life's crucial choices. And on that basis it was defended.

To disenchanted parents, however, the relation between mental growth and this type of values program is of an entirely different nature. It deepens their despair over the intellectual quicksands into which the schools have now sunk, where each step taken to solve a problem seems to make things worse. They say that in regard to rationality, the effect achieved by methods like V.C. is the opposite of what is claimed; that the desire for knowledge and delight in reasoning, naturally budding at that age, may be channeled into something else: an endless sequence of games, of questions and answers that place the trivial and the profound on equal footing. The student is stupefied to a point where he is not likely to stop and think—or object—when after innumerable other queries he comes across, " . . . enjoy watching movies on T.V.? . . . *enjoy go-*

ing to church or synagogue? . . . enjoy going on a picnic?" (Emphasis added.)

The long-term intellectual effects of holistic elements in the curriculum are always hardest to deal with, and in this area parents have the greatest difficulty making themselves understood. Often they hear: "Do you mean that this innocent little question will corrupt your child? You can't be serious." But these parents are serious, and answer: "Values Clarification mocks the educational process."

Parent vs. school

For some families, no doubt, V.C. was the last straw, especially in view of the school's response to their considerable and initially hopeful efforts. This response—or rather, the response of the education system at its many levels—when faced with inquiry and criticism, is itself a matter that must receive special attention.

The first reaction was, unfortunately, a denial that any such thing as Values Clarification was included in the curriculum—an inauspicious beginning, immediately rupturing the trust between the school and the community. Unconvinced, some parents began their own education, gradually acquainting themselves with the basic texts of the V.C. movement. It was not long before they could place on the table the handbook by Simon, Howe, and Kirschenbaum, and beside it definitions, voting sheets, and tests that children brought home. From then on, the source of these lessons was never in doubt.

There followed months during which letters of protest and dissent appeared in almost every issue of the local weekly. Not all were restrained, or thoughtful, or distinguished by sensitivity to the teachers' unenviable position—letters to the editor being what they are. It is significant, however, that leaders of the protest group clearly set forth arguments paralleling those in the academic literature —a literature with which they were still unfamiliar. That scholarly criticism of values programs is not as easily found as the many volumes written by proponents was certainly a factor in these events.

The second phase of the school's reaction was to say, in effect: Well, yes, we use this "technique," but what of it? Many school systems do; it is state-evaluated, government funded, and approved by the best educators and universities. Then it was possible to quote Lawrence Kohlberg,[7] use a few psychological terms, mention the formidable name of Harvard, and so on—making it quite clear that behind the local course stands a vast professional world of *science*, prestige and official recognition, in comparison with which the doubting parent is a stumbler, at best. And to insure the final effect, there followed, at a public debate in 1978, this impressive counterthrust:

> Now I want to know who are *your* sources. . . . Where do you *get* these ideas? . . . You made very strong allegations against the school. . . . On what kind of *research* are these statements based, and *where* does this research come from?

Alas, at this point the spokeswoman for the parents' group could cite only the texts of V.C. itself—the books speak for themselves, don't they? How could anyone read this and *not* see what we see?

What happened instead was totally unexpected by the parents. In the third phase it was they who stood accused:

> We are witnessing an attack by an organized group . . . led by extremists from the far right who would like to see a little more hate than already exists in the world. The philosophy espoused in recent letters is embraced by the John Birch Society, the Heritage Foundation, the Conservative Caucus, the National Conservative Political Action Committee, and other ultra-conservative organizations.

This published outburst from a Spencer citizen became the keynote for much of what followed. The critics were described as anti-intellectual, simplistic, and opposed to independent critical thought. They were charged with "lifting" ideas from outside sources, and their actions were blamed for "dividing" the community. The insights of humanistic psychology and advantages of "process methods" seemed far beyond their understanding. But that was hardly the worst of it: The teachers' spokesman—head of a recently formed "Academic Freedom Committee"—warned of possible "links with the new right coalition in the country, one aim of which is to do away with the public schools." [8]

Actually, the situation was quite different. In over two years of controversy, no evidence of any ties to an extremist organization was uncovered, though at least one Ithaca newspaper went to the trouble of "acting on local tips" and conducting its own investigation. "Are you now or have you ever been a member of the John Birch Society?" was asked of a member of the Board of Education.

In the beginning, lacking political experience, the letter writers did avail themselves of whatever materials seemed to indicate a shared concern—and these, it is true, do not all conform to the highest standards of scholarship. Still, such fragments as appeared in Spencer could not in seriousness be called extreme or "ultra." (Of "outside sources" serving as a true inspiration here, C.S. Lewis' *The Abolition of Man* was one, and the Harvard speech of Alexander Solzhenitsyn another.) Thus the school critics of Spencer-Van Etten acquired a bad name: "We have become the target of much criticism, mockery, segregation . . . not only as a group, but as individuals as well. We are not enjoying this role." And a bad name is not easily shed.

Much later, when the relevant scholarly papers were discovered, when academics came to town and long discussions were held privately and publicly, and when highly respectable professional criticism was offered to the community, the labels still stuck. Repeatedly, the critics had to ask for attention to the substance of criticism, not its alleged sources:

> I am very concerned about being labeled "extreme right wing". . . . If you think what we are saying is wrong, then *talk* to us about those issues, don't call us names. . . .

And even when a scholar experienced with the problem (Professor Baer, of Cornell) came to the aid of the parents' cause—with detailed analyses, and lots of patience—that only discredited the scholar! "An avowed enemy of Sidney Simon," was the teachers' reaction. "Why has an outsider stepped into our local controversy?" asked the president of the Board of Education, "his remarks were . . . an affront to our local people."

Here the issue stands. Those parents who out of religious or moral conviction do not wish to have their child's values "clarified" can with some effort avail themselves of a special procedure: The pupil is separated from his class and placed in study hall. This was the main concession brought about by the protests. Though parents point out the possible psychological harm, the injustice, and the educational waste of such a policy, no further accommodation has been offered. However, as people in this community continue their criticism—drawing in more detailed, credible support—the aura of unquestioned legitimacy surrounding the values program is dispelled. Since the election of June 1980, at least one third of the Board of Education is sympathetic to the case of the protesters.

Six unsettling questions

The controversy described obviously touches on issues of greater significance than a particular program used in one community. A critique of the Values Clarification method as such will not be given here. Rather, my aim is to reflect on a few of the more important problems brought to light by the Spencer-Van Etten story; and to pose, in the case of each problem, the basic question involved.

It is perhaps not accidental that the first difficulty encountered in Spencer-Van Etten, that which caused the earliest complaint and much bad feeling, had to do with the question of *truth*—not the problem of what to teach children about truth, but whether the school is telling the truth. Certainly access to fact was hard to obtain for those whom these facts affected most—the families of pupils, the "consumers" of education. A controversial program was part of the required curriculum, but parents were told it was not. When they discovered otherwise, they were assured it played a minor role; when they perceived it was the basis of courses in decision making, the explanation was that no educator could be found to oppose the approach; and when they brought to town scholars who did oppose it—things turned nasty.

We have here a new kind of credibility gap, involving not merely the schools' shortcomings, but their very intentions. And this misinformation or lack of information regarding programs likely to be found objectionable is not unique to the towns we have focused on. It is reported of a district in Anne Arundel County in Maryland that the Board of Education itself "had no idea" of the use of V.C. in their school, and the revelation was "positively electrifying." [9] In a New Jersey course, Transcendental Meditation was apparently practiced with incense, chanting, and invocations to Vishnu, but that did not prevent school officials from blandly denying a religious content. "Inexcusable ignorance . . . bordering on deception," replied parents; a legal suit was needed to eliminate the program.

Did the response in Spencer-Van Etten also border on deception? Many people believe just this. Unfortunately, the V.C. handbooks lend support to that suspicion, since total frankness is not encouraged. What parents see, teachers are told, should be *carefully selected*. Trainers themselves prejudge the source and nature of objections in a way that corresponds exactly to what happened in our story.[10] The patronizing attitudes, so bitterly resented by parents in this case, are less surprising therefore.

National attention is now directed to problems of "truth in lending," "truth in advertising," the Freedom of Information Act, and so on. But "truth in education"—in the same sense—seems to have been taken for granted. Thus, our first question:

1. *Is it acceptable that families of pupils in public schools be denied access to any information regarding curricula, school activi-*

*ties, or teacher training? Or that the standard of veracity for teach-
ers and school officials be lower than that for auto makers, bankers,
or the Department of Justice?*

The second point may also be seen in a consumer's perspective:
Not only the purpose of a product has to be considered, but unintended results also. Cigarettes, energy use, and certain medicines
have taught us that some side-effects are cumulative, long range,
and hard to detect. Such experience supports the demand that on
every new product or "system" introduced into society there be imposed bounding conditions within which the designers must solve
their problem. And to insure not only that positive claims are justified, but that these conditions too are met, *time* is required.

How do matters stand in education in this respect? When Values
Clarification was introduced in Spencer-Van Etten in 1974, and the
Handbook of Practical Strategies was beginning to be used there,
this fundamental text of the movement was barely two years old.
"Research" on the effectiveness of the approach was "far from conclusive"—by the authors' own admission—and side-effects were not
even mentioned. In the following year, evaluators termed these
studies "relatively unsophisticated"; [11] and the first systematic appraisal of even this doubtful evidence—which did not appear until
1978—essentially refutes the positive claims of the proponents.[12]
Thus, when the program was initiated in this school district, detailed professional criticism of Values Clarification had not yet begun. But advocacy by the developers was loud, their materials
flooded the libraries, and their activities were gaining favor with
the State and the teachers' union.

This situation gave rise to an especially instructive though predictable phenomenon. There was a time—some parents believe—
early in the protest, when the protesters were being "listened to"
by their community, and indeed by a fair number of the teachers
themselves. It was their inability *at that time* to produce unim-
peachable professional critiques, supporting at least in part their
own objections, that largely determined the ensuing course of sentiment. In the absence of scholarly judgment, the charge of "right-
wing sources" dominated the atmosphere. And once public positions were adopted, and commitments made, no amount of credible
evidence could alter the outcome, for then a powerful new element
had entered the picture—personal prestige.

Whether we take a "consumerist" viewpoint, or that of scholarship
and science, the implication is clear: Criticism *follows* innovation; a decent pause between proposal and full-scale use is there-

fore indispensable. The lack of thorough, many-sided evidence invites leadership by selected expertise and half-baked professionalism, and in such a context the ideal of local control of education through elected boards is hardly meaningful. Our second question, therefore, is:

2. *What checks and balances, if any, exist within the educational system to prevent questionable practices from being "sold" to the school before competent evaluation has taken place? What mechanisms are there for communicating to the schools and their communities all aspects of such evaluation at the time they are needed?*

Now suppose a new program is in fact developed at the universities and widely implemented—and it does engender opposition. What then have we a right to require of the educational system?

Nothing was more evident, and more embarrassing to the teaching profession, than this fact: After a year of discussion and debate, the protesting parents were in possession of more knowledge, more documentation, and deeper understanding of the subject at issue than were the teachers defending the school's position. The parents, not the school, informed the community of the relevant literature, and brought in scholars to speak. Teachers involved in the controversy seemed caught off-guard, frightened, and badly prepared to handle the intellectual substance of the protest. Perhaps this explains why they never did come to grips with that substance, but concentrated instead on other replies.

"My intention here tonight is to get the facts out, and to demonstrate to you what we have found in our research." So began the teachers' representative in a public forum in Spencer-Van Etten. His posture is flawless. It is indeed the teacher's job to supply facts and dispel prejudice. What followed, however, was breathtaking: "I teach a college course in adolescent psychology and moral development . . . and the only place that I find the statements you people make about Values Clarification is in this right-wing literature." When this statement was made in December 1978, the *Moral Education Forum* had been reporting professional opposition for about three years, and a special issue of *Phi Delta Kappan* featured debates on the same kinds of objections local parents were raising.

The conclusion in Spencer was inescapable: Either school employees knowingly withheld critical opinion from the community, or they honestly did not know of it and could not find it even with effort. In any case, the professional training of these educators is called into question, and the responsibility of the academic world in such controversies reveals itself as greater than commonly assumed. Criticism of teacher education is nothing new, but the expansion of public schools into the realms of morals, sex, death, the self, and "decisions" in general, raises additional questions.

Can the average teacher with the average training be a "teacher" —or "facilitator"—in such deep waters without comprehensive additional education in ethics, moral history, theory of knowledge, and the like? May we not expect that these modern "teachers of virtue" will themselves have had an education commensurate with the task? It does not inspire confidence to be lectured by an instructor in "moral development" who does not even possess the basic skill of a "library look-up" in his own field.

Unfortunately, most developers of these programs are far more engaged in stocking a veritable supermarket of materials—with films, tapes, games, numberless "strategies" and "moral dilemmas"—than the in-depth education of the teacher. Values Clarification, which recommends itself as "easy to get started," is especially culpable in this respect; to become a practitioner, the novice is assured, "a relatively short training program, as short as a few hours," will suffice! Summing up this side of the problem, then, we ask:

3. *Do the universities—and does society—feel comfortable with a situation in which millions of children in thousands of schools receive systematic moral education from teachers whose study of the subject consists of no more than a one-week workshop and a handbook of strategies?*

Morality and process

In discussions of whether moral education belongs in public schools at all, two questions always arise. Can you really avoid moral problems? And wouldn't prohibition violate a basic freedom?

Again the drama of Spencer-Van Etten casts the issue in a new light. The controversy there began in earnest not because an individual teacher made an isolated remark or gave a personal opinion, but when parents discovered exercises, questionnaires, and definitions, taken from *handbooks* and systematically applied in classes, and when they realized that this methodology projects a meta-ethic fundamentally different from the universal recognition of objective value and "common human law"—what C.S. Lewis called the "Tao."

Teachers' freedom to express personal views on moral questions, when these questions arise naturally in subject matter or discussion, was *not* contested here. And of course such "dealing" with moral issues cannot be avoided—nor is it. Nor does any serious person suggest it should be. The crucial question seems, rather:

4. *Is the issue of "free speech," when each individual teacher responds on the basis of his own unique background and convictions, the same issue as when a whole school, or district, adopts this or that developer's system of moral education, complete with hardware, software, "trainers," and gurus? In the latter case, may it not actually be a restriction on moral dialogue?*

The opposition in Spencer-Van Etten did indeed believe that a narrowing of moral vision had been imposed. Parents usually find the nature of this narrowing difficult to articulate in a form acceptable to educators, but in this community one school board member rendered the gist of it concisely: "We're not saying our precepts should be taught, but if ours are left out, then leave out all values."

The statement deserves attention. What is meant by "our precepts"? It is not, as sometimes charged, "our religion." The Constitution's stricture in this regard is well known here and not challenged. We arrive therefore at a point where the pervasive effect of *meta-*ethics comes to the fore—the foundation of ethics, its origin, its categories. What is clearly felt by many parents is the exclusion—from the explicit methodology—of a whole realm of moral categories not specific to one religion, but part of that "Tao" encompassed by the heritage of both East and West: the *good*, the *true* (objectively), the *just, soul, faith, courage, moral rebirth*, (or "turning," or "enlightenment") . . . etc. What they see instead is a new set, including such concepts as *self-image, life-style, rich experience, decision-model, risk strategy, maturity, self-actualization*, and *rationality* (in the hypothetico-deductive sense). The only element from the older list often kept is *justice*.

Granted that such a shift in ethical categories accords with trends in psychology and operations research, are there valid grounds for *excluding* from public education the more traditional set? Well . . . there may be. There may, indeed, be—*if* such language is in itself deemed to be religious, and its inclusion unconstitutional. But this raises perhaps the most fundamental question of all:

5. *If the systematic teaching of morals within the bounds of the First Amendment requires systematic exclusion of a whole realm of meta-ethics underlying moral thinking in our society, isn't this in itself a distortion of ethical discourse in the intellectual sense, and injustice in the social sense?*

Yet systematics is the main feature of the values teaching movement today; it meets the requirement that morals too be seen as *skill,* that here also a *science* legitimates. Let us look at the point from a humanist perspective.

The word "humanism" is, of course, ambiguous. One usage,[13] relevant here, connotes by "human" what is distinct from "mechanical." The "knowledge factory" and "mega-machine" embody its opposite. It is this anti-mechanistic, anti-rule-following inclination that led reformers to indict so-called traditional education, and to introduce a whole series of reforms to free the schools from needless stifling formalism. And this aim one can easily accept.

But today a curious reversal seems to be occurring. Humanist educators increasingly press to systematize the few realms that have so far escaped this fate. "Traditional" education assumed certain values axiomatically—and for that very reason had no need to explicate them through a system. If a child cheated on a French test, for example, he lost face with his peers and his teachers—and this is how the value was *supported* (not "reinforced," not taught!). Now, however, a pupil is asked whether, according to someone's criteria, that "decision to cheat" is or is not a "critical" one. Again, a child is tempted to "drop a friend who is being made fun of by other kids at school." In a traditional environment, chances are a youngster would *recognize* that act for what it is; but today in Spencer he is *taught*—to identify which of the four "main risk-taking strategies" this decision represents.

Science, by definition, systematizes what it deals with, it formalizes its subject. And the formalization of decision making along the lines of management and computer models, if applied to morals, must obviously reduce that also to a system. It is fair at this juncture to ask, of humanists especially:

6. *Is it good "strategy," in the long run, to humanize our "knowledge factories" by replacing the axioms and disciplines of one era with the systematics of another? Is rule-following in "how to decide" really less mechanical than rule-following in regard to ends? In short, is an automatic "value-driven decision system" the proper model for a more moral, more humane society?*

A warning, ancient and modern

The final point is not a question at all, but a reminder. The values education movement has justified its mission partly by the rapid social change occurring in our time—the "collapse of the old morality." True, the change is great. It lends urgency to the work of the developers; to do nothing seems dangerously complacent. That is one horn of the dilemma of values education. But in thinking about man, as about nature, there generally has been equal concern with the *invariants,* as science calls them—that which remains constant in the midst of all change. Compare now the dialogues from Tioga County that have occupied us here, with those of another, "simpler," age. In the invariant lies the second horn of the dilemma.

Protagoras, the Sophist, is come to town. And the young Hippocrates is all on fire—for this teacher, famous in all the cities, promises his student not the "drudgery of calculation, and astronomy, and geometry, and music," but "prudence in affairs private and public . . . to speak and act for the best." He has a special method, it is told, and all the youth and would-be teachers throng about him like a king's entourage.

But wait a minute, says Socrates—how do we know it's all true?

> When the soul is in question, which you hold to be of far more value than the body, and upon the good or evil of which depends the well-being of your all—about this you never consulted either with your father or with your brother or any one of us. . . .
>
> Surely . . . knowledge is the food of the soul; and we must take care, my friend, . . . that the Sophist does not deceive us when he praises what he sells, like the dealers wholesale or retail who sell the food of the body. . . . In like manner, those who carry about the wares of knowledge, and make the round of the cities, and sell or retail them to any customer who is in need of them, praise them all alike; though I should not wonder, O my friend, if many of them were really ignorant of their effect on the soul. . . . If, therefore, you have understanding of what is good and evil, you may safely buy knowledge of Protagoras, or any one; but if not, then, O my friend, pause. . . . For there is far greater peril in buying knowledge than in buying meat and drink. . . . You cannot buy the wares of knowledge and carry them away in another vessel; when you have paid for them, you must receive them into your soul and go your way, either greatly harmed or greatly benefited. . . .
>
> Plato, *Protagoras*

And today:

> "You are what you eat," most of us have heard that expression.
>
> There are those who are very concerned about "junk" being served through the school breakfast and lunch programs. They believe as adults we are responsible, and should be choosing nutritious food for school children. . . .
>
> I have heard the phrase, "You are what you think." This also has clear meaning to me. What I think is eventually manifested in my character; the things I say and do. Shouldn't I be equally concerned

with the nutritional value of what enters my mind? Shouldn't I be even more concerned as to my children's choice? . . .

Theresa Rimbey
Spencer Needle
August 10, 1978

NOTES

[1] *Goals of Elementary, Secondary and Continuing Education in New York State* (The University of the State of New York, 1974).

[2] For a general introduction and critique, see William J. Bennett and Edwin J. Delattre, "Moral Education in the Schools," *The Public Interest,* 50 (Winter 1978).

[3] Sidney B. Simon, Leland W. Howe, and Howard Kirschenbaum, *Values Clarification: A Handbook of Practical Strategies for Teachers and Students* (Hart, New York, 1972). This is a widely used text.

[4] For example: John S. Stewart, "Clarifying Values Clarification: A Critique," *Phi Delta Kappan,* 56, No. 10, 1975, and other articles in that issue. Alan Lockwood, "A Critical View of Values Clarification," *Teachers College Record,* 77, No. 1, 1975; and "Values Education and the Right to Privacy," *Journal of Moral Education,* 7, No. 1, 1977.

[5] Professor Richard A. Baer, Jr. (Cornell University). See also his "Values Clarification as Indoctrination," *Educational Forum,* XLI, No. 2 (January 1977).

[6] September 14, 1978, p. 7. Most of the local quotations given in this article appeared in the *Spencer Needle* during 1978 and 1979.

[7] Lawrence Kohlberg has criticized Values Clarification for some of the same shortcomings as have the parents of Spencer-Van Etten. But since he has defended the use of V.C. in public schools, his name was used here in support of the controversial course. See "An Exchange of Opinion between Kohlberg and Simon," in *Readings in Values Clarification,* Howard Kirschenbaum and Sidney Simon, eds. (Winston, Minneapolis, 1973).

[8] *Ithaca Journal Magazine,* January 27, 1979, p. 1.

[9] Private communication. See also *Maryland Gazette,* July 30, 1979, p. 1, and *Sunday Sun* (Baltimore), May 27, 1979, p. A-1. In Anne Arundel County, parents apparently won some legal restrictions on the use of V.C.

[10] Howard Kirschenbaum, *Advanced Values Clarification* (University Associates, La Jolla, 1977), Chapters 4 and 13.

[11] Douglas Superka and Patricia L. Johnson, with Christine Ahrens, *Values Education: Approaches and Materials* (Social Science Education Consortium Inc., Boulder, Colorado, 1975).

[12] Alan Lockwood, "The Effects of Values Clarification and Moral Development Curricula on School-Age Subjects: A Critical Review of Recent Research," *Review of Educational Research,* 48, No. 3 (Summer 1978).

[13] But "humanism" also connotes an opposition to *theism*: in our culture, Judaism/Christianity. The confusion of the two meanings of the word greatly exacerbated the conflict in this communty, and elsewhere.

Private schools, public schools, and the public interest

JAMES COLEMAN

THERE is not one private school policy issue today, there are two. Certain proposed policies would expand the role of private schools in American education or at least make it easier to attend them; other policies would inhibit their use. Thus, there is the unusual situation in which conflict is so strong that support exists for policies that would go in exactly opposite directions. The principal examples of policies that would aid private schooling are tuition tax-credit legislation at the federal level, such as the Moynihan-Packwood bill currently in the Senate, and tuition vouchers at the state level, such as the proposal designed for California by John Coons, Professor of Law at Berkeley. The principal examples of policies that would restrict private schooling are attempts by the Internal Revenue Service to impose some form of racial-balance criterion on private schools in order for them to maintain tax exempt status. Opponents of the first set of policies argue that those policies would destroy the public school system; opponents of the second set argue that those other policies would destroy the private school alternative to the public system.

Another unusual aspect of the private-public education conflict, especially in its voucher incarnation, is that it cuts across traditional liberal-conservative lines. John Coons, for instance, was also the principal moving force behind the Serrano case in California, which brought equal financing to schools in California and elsewhere. Vouchers have been supported or proposed by conservatives like Milton Friedman and liberals like Christopher Jencks. Still another curious aspect is that the conflict separates action from advocacy for a number of persons: There are many who vigorously oppose making private school attendance easier and at the same time have their own children enrolled in private schools; and there are many who support private schools and still have their children in public schools.

The principal arguments of those who favor aid to private schools are that: (a) private schools provide better education; (b) attendance at private schools is available only to those who can afford it; therefore, (c) reducing costs of private schooling will make the better education of private schools more equally available to families of different incomes. What may be questioned in this argument is the assumption that private schools provide a better education. This assumption is one of the two central questions studied in the research to be summarized here.

The principal argument of those who support constraints upon private schooling, or oppose making it easier to attend them, is that private schools segregate different segments of the population, due to the "self-selective" character of these schools. The specific arguments differ. One, the oldest, is that private schools draw off the most economically affluent from the public school system, and then engage in further economic stratification among schools within the private sector, resulting in economic elitism in the schools. Another argument, the most recent, is that private schools segregate racially by drawing off whites from the public sector, and then further segregate among schools within the private sector as whites choose certain schools and blacks others. The only solution is for students to be assigned to particular private schools, as is ordinarily done in the public sector. One final argument is somewhat different. This argument says that assisting private schooling, by any public means, constitutes "establishment" of a church and thereby violates the church-state separation provision of the Constitution.

What is subject to test in these arguments, except the last, is the fundamental assumption that private schools do segregate different segments of the population. The truth of this assumption appears at first self-evident, but the matter turns out to be more complex: Public schools are themselves not perfectly integrated on these economic and racial dimensions, and there is already social self-selection within the public sector when people choose where to live. The question is whether the education system as it now stands, containing private schools, is more segregated along income, racial, or religious grounds than would be a system without private schools. Or to put it differently: Does the choice which results from the existence of private schools lead to greater segregation than the choice that exists within the public sector?

A study of school differences

To help address these important questions about private-public school differences, the National Center for Education Statistics held a conference in April 1981 at which the first reports of its "High School and Beyond" study of high school sophomores and seniors were presented and criticized. Both analyses had to do with comparisons of public and private schools, but the first one, conducted by Andrew Greeley, was focused mainly on the role of Catholic schools in the education of blacks and Hispanics. The second analysis ranged more broadly over the issues of achievement and segregation that I discussed above, and was conducted by Thomas Hoffer, Sally Kilgore, and me.[1]

As has become evident from the intensity of the response to these reports, the issues they addressed touched some very sensitive points—more sensitive than was anticipated by any of the authors, and certainly more than was anticipated when the reports were initially planned in the Spring of 1980. For this reason, it is useful to briefly review the results of the Coleman-Hoffer-Kilgore report here—an action which may also help to dispel the confusion created by what has appeared in the media—and to suggest something about the deeper and more sensitive questions which this report touched.

First of all, it is useful to give a sense of how schools in the public and private sectors differ. Public high schools (grades nine through twelve) enroll over 90 percent of the total high school population and have an average of 750 students, while the Catholic schools enroll about 6 percent and average about 500 in size, and the other private schools enroll between 3 and 4 percent and aver-

---

1 The Coleman-Hoffer-Kilgore report was written in August 1980, and initially planned for release in the Fall of 1980. However, delays in the reviewing-and-revision process led NCES to defer its release until April 1981. The Greeley report was written in early Fall 1980, and also initially intended to be released in Fall 1980. A fuller outline of overall study is given in the research note at the end of this article.

age only about 150 in size. The pupil-teacher ratios in Catholic and public schools are very similar but in the other private schools they are less than half as large.

Students and principals in Catholic schools are much more likely than students and principals in public schools to report that their schools have rules about student dress and that students are held responsible for damage to school property; students and principals in the other private schools report this more frequently than in public schools but less than in Catholic schools. Students in Catholic schools are much more likely than public school students to report that discipline in their school is effective, with the other private schools again in between. And both Catholic and the other private school students are somewhat more likely than public school students to say that school discipline is fair. Overall, *the evidence shows that discipline in the Catholic and other private schools is both stronger and fairer than in the public schools,* with discipline in the Catholic schools being strongest and that in the other private schools most fair (as perceived by the students).

Students in Catholic schools are much less likely to be absent or to cut classes than are those in public schools (again with the other private schools in between and closer to the Catholic schools) and public school principals are much more likely to report that absenteeism constitutes a problem in their school than are either Catholic or other private school principals. On other measures of student behavior as well, *students in the Catholic and the other private schools show far fewer "problems"—as reported either by the students themselves or the principals—than do those in the public schools.* Catholic school students do about half again as much homework as do public school students, and students in the other private schools do even more.

In all the above respects, Catholic schools are the most homogeneous, differing least from one another, while the other private schools are most heterogeneous, showing greatest variation in discipline and student behavior.

Achievement—public and private

This sketch of the differences between schools in the public, Catholic, and other-private sectors gives an indication of how these schools differ in their everyday activities. But it says nothing about the central policy questions. The question of whether there is higher average achievement in the private sector than in the public sector is answered very simply through a comparision of scores on standardized tests in the two sectors. The answer is that in the areas in which both sophomores and seniors were tested (in reading, vocabulary, and mathematics), students in Catholic schools and students in other private schools scored about two grade-levels higher than did students in the public sector. But this is not the question asked by the parent choosing between a public and private school, or legislators deciding whether to support a bill assisting attendance at private schools. They ask a question asked of me by a colleague shortly after the report had been released. He asked, "How can you determine whether the *same* child would achieve more highly in the private school? Couldn't the achievement difference be solely due to selection?"

This question—which asks whether the school itself really makes a difference, and if so, how much—is as difficult to answer as the first one is simple. But it is not impossible. An extreme way would be illustrated by pairs of identical twins with one twin from each pair assigned to School A, and the other to School B. If the achievement of the twin assigned to School A was consistently higher, this would be strong evidence that School A brings about greater achievement.

A study of identical twins assigned to different schools, or even a study of non-twins assigned randomly to different schools, could test the effect of the schools on achievement. With random assignment of non-twins, a larger number of children would be necessary for statistical reasons—but the conclusions could be just as strong. Absent this kind of evidence—a problem which is characteristic of research in the social sciences because of ethical constraints on "arbitrary" assignment (and random assignment is certainly arbitrary) to different settings which might have long-term consequences—other methods must be used to separate the effects of selection from the effects of the school itself.

We used three methods in our study. The first was to "control" the background characteristics of students through multiple regression analysis, in effect comparing achievement for students who have similar background characteristics. Seventeen background characteristics were used (including some which might be consequences rather than causes of achievement) in order to control as fully as possible, even to the extent of overcompensating, for selection into the schools. These background characteristics ranged from things like family income, to each parent's education, to ownership of a pocket calculator, to each parent's aspirations for the child's education. The result of this analysis showed that about half of the original difference in achievement is due to selection, and about half the original difference remains. Less remains in reading and more in mathematics, and slightly less remains in the other private schools than in the Catholic schools.

A second method of analysis examined differences between the sophomore and senior groups (adjusting for dropouts) and used the two groups to measure gains and learning rates between sophomore and senior year. *This method showed higher learning rates in the other private schools than in public schools in all three achievement areas, higher rates in the Catholic schools than in the public schools in vocabulary and mathematics, and equal Catholic and public rates in reading comprehension.* Learning rates in the other private schools were higher than those in Catholic schools in reading comprehension and mathematics, but the two sectors were alike in vocabulary.

This second method roughly confirms the public-private differences in the first analysis, though it shows achievement growth in the other private schools to be somewhat higher than that in the Catholic schools, while the first analysis showed the sophomore achievement levels to be slightly higher in the Catholic schools.

Better schools do better

Both of these methods for discovering differences among schools in their effects on achievement contain a potential flaw: There may be some *other* uncontrolled background factor which determines whether, even among students alike in all the characteristics that are statistically controlled, the better-performing students are selected into the private sector and the less-well-performing students remain in the public sector. This seems possible or even likely for those private schools which select entrants using admissions tests, but these constitute only a handful of schools, a tiny fraction of the more than 6,000 private schools with secondary grades in the country. It seems less likely for the vast majority of private schools in which admission depends on the parents' ability to pay.

Despite the improbability of selection accounting for the remaining differences, we carried out a third analysis. And it is this analysis which carries special implications for public education. The argument is as follows: *If* Catholic or other private schools bring about higher achievement for comparable students, and *if* they do so through those attributes measured in the research which distinguish

Catholic and other private schools from public schools, *then* we should find achievement differences among schools within any sector, public or private. In other words, those schools within any sector which are like the Catholic and other private schools should have students performing at levels comparable to those in the Catholic and other private schools, while those schools in any sector that are like the public schools should have students performing at the public school levels.

The major measured differences between the public and private sectors, other than size, are those described earlier: differences in disciplinary climate, in academic demands, and in student behavior. Further, even when the backgrounds of students are statistically controlled, much of these differences remains—differences in homework, in student attendance and in-school behavior, and differences in the disciplinary climate perceived by students. These differences can reasonably be attributed to differences in school policy rather than student background.

When we examined, wholly within the public sector, the performance of students similar to the average public school sophomore, but with the levels of homework and attendance attributable to school policy in the Catholic or other private schools, and those levels of disciplinary climate and student behavior attributable to school policy in the Catholic or other private schools, the levels of achievement are approximately the same as those found in the Catholic and other-private sectors.

The first implication of these results is that they strongly confirm the school-effect results found by the other two methods. For the selection hypothesis necessary to account for these differences must be especially tortured, operating not only between sectors but also to the same degree within sectors, and operating to select students, on the behavior variables indicated above, into schools with particular disciplinary climates. Thus, the validity of the private-sector effects is strongly confirmed by these results.

A broader implication holds as well: that *these attributes described above are in fact those which make a difference in achievement in all American high schools no matter what sector they are in.* Schools which impose strong academic demands, schools which make demands on attendance and on behavior of students while they are in school are, according to these results, schools which bring about higher achievement. This is not to say that such policies are easy to institute in all schools. Public schools have greater constraints on suspending or expelling students than do private schools, for example, and quite beyond that, a public school principal may have less autonomy from the district in establishing a particular educational and disciplinary philosophy than does a private school principal. Rather, it may be said that in those schools where these policies *do* exist, students achieve more on average than in schools where these policies do not exist.[2]

Besides the overall difference between the public sector and the private sector in effects on achievement, there is another strong achievement-related difference—this time between the Catholic schools on the one hand, and the public schools and other private schools on the other. This is in the *homogeneity* of achievement: Catholic schoolchildren of college-educated and high-school-only parents achieve about the same, as do whites and blacks in those schools, even after other background characteristics are statistically controlled. This means that Catholic schools in general do less for students from the most advantaged backgrounds, and more for students from the most disadvantaged backgrounds, than do schools in the other-private sector. In both the public sector and the other-private sector there is a wide range of schools from the benighted to the elite; there is far less variance in the Catholic sector.

Do the private schools segregate?

The second major policy-relevant question examined in the report is whether private schools increase segregation. Segregation operates as the consequence of two different mechanisms: first, the segregation *between* sectors (that is, through high-income or white students going to the private sector), and second, through internal segregation within each sector. The segregation in American secondary education as a whole is a result of both between-sector and within-sector segregation.

As it turns out, the impact of the private sector on segregation differs in the religious, economic, and racial dimensions. Examining only segregation between Catholics and non-Catholics, the proportion of Catholics is, of course, sharply different in the Catholic, public, and other-private sectors—about 90, 30, and 17 percent,

---

2 Nor is this to imply that the same factors would be critical in other settings or at other times in American schools when discipline would be taken as given. Results of the sort discussed here, while they point to factors that affect achievement in a given population of schools, will not hold in a population of schools which varies much less on the factors found to be important, or more on others. Twenty-five years ago, when discipline in American public schools was far less problematic than it is now, the results found here might very well not hold.

respectively. This means that the between-sector segregation is very high. Within each of the three sectors, *given* the proportion of Catholics in the sector, the within-sector segregation is quite low. Taking together the high between-sector segregation and the low within-sector segregation, *the overall effect of the private sector is to increase somewhat the degree of religious segregation in American secondary schools*, relative to that which would exist if Catholic and non-Catholic students from the private sector were distributed into the public schools as Catholics and non-Catholics are now distributed in those schools.[3]

The impact of the private sector on economic segregation is somewhat different. Both the Catholic and other private schools have somewhat higher proportions of high-income students than do the public schools, and smaller proportions of the lowest-income students. The economic differences between sectors are not, however, especially high, with median incomes reported as $18,200 in the public sector, $22,700 in the Catholic sector, and $24,300 in the other-private sector. The economic segregation within each sector is also low, though there is more economic segregation in the public sector than in either of the private sectors or in both taken together. *The combined result of the between-sector and within-sector economic segregation is to give a degree of overall economic segregation that is not high, but is slightly higher than is found in the public sector.* In other words, it is slightly higher than would exist if private school students were redistributed among the public schools.

The impact of the private sector on black-white segregation is still different.[4] There is a substantial difference between the proportion of blacks in the public sector, the Catholic sector, and the other-private sector: about 14, 6, and 3 percent, respectively. *Within* the public sector, segregation is much higher than the black-white segregation in either of the private sectors or in the total private sector combined. *The joint result of the substantial between-sector segregation and the substantially lower private within-sector segregation is that there is no overall impact of the private sector on black-white segregation.* If whites and blacks now in private schools

---

[3] The results of such a "redistribution" are obtained very simply, merely by assuming that the public sector was expanded to cover all students, maintaining the same level of religious segregation now found in the public sector.

[4] There is no effect on the Hispanic/non-Hispanic segregation because the private sector has about the same proportion of Hispanics as does the public sector, and the degree of segregation within public and private sectors is about the same.

were redistributed into the public sector in just the way whites and blacks are now distributed in that sector, there would be no greater and no less segregation than currently exists. This result may go against intuition, which sees the private sector as a haven used by whites when desegregation rulings are passed; but intuition overlooks the fact that suburban schools within the public sector are used as a haven to a much greater extent than is the private sector. Eliminating the private sector would hardly deposit whites back in the public schools they were attending, even those who had used a private school as a haven in the first place. It is probably less true to say that private schools increase the degree of racial segregation in education than to say that private schools permit a greater degree of residential integration by race than would exist in their absence.

Tuition as "tariff"

The results of this report, as I have described them above, are generally favorable to private schools. Further results in the report not described here are also generally favorable to private schools. A common response of some people, when confronted with these results, is the question, "But is the public interest served by assisting enrollment at private schools?" This is a question that merits serious attention, for private schooling on its face negates the classic American ideal of the public school.

I believe the matter can be usefully examined by viewing private school tuition as a protective tariff relative to tax support for free public schools. Just as a protective tariff on automobiles would protect the American automobile industry from foreign competition, private school tuition, measured against the free tuition at public schools, protects the public schools from competition by private schools. As students in first-year economics have learned, protective tariffs are generally inimical to the public interest. They benefit producers at the expense of consumers, but the producers they benefit most are those that would fail without the tariff—that is, the least efficient firms and industries. Protective tariffs keep resources employed inefficiently, lowering the general level of welfare, and opposing the general public interest. Furthermore, protective tariffs harm the interests of the least well-off, for the increase in prices relative to incomes (which is what protective tariffs bring about) hurts most those with the fewest dollars.

The effect of private school tuition and other barriers to attendance at private schools is very much the same. It protects the public schools to which students are assigned, and it protects most the worst public schools, those public schools that would be most depopulated by families' freedom to choose. It harms the consumers of education (the children and their families) and it harms most those to whom the price of tuition or the choice of school by moving residence is the greatest barrier—that is, the low-income family that is least able to leave a bad public school, and the black family that confronts the greatest barriers to moving elsewhere. (The evidence that this has occurred in American high schools is most fully seen in Greeley's report, which I have not discussed here.[5])

There are some conditions under which protective tariffs can be beneficial to the public interest—though as economists are quick to point out, these are rare, far less numerous than the arguments of certain producers would lead one to believe. In the same way that one must be suspicious of these arguments, one should be suspicious of public school arguments for maintaining their protective tariff. The most frequent condition under which protection is beneficial is when "infant industries" need a period of protection to get started.

Public schooling is not an infant industry, but a somewhat different argument could be made: There is a public interest (or perhaps a community interest or a national interest) in broad participation in common institutions. The same kind of argument could be (and sometimes is) made for the military draft, or for non-military national service. The same kind of argument could be made against "private schools in the public sector"—that is, homogenous elite public schools in homogenous suburbs. But there are two points of importance about this argument as it applies to private schools. One is that the public schools are no longer a "common" institution. Residential mobility has brought about a high degree of racial segregation in education, as well as segregation by income. The second point is that the public interest in common institutions is not an *overriding* public interest. It is a relatively weak public interest when measured against the public interest in helping all children, particularly those of the disadvantaged, receive a better education. It is a relatively weak public

---

⁵ An interesting proposal that would give tuition vouchers, but only to children who do badly for a period of time in public schools, has recently been made by Barbara Lerner in *Minimum Competence, Maximum Choice: Second Chance Legislation*. This would eliminate the tuition tariff barrier in those schools which are doing worst for those students who are most harmed by the barrier.

interest when measured against the interests of children who are being directly and manifestly harmed by the school environment in which they find themselves, but who are unable to escape that environment. That plight is a poor family's plight, not one that policy-makers find themselves in. It takes sympathetic identification beyond their own experience to recognize this plight.

Some part of the plight is of very recent origin, for it is only very recently that control of a community's schools has been taken largely out of the community's hands by federal (and to a lesser extent, state) intervention. Public schools have become an over-regulated industry, with regulations and mandates ranging from draconian desegregation to mainstreaming of emotionally disturbed children, to athletic activities that are blind to sex differences. It is in part these regulations, imposed on the community and the school, which are responsible for the slackening of academic demands and the breakdown of disciplinary climate that many public schools have experienced in recent years. And it is the disadvantaged who are least able to select a school, in the public or private sector, that continues to function reasonably well.

There may be a rationale for some protective barriers to encourage participation in the public schools, but certainly not those that exist now, which harm most the interests of those least well-off and protect most those public schools that are worst. In short, the tuition barrier to private schooling as it exists now is almost certainly harmful to the public interest, and especially harmful to the interests of those least well-off.

RESEARCH NOTE

The study from which these data were taken, titled "High School and Beyond," is designed as a longitudinal study of a national sample of high school seniors and sophomores of 1980. The study is sponsored by the National Center for Education Statistics of the U.S. Department of Education, and has been conducted by the National Opinion Research Center of the University of Chicago. The first wave of data, on which the results described in the article are based, was collected in the Spring of 1980. The sample of schools consists of 1,015 high schools, the sample of seniors in these schools (randomly drawn from the list of seniors in each school) consists of 28,465 students, and the sample of sophomores, drawn in the same way, consists of 30,263 students. The study is designed for examining a number of policy questions, perhaps the most central of which are those involving the transition of youth from secondary education to a variety of post-secondary activities and into adulthood. The data set, which will be augmented by subsequent waves of questionnaires at approximately two-year intervals, is publicly available for analysis from NCES. The two reports which have been released to date are "Minority Students in Catholic Secondary Schools" by Professor Andrew Greeley of the University of Arizona and NORC, and "Public and Private Schools" by James Coleman, Thomas Hoffer, and Sally Kilgore at the University of Chicago and NORC.

Power to the parents?— the story of education vouchers

DAVID K. COHEN & ELEANOR FARRAR

EDUCATION vouchers were the *enfant terrible* of recent school reforms. Yet the idea seemed appealingly innocent: Instead of giving money to public schools and thus requiring either mandatory attendance or additional outlays for private schools, vouchers would directly aid families so that they could enroll their children in schools of their own choice. The idea of vouchers gained the attention of many reformers in the 1960's because it promised to solve so many educational problems. Christopher Jencks and other radical critics thought vouchers would improve ghetto education by offering parents and teachers alternatives to the failing public schools. The country's impatient youth liked the idea because it would enable more people to afford their "free" schools. Some Catholics thought vouchers might boost enrollments in parochial schools, which were sagging under the pressure of rising costs and shifting values. And Milton Friedman, searching everywhere for some vestige of capitalism in mid-century America, discerned a market mechanism in parent choice and promptly pronounced vouchers the only hope for educational efficiency.

The idea was attractive partly because it seemed to address such disparate hopes. But everyone agreed that vouchers would promote "competition," which would loosen up public school systems grown rigid with age, size, and professional power. The fear of losing students and revenues would move schools to improve curricula and increase responsiveness.

One might think that a notion with such diverse appeal would take the country by storm. Instead, it stirred up a hornets' nest of opposition. Teacher organizations viewed competition among schools as an invitation to union-busting—a fear that Professor Friedman's endorsement did nothing to relieve. Administrators were afraid of losing control over budgets and appointments. Civil libertarians were apprehensive that the flow of public monies to sectarian schools would represent a breach of the constitutional separation between church and state—a concern that was not alleviated by Catholic support for vouchers. Civil-rights advocates were in favor of allowing urban blacks to choose their own schools, but balked at the prospect of granting whites the same freedom of choice—which, they held, would be a disaster for desegregation. Finally, many thought that vouchers would eviscerate one of the nation's few egalitarian institutions by paying for private education at the taxpayers' expense; public schools would then become the alternative of last resort, reserved for those without the wit to go elsewhere.

Whereas most federal educational programs are launched with Congressional hoopla and Presidential panegyrics, vouchers were thus introduced in an angry political atmosphere. The idea excited visions of change in the minds of both radical and conservative theorists, but it produced only nightmares for the moderate masses known despairingly as "liberals" six or eight years ago. Given their fears, the wonder is that the idea of vouchers was not stillborn.

It wasn't, partly because it was conceived in something of a political vacuum. The idea had caught the fancy of the few left-wing bureaucrats still remaining at the Office of Economic Opportunity (OEO) while the Johnson Administration was coming unstrung over Viet Nam. Partly as a result of their help, Jencks and several of his Cambridge colleagues were awarded a grant to study the feasibility of vouchers. The result was a thick report that—like many studies—solemnly announced that the ideas of its authors were indeed feasible. In fact, there was even a plan describing how vouchers would work (*Education Vouchers: A Report on Financing Elementary Education by Grants to Parents,* Center for the Study of Public Policy, 1970), which was duly dispatched to Washington.

By that time the Nixon Administration had begun reshaping OEO: Tired old liberal ideas and big give-away programs were out; modest experiments were in. The new OEO staff knew the difference between Milton Friedman and Christopher Jencks, but they read the report, and after some exploration—and a bit of urging from the authors and their friends in the Administration—decided to give vouchers a try.

Support for vouchers by the Nixon OEO did not exactly assuage the fears and suspicions of liberals, who responded with a barrage of criticism delivered through the mails, the media, lobbyists, and Members of Congress, and in some often nasty confrontations euphemistically known as "briefings." The new OEO staff were somewhat taken aback by the ferocity of this response, but stuck to their commitment to social-science experiments: All they sought, they said, was a dispassionate test of the idea. They didn't favor vouchers —just new alternatives. If vouchers were half as bad as everyone said, then they would deservedly sink without a trace; if not, then who knows—perhaps they merited consideration. A curious collection of conservative theorists, radical reformers, Republican politicians, and social experimenters thus managed to persevere under the banner of science. In 1969 a federal effort was launched to test education vouchers. It was a frail craft, but it did float.

Eight years later, it still does. In the meantime a good deal of evidence has been accumulated—some of it from a single school district in Alum Rock, California, which has operated a trial program for several years; some of it concerning the extensive efforts to get other areas to try vouchers. One wonders what might be learned from all this evidence. It would be a mistake to anticipate a definitive verdict, for the experience has been limited. Anyway, no decision could be conclusive about something as interesting and problematic as education vouchers. But the experience so far does illuminate several points of interest. Does the diagnosis of school problems still make sense now that the prescription has been administered and the patient observed? And what has become of federal efforts to improve education by experimenting with political reforms? We will address these questions on the premise that something may be learned—both about "what is wrong with schools" and about federal efforts to "set things right."

Implementing a test

Education vouchers seemed an appealing way to correct the balance of power in education, to reduce the sway of professionals and increase the influence of parents. It was hoped that if parents could exercise free choice, schools would compete by undertaking new educational ventures, which would presumably succeed only if they truly reflected the wishes of the parents. The mere existence of competitors, it was reasoned, would weaken the monopoly in education by encouraging schools to be responsive to the public.

This idea made sense to both radical and conservative reformers because it placed responsibility for school problems squarely on the public education monopoly—a large, clumsy, and perverse creature that had become by 1968 a popular political scapegoat. Professionalized bureaucracies, it was held, had become calcified, unresponsive, insensitive to cultural variations, and capable only of doing the same dreary things, year after year.

This was a trendy diagnosis of school problems, but hardly a promising prognosis for a voucher test. After all, the educational bureaucracy presumably was in charge everywhere, from Albuquerque to Xenia. Why should the established authorities tolerate an idea designed to diminish their power and make their lives much more uncomfortably competitive? The federal sponsors of the voucher test program never had a clear answer to this question, but they began with efforts to organize local parents and citizens. The notion was to pressure the local monopolists from below: It was hoped that if enough grassroots support could be mustered, school boards and professionals would have to cooperate with a test.

But this approach didn't square with the reformers' diagnosis of school problems: Local authorities could be expected to resist such a challenge, and Nixon's OEO was in no position to agitate against them. At that time, OEO was slathering itself in social science; and besides, there was Daniel P. Moynihan, then the President's counselor, who had just published a book about how OEO had made social problems worse by stirring up local communities. So organizing communities to force a voucher test seemed uncomfortable in principle.

Worse yet, it did not work. The insurgent forces were never powerful enough to produce a voucher experiment, and as a result federal reformers began again at the top. Enlisting administrators and board members seemed more appropriate, but it did not help much either. Aside from the fact that educators sympathetic to vouchers were hard to find, turning to them did not solve the political problems, for in almost every case, local administrators lacked the power to mount a test. After all, they had boards, teachers, principals, and parents to worry about, none of whom was ecstatic about vouchers. So the same difficulty kept turning up in different forms. The federally organized local forces were too weak to succeed without support from within the school power structure, and administrators within the bureaucracy were impotent because they lacked outside support. The ensuing story illuminates a problem that has plagued so many federal agencies and faddish foundations: how to produce political reform in somebody else's town with only bright ideas, some outside consultants, and a little free cash.

Groping at the grass roots

The voucher plan drawn up by Jencks and his associates at the Center for the Study of Public Policy (CSPP) was cautious and carefully hedged. It favored individual choice, but in harmony with several competing values. The plan sought to shield minority and poor students from discrimination, to ensure maximum protection for consumers against the claims or indifference of schools, and to prevent public schools from becoming the alternative of last resort. The resulting idea for a "regulated compensatory voucher" was thus a complex and cumbersome creation—an effort to promote freedom of choice, equality, and due process all at once, while radically revising public schools.

The voucher plan was thus something of a Rube Goldberg contraption. It supplied fiscal incentives for schools to enroll poor children and to prevent economic discrimination. It provided detailed admission policies permitting applicants their choice of schools, schools their choice of applicants, and applicant lotteries—all at once—to protect the families' desires to select schools, the schools' desires to select their students, and the authors' desires to prevent discriminatory admissions. And the scheme included an elaborate plan for an Education Voucher Agency, independent of the participating schools, to administer voucher distribution and accounting, oversee school quality, and provide consumers with information to make informed choices.

CSPP, then, did not propose a simple idea. Milton Friedman had argued for simplicity, favoring a laissez-faire approach on the view that regulation would interfere with operations. But the authors of the CSPP plan demurred: They argued that vouchers could take many forms, but nearly all would be an absolute "disaster" for education. Besides, they were not convinced that operations would ever get underway unless the plan included safeguards to mollify angry opponents. Avoiding trouble, they said, would require dispensing with the simplicities of Friedman's free market, and faithfully following their plan. But as a result, the CSPP voucher project embraced the worst of both worlds. On the one hand, although the plan strained to protect equality and avoid discrimination, these efforts neither appeased the liberals nor reduced their opposition. On the other hand, making what had been a simple idea infinitely complex impeded easy discussion, quick comprehension, and local adaptation.

OEO hired CSPP to stimulate the local discussion and adoption process, but there were two problems. First, the CSPP staff was a rather implausible group for such work: Its members were bright, but few had been in a school since they were students (several had been schooled at such places as Andover and Choate). They were inclined to believe that the people who ran public schools were either dim or nasty—or both. Second, although CSPP staffers tended to be partisans of "community organization," they rather liked living in Cambridge. This posed a few difficulties when it came to inciting the masses in Peoria.

The situation in Washington did not help. Vouchers were new and controversial, and lacked a real constituency within the government. By contrast, the other big OEO experiment, the negative income tax, had taken years to percolate through the higher civil service in the 1960's; much of the bureaucracy remained intact and supportive after the Republicans took over. In addition, there was Mr. Moynihan, an articulate and powerful negative-income-tax advocate close to a President who wanted to make something like the tax experiment into law. Vouchers, however, had no such support. Moynihan more or less liked the idea, and he liked the people at Cambridge who liked it. But few others in Washington did, and many did not. Vouchers were thus something of a political albatross for OEO.

As a result of all these difficulties, voucher projects did not take fire in local communities.[1] The chief reason was that no stable or cohesive support for the plans ever developed in any of the cities. One possible source of support was the Catholics, but they preferred other approaches to parochial-school aid. Worse yet, most of the other local participants who favored vouchers did not favor Catholics. The CSPP report was uneasy about the Supreme Court decision permitting vouchers in church schools; the CSPP organizing staff was reluctant to see its pet project tainted by parochial affilia-

---

[1] Interestingly, the written analyses of the efforts to organize and promote vouchers are not available. OEO and the National Institute of Education (NIE) funded such histories, but so far they remain unavailable to anyone but NIE and the authors. This article is thus based on interviews with participants in many of the prospective sites, on the CSPP and NIE files, and on interviews with NIE, OEO, and CSPP staffers.

tion. So even when Catholics were supportive, they were encouraged to be discreet.

CSPP and OEO expected the poor and minorities to be another natural interest group. Their children, after all, were being so badly served by the schools; surely these parents would welcome alternatives. But the poor were mostly unorganized; any effort to turn them into an active interest group would have required vastly more time, energy, and personnel than CSPP had. Its part-time and episodic contact with local communities meant that CSPP could deal only with organized groups, or coalitions of such groups, or leaders who seemed likely to invent or recruit groups for themselves.

Blacks were organized, but their ideas about school reform had been shaped by decades of civil-rights struggle over education. In seeking to desegregate schools they had learned to distrust any scheme that either placed the burden on minority choice or allowed whites not to choose minority schools. So when a group of white academics proclaimed vouchers to be a new solution to black school problems, established black organizations were either hesitant or hostile. Local organizing on behalf of vouchers quickly became entangled with local political conflicts over race and education. In Seattle and Rochester, for example, integrationists saw vouchers as a way out for whites; consequently they opposed a test, which they regarded as either a racist trick or sabotage. CSPP pleaded that its plan would protect integration, but local civil-rights advocates—given their experience with "freedom of choice" and their knowledge that vouchers were sponsored by the same Nixon Administration that opposed busing and favored neighborhood schools—were either hostile or skeptical. Worse yet, although the pledges of CSPP failed to placate the integrationists, they were sure to offend potential voucher supporters who opposed integration. Either way, the organizers lost.

Another reason for the lack of local enthusiasm was the fragmentation of political power in the cities. The voucher-project staff labored under a delusion widespread among recent school reformers: that political power in urban education is centralized and monolithic, and that organized grassroots power is needed to overcome resistance.[2] But although there was often little change in city schools, this resulted more often from decentralized and fragmented local power structures. The voucher field staff found the power of urban superintendents seriously hampered by politically divided

---

[2] Christopher Jencks, "Is the Public School Obsolete?" *The Public Interest,* No. 2 (Winter 1966), pp. 18-27.

boards, by the autonomy of principals and district administrators, by the power of organized interests inside and outside the schools, and by bureaucracies with powers and minds of their own. While it was possible to keep school systems running through complicated treaties among these groups, it was difficult to change the rules in any important way without throwing the agreements into doubt— and the parties into a mild panic.

Vouchers, of course, were not just any change: They would have required the renegotiation of all treaties binding a city school system together. The idea thus raised anxieties all around; when vouchers appeared in cities like Seattle, San Francisco, and Rochester, many principals were opposed, teacher organizations were skeptical or hostile, most central administrators were dubious or completely negative, and school boards were divided. The problem was less monolithic resistance than decentralized uneasiness.

Working from within

Since there was little indigenous support for education vouchers, OEO and CSPP were gradually moved to try a different tack—organizing a test by gaining the support of local boards and superintendents. Several sites with interested administrators or board members were duly found. These school districts were much smaller and, for the most part, much more homogeneous than the cities in which earlier work had been done.

But support from the top, even in such relatively manageable places, was no more effective politically than pressure from below had been elsewhere. Once again, a major problem was the fragmentation of political power. The superintendent in East Hartford, Connecticut, for example, was personally quite committed to vouchers, but many teachers and principals were opposed. Given the explosiveness of the voucher idea, the superintendent then grew cautious. The chairman of the New Hampshire state board of education, a devotee of Friedman's economics, was also a strong supporter of vouchers. With a clear majority of the board, he got a state planning grant for a "free market" voucher test from an unwilling OEO (the Nixon White House helped), but then had problems lining up local districts. Only after securing extra federal money and promising local districts the chance either to influence decisions or to bail out, did he manage to persuade five districts in the southern part of the state to allow preliminary planning. As time went on, of course, even these districts became aware of the practical implications of vouchers; finally, they dug in their heels, and would not buy a test.

The other major reason that efforts to work down from the top failed was that state and local leaders were committed to vouchers because they liked the idea—not because there were real local problems that vouchers might solve. It was easy to favor competition and choice, and to oppose the bureaucracy, but in practice choice and competition turned out to have hard and nasty meanings: Parents could choose some local schools and not others; some schools would be forced either to expand to meet demand, or to turn away interested parents; other local schools could shrink or close, costing the jobs of teachers and principals. All this meant there would be some very angry teachers and principals—and that meant trouble.

None of these possibilities was entirely clear at the outset. But as planning progressed, local administrators gradually realized that they were being asked to sacrifice a fairly comfortable situation in favor of a much more prickly and unsettled one. In New Hampshire, the local administrators responded by trying to remove the sting from vouchers by redefining the plan, removing most of the choice and competition with an engaging Yankee directness. The superintendent in East Hartford also tried this, and avoided decisions whenever possible. In both cases, local administrators grew ever more unwilling to meet the bare minimums of a local voucher test: They became increasingly allergic to encouraging choice, supporting new alternatives, allowing unchosen schools to fail, or permitting a strong and independent voucher agency. Equivocation and compromise took over. The more local leaders learned about this dream of reform, the more nightmarish it seemed.

As a consequence, efforts to secure test sites were often makeshift operations. Almost nothing ever happened on time; almost nothing was done well. Indeed, it often seemed that almost nothing would have happened at all had not CSPP and NIE kept up a constant stream of bureaucratic and technical support. CSPP wrote the local proposals to get the NIE money. In both New Hampshire and East Hartford, CSPP helped to draw up schedules and then harassed the locals into heeding them. CSPP designed training programs for teachers, put together community information campaigns, wrote letters for the administrators, and in many other ways did the work for the locals. Without such "technical assistance" the local efforts would have fizzled out early on. As things turned out, all that help only postponed the inevitable. By 1976 all the potential test sites had failed.

Working from within thus proved as unsuccessful as groping at the grass roots. Insiders and intellectuals saw vouchers as a solution to vague and abstract problems, such as monopoly power in education—not as the solution to the day-to-day problems of running a school system. But contrary to the received doctrine of contemporary school reformers, local communities were not primarily concerned with power, choice, and participation. As a result, they did not work themselves into a sweat of enthusiasm for vouchers, and there was thus no real pressure for change—even when the opportunity fell into their laps.

The Alum Rock experience

But in Alum Rock, California, by contrast, administrators at least fancied there were real local problems that vouchers would help to solve, which helped generate political and administrative support for a test. The schools in Alum Rock were in poor financial shape in 1971, and Superintendent William Jefferds thought they had other shortcomings as well.[3] They had long been run tightly from the top; there had been little flexibility within the system for some time; and the same old jobs were being done in the same old way. Jefferds felt that the system was in danger of stagnating and that education for the numerous black and Chicano students needed to be improved.

The superintendent of this small school district thus wanted a voucher test because he wanted to decentralize the Alum Rock schools and because he needed money. But if decentralizing the schools struck top administrators as the right course, no one knew how to pay for it. At the same time, OEO was fresh from several stunning defeats in other cities, and feared that without a working demonstration the whole voucher project might soon sink. At first, Alum Rock excited no one: It was a smallish district near San Jose composed largely of minority and poor families, with little promise of diversity in its schools or interest in its community. But in the early discussions, Jefferds quickly learned that OEO and CSPP

---

[3] This section of the article is based on several sources: the published reports of the Rand Corporation (the evaluator of the Alum Rock effort); interviews with staff at NIE and Alum Rock; and interviews with Rand researchers. The Rand publications most useful are E. Levinson, with S. Abramowitz, W. Furry, and D. Joseph, "The Politics and Implementation of the Alum Rock Multiple Option System: The Second Year, 1973-74," *Analysis of the Education Voucher Demonstration, A Working Note* (May 1975); Stephen S. Weiner and Konrad Kellen, "The Politics and Administration of the Voucher Demonstration in Alum Rock: the First Year, 1972-73," *Analysis of the Education Voucher Demonstration, A Working Note* (August 1974); Daniel Weiler, *A Public School Voucher Demonstration: The First Year at Alum Rock* (June 1974).

needed him more than he needed them, and OEO and CSPP found an avid enthusiast for parental involvement and innovation at the school level.

The ensuing negotiations were not easy. One reason was that some Washington and Cambridge staffers still felt that Alum Rock was a silly place to try anything. Another was that Jefferds nearly lost to the local opponents of vouchers on one occasion, and barely avoided defeat by postponing everything for several months. A third reason was the failure of the California legislature to pass quickly a bill permitting public monies to flow to private schools, something everyone regarded as necessary for a voucher demonstration.

The most important problem in the negotiations, however, involved differences between the priorities of OEO and Alum Rock. OEO wanted a test of consumer sovereignty, while Alum Rock wanted OEO support for its decentralization plan: OEO had the money, and Alum Rock provided a potential test site. OEO didn't like the idea of such an "impure" test, but OEO had to take what it could get. Jefferd's superior bargaining position became obvious when he got OEO to produce some money for his decentralization program even before Alum Rock agreed to the voucher test. As is so often the case with professional reforms, the only way to get anything done is to let the locals do what they like—as long as they say they are doing what the reformers like. The reformers are really at the mercy of those they are reforming.

Cooking up the voucher test thus began with one small and dusty California school district, poor and discontented. To this were added two rather different recipes for political reform, a dollop of federal dollars, and intermittent doses of outside advice. With such ingredients and so many contending cooks, it is no surprise that the result was eventually something of a stew. But if Alum Rock did not test a single clear plan, its experience does throw some light on how vouchers worked in practice—if not how they might have worked in principle.

What happened when Alum Rock tried to reform its schools? Did more diverse educational offerings result? Did schools become much more responsive to parents? Did the power of professionals wane while that of parents waxed? Were families more satisfied? Was schooling improved?

The central theme in our answer to these questions is that the Alum Rock voucher test confounded almost all expectations—from the cautious hopes of Christopher Jencks to the dire warnings of

Albert Shanker. There was indeed more consumer choice, but not consumer sovereignty. Parents had more freedom to choose among more varied educational offerings, but as far as anyone can tell, they gained little power. Only the school-level professionals gained in that respect. Not only did teachers and principals inherit power from the central office as a result of decentralization, but they also acquired influence from the greater flexibility, uncertainty, and fiscal leeway that followed from parent choice.

Limiting choice and restricting competition

One point of the reforms in Alum Rock was to offer families more options for their children and to give professionals more latitude in defining school programs. But these choices created uncertainty, and unsettled parents and professionals. In a meeting to discuss proposals called by the district in the spring of 1971, parent representatives worried that children might not be able to attend their neighborhood schools. They sought and obtained a "squatters' rights" agreement whereby children already enrolled could attend neighborhood schools if they liked. Parent representatives also saw to it that every voucher school would offer at least two alternative programs, to prevent children from being forced out of a local school by distaste for the program offered. (OEO sought a compromise after the first year of the demonstration, guaranteeing everyone his first-choice school for the following September—if he signed up before May.) Thus rather than seizing the initiative to expand choice or to enhance power, parents tried to make sure that neighborhood attendance was secure and that neighborhood schools would not be overly innovative.

It was expected that once parents were given the wherewithal to choose among schools, educators would vie to expand their enrollments and incomes. School professionals, however, were concerned with protecting their jobs. It was thus agreed that teachers who left a voucher school for reasons associated with the demonstration would be given priority in assignments to other schools, or that OEO would cover their salaries while they were assigned to headquarters. No one was to be put out on the street by consumer preferences.

This eased things for teachers who did not succeed, and at the outset no one worried about those who did. As it turned out, however, even success was no bed of roses. Teachers in schools that recruited more students were not rewarded with higher salaries:

Although their school would receive more in tuitions, the money was to be spent for more teachers or materials. As a result, competitive success only produced more of the problems teachers struggled with every day: more children, more planning, more meetings, more colleagues, more noise at recess, more disruptions at lunchtime, and so on. Success brought more bother than benefit.

This nicely illuminated the great discrepancy between the ways teachers and voucher advocates thought of school problems. Teachers wanted better working conditions: room to breathe, to prepare, to teach, perhaps even to invent. Voucher advocates wanted better market conditions: to improve educational performance by turning up the competitive heat. Although teachers were hungry for more of the things professionals habitually crave—autonomy, more resources, and less pressure—reformers thought they already had a surfeit.

It is hard to imagine more of a mismatch. Had anyone noticed it, he might have suspected that competition would fail, or would have crazy consequences. But the reformers scored low on both sociology and school experience. The real surprise is that they scored so high on economic mythology. It is quite a testament to the continuing power of capitalism in American culture that liberal reformers not only failed to notice the obvious in education, but so thoroughly ignored the evidence concerning the effects of economic competition that littered the social landscape.

In any event, Alum Rock professionals were under no such illusions. Before the demonstration was half over they changed the market aspects of the voucher scheme to suit their purposes. The first step was to restrict demand by making it impossible for schools to expand indefinitely to meet enrollment pressures. After a year's trial with such expansion, teachers and administrators insisted that each school be given enrollment limits. From that point on, schools only needed to maintain enrollments at capacity levels, which assured the usual income without producing more than the usual strain. And since such limits meant that the less appealing schools would get the overflow from the more appealing schools, the chances for "success"—measured by enrollment—increased vastly all around.

However, the mere fact that public schools agreed to ease competition among themselves did not mean that nonpublic schools could not seek a share of the market. OEO had expected nonpublic school participation, but at first the California legislature would not permit it. OEO and Alum Rock therefore agreed to begin the demonstration as a "public-school-only" effort. Initial work focused on creating diversity within the public sector by encouraging differentiation and competition among "mini-schools" within existing buildings.

In the fall of 1973, the legislature finally enabled nonpublic schools to enter the demonstration. But partly because of the efforts of such public-spirited groups as the California Teachers Association, the legislation was quite restrictive. It permitted public monies to flow only to schools under the "exclusive control" of the local authorities, and it provided that the local certified employee councils (the professionals' bargaining agent) could formally review all policies in each voucher demonstration. In addition, it required that all participating schools be subject to district rules concerning teacher certification, curriculum standards, and student discipline, as well as other general rules and regulations.

Since Alum Rock was a poor district, it had no established private schools, and there were thus no disappointed private educational entrepreneurs. But a few months before the enabling legislation was passed, a group of four young teachers interested in "free schools" set out to organize an alternative school within the demonstration. The prospective school (called "Gro-Kids") got a small planning grant in the spring of 1973, and operated an after-school program the following fall.

The omens were not auspicious for Gro-Kids, however; the district leadership was ambivalent, and the teachers' organization was hostile. As a result, the certified employee council took the view that private schools could enter only if they met most of the operating standards of the public schools. This meant that Gro-Kids would be obliged to hire certified teachers and provide roughly the same staff/student ratios, salaries, and fringe benefits.

These conditions meant that private voucher schools in Alum Rock could differ from public voucher schools only in the ways public schools differ from one another. This left room for important differences, but they would be pedagogical and philosophical. The voucher idea had once again been radically revised. Although the organizers of Gro-Kids persisted and the school board voted to admit the new school in the winter of 1974, momentum had been lost. When parent choices for the following school year were made, no one selected Gro-Kids. It promptly vanished.

Alum Rock professionals thus sharply reduced the scope of economic competition, making life hard for private schools, eliminating school expansion, and protecting individual teachers from competitive failure. The voucher plan was drastically modified because schools are presently governed more by political than market forces; in Alum Rock, economic competition had no effective advocates. Such competition might have had a chance if it offered something to at least some of the participants, but it didn't.

Protecting roles and power

The failure to promote economic competition among Alum Rock schools still left plenty of room for other kinds of competition. But there was less than might have been expected, largely because of the effects of the district decentralization program. Some time before the voucher demonstration, decentralization had begun in six schools whose principals had expressed a desire for more authority. Superintendent Jefferds had procured OEO funds to prepare the six principals for more power through team-building and sensitivity training. The principals went into the training with a common interest in more authority, but they came out of it with a strong sense of group identity and an even stronger desire to get more power from the central office.

It was in precisely these six schools that the voucher experiment began. Conflicts between the goals of vouchers and decentralization—between parent power and principal power—developed almost instantly. The principals were extremely sensitive to anything that might tend to divide them, and competition among schools was exactly such a policy. They could accept programmatic differences, but they resisted such competitive devices as advertising, comparative evaluations, and the like, which would draw attention to the differences and encourage parents to act on them. Thus, the commitment by the district to increase the power of the principals through decentralization was in conflict with the commitment by OEO to encourage parent power by extending choice.

The Sequoia Institute was one focus of this conflict. Sequoia was directed by a former CSPP staffer, and the rest of its top staff were either Chicano or black. It was a bastard child of the Education Voucher Agency proposed by CSPP, an independent non-profit organization under contract to the school district, which Jefferds and OEO agreed would help set voucher policy and manage certain aspects of the demonstration. From Jefferds' point of view, Sequoia would legally be part of the district and under his control, even though it was an autonomous organization. But OEO hoped it would be more independent, effectively acting as an advocate for vouchers and parents: to provide parents with counseling and information, to speak for parents at all levels of the demonstration, to evaluate the performance of schools and students and disseminate the information so that parents could make informed choices, and to help monitor the project and insure that vouchers were not abused or misused.

Sequoia and the principals were incompatible from the start. The principals began by opposing the mere existence of the institute on the grounds that any addition to the bureaucracy would erode decentralization. They also objected to its view of parent advocacy and evaluation, and vigorously resisted publishing comparative information that might encourage competition among schools.

When Sequoia tried to press ahead with evaluations in the first year, the principals blocked the effort. During the second year, the Sequoia staff counterattacked and won permission to proceed, but by then it was so late that the information could only be used in the third year. And even then the principals made sure that parents were only provided information on the mini-schools attended by their own children. Information on other mini-schools —necessary to make comparisons—would have to be requested by each parent.

A similar struggle took place over the effort by Sequoia to provide counselors to help parents make choices and deal with school staff. The principals argued that if parents wanted information or help they should come to the schools' professional staff members, not some outside group. For the first year the Sequoia counselors thus lived in limbo; then they were assigned to individual schools, as principals had demanded. Their advocacy role was redefined by changing the job description, the place of work, and the chain of command.

In fact, this was the pattern throughout the history of Sequoia: New roles were redefined and transformed into old ones. Sequoia's assistant director for evaluation became the district's director of evaluation; Sequoia's director became a district administrator; the parent counselors became school registrars (some said clerks); and Sequoia became part of the district administration. In each case, the role that had initially been conceived as a reform was progressively redefined until it was hardly distinguishable from long-established and accepted practice. Not surprisingly, Sequoia did not work as OEO hoped. The reform that Alum Rock administrators wanted proved more durable than the reform they were paid to adopt.

Parent power

A similar story can be told about parent power. Parent advocacy groups were established for each mini-school and an overall Education Voucher Advisory Committee (EVAC) was created at the district level. These groups were purely advisory, having neither resources nor any formal role in decision-making. By contrast, EVAC had not only legitimacy but visibility, its own budget, defined powers, and potential for affecting the conduct of the experiment. Still, its parent members were neither aggressive nor particularly effective. They took an active role only on matters that directly and obviously affected them, such as neighborhood attendance, and even then they were far from consistent. The parent members generally tended to be absent, poorly informed, and deferential to the professionals holding EVAC seats. Parents simply did not take advantage of the opportunities for gaining power. Like the district professionals, they accepted existing roles.

This might be explained by the fact that parents were at a real disadvantage in EVAC; expecting them to act effectively in such circumstances may be foolish. Evidence of how parents used the voucher scheme to become more powerful might better be found in areas more familiar to them—choosing schools, discovering the available options, negotiating transfers, and the like. There is, for example, the encouraging fact that all parents in the voucher demonstration made choices. But the trouble is that the project was organized to force choices upon everyone: Even parents whose children remained in a neighborhood school had to choose a mini-school within it.

Something can be learned, though, from the proportions of parents who chose schools outside their neighborhoods. In the first year, a negligible fraction did so, but this probably can be ascribed to the late start of the demonstration. During the second year, about 10 per cent chose non-neighborhood schools, and after that the proportion rose again to about 18 per cent—a distinct increase in parent initiative, but involving only a modest number of parents.

The choices parents made within schools are also quite illuminating. One might expect that high transfer rates among mini-schools signalled parent initiative or discontent, or both. The transfer rate within schools, for example, rose by about 11 per cent between 1973 and 1974—not astronomical, but clear evidence that a modest proportion of parents did exercise choice. Likewise, a fair proportion of parents chose innovative mini-school programs. At first, most chose traditional programs; among those who selected the more modish programs, higher-income families were considerably over-represented. The proportion of children in traditional programs did decrease by about 18 per cent, however, between 1972 and 1975.

A similar pattern characterized parents' knowledge about schools. During the first year a modest fraction did not even know which mini-school their children were enrolled in, and many more who did knew nothing else about it. In the course of the demonstration parents learned more about their children's programs, but their knowledge about the system remained fairly shallow. Most parents learned about schools from official communications, a small fraction gained information on their own, and almost all reported satisfaction with what they knew. With a few exceptions, parents involved in the Alum Rock demonstration were content to learn just as most parents do—by being told by professionals.

This is reasonably typical of American education. A small proportion of parents are active, but most are not. The voucher demonstration appreciably increased parent choice among educational alternatives, but most parents failed to become more autonomous, powerful, or involved. The existing roles may not have been entirely satisfactory, but they seem to have been sufficient to forestall much of a search for alternatives.

Programs and pedagogy

It would be a great mistake, however, to imagine that nothing happened in the voucher schools. This would make sense only if one believed that schools suffer the blahs because they are not sufficiently accountable. The absence of increased accountability did not imply stagnation; considerable change seemed to take place in many Alum Rock voucher schools.

The most obvious change was more diversity. Where before a uniform curriculum had lain over all the schools, there were now Spanish-English bilingual programs, an arts-and-crafts mini-school, several "open classroom" mini-schools, and a number of innovative approaches to reading. Some of these programs retained the regular grade-level organization of elementary schools, but others were more flexible. While some schools made few curriculum changes, others made modest revisions and still others made more serious departures. Three years after the demonstration began, voucher classrooms were certainly more different than they initially had been.

Probably the most striking change in the voucher schools was the increase in the independence of the teachers. The curriculum had previously been set by the central-office staff, but with vouchers decisions were primarily made by teachers, who even had the resources (thanks to the extra funds provided by compensatory vouchers) to support their choices. Administrators were no longer quite as important; teachers had more freedom to arrange their working conditions than before; more flexibility in grouping students was possible; and teachers could create smaller working groups for themselves. The program was thus easier to revise and adapt as teachers went along.

Innovation at the school level was thereby supported and encouraged by decentralization, the mini-schools, and the compensatory-voucher monies—not by competition. If one were to speculate about innovation based on the Alum Rock experience, one would have to say that social and economic encouragement were more important than competition or political power.

But the voucher demonstration was not exactly easy for Alum Rock professionals. For one thing, it was temporary. Everyone knew things would revert to the old system in a few years, which did nothing to ease the problems of change. For another, the demonstration meant much more work: Administrative and fiscal procedures were redesigned, new budgeting systems were created, and mini-schools curriculums were established, placing greater burdens on teachers and principals. Many teachers reported they had never worked so hard and had not expected that the demonstration would require so much effort. Especially in the early stages, there was an avalanche of meetings, and many teachers felt overwhelmed and exhausted.

Thus although the working conditions of the teachers improved in some respects, in others they declined. There was more work and more worry, but no less teaching, nor more hours in the day. And while there was more money to spend on materials and resources, teachers were not paid much more for their extra duties. They received some compensation for in-service training, but it amounted to a very modest annual salary increase over the course of the demonstration. If this was an incentive, it certainly was not awfully enticing. Indeed, the whole demonstration was a terrible tease: It offered some opportunities and encouragements to teachers, but made only marginal allowances for the personal and professional sacrifices involved.

It was no surprise, then, that as the demonstration progressed energy flagged. Teachers had less time for meetings, less patience for the demands of innovation, less desire for the rigors of collaboration, and more appreciation of the lives they could once again lead separately and individually behind classroom doors. Because the voucher demonstration offered some encouragements for innovation, and because many professionals desired change, things began with energy, hasty improvisation, and excitement. But because the scheme had not been designed with much appreciation of the classroom experience of teachers—because it assumed that teachers should be reshaped by a stiff dose of competition—there were only partial and sometimes accidental incentives for professionals. As the demonstration moves toward a close, many innovations have begun to slip away.

Confusing symptoms with causes

One lesson of the voucher saga seems to be that if parent choice and educational alternatives make sense for public schools, it is not for the reasons contemplated by the reformers. The assumption underlying the original scheme was that schools were bad because parents were powerless, and that parents were powerless because they had been excluded by professionals anxious to protect themselves from popular control. If parents had more power—which in this case was to be gained by control of school funding—it was expected that professionals would then be accountable and that schools would thereby be better places for children. But when some barriers to parental involvement were removed, power distributions did not change appreciably.

One explanation for this may be that the existing power imbalance between parents and professionals is great enough to require even more support for parents before they can participate effectively. If this is correct, it raises questions about participatory reforms that assume that parents have been excluded and that given the opportunity to use power, they will. When they failed to, as in the case of EVAC, some observers argued that even more training, support, and professional advocacy were needed. But this argument redefines citizen participation: It no longer involves releasing the political energies of excluded citizens by providing greater access to power; it now consists of paying professionals to train, speak for, and support citizens. This view seems both plausible and puzzling. One is not sure whether to agree because implementation was only partial, to wonder why a larger dose would do more when a partial dose failed to help much at all, or to marvel at the need for even more professional help in the effort to overcome professional power.

The chief defect of this analysis is a confusion of symptoms and causes. There are real political imbalances in the governance of American schools, which contribute to the poor performance of political reforms to increase participation. But the real imbalance is not political in origin. It results more from a social division of labor that encourages the specialization of work, the professionalization of roles, and the partitioning of authority. In advanced industrial societies this solidifies professional power in education, as well as discouraging active parental involvement. Parents used to have more to do with education simply because there often was not much formal schooling available. It was not uncommon in the 18th and early 19th centuries for children to get much of their education from a parent—or from a job, in church, in an apprenticeship, or in other informal settings.

With the rise of schooling, education increasingly became the province of trained specialists. Professionals gain economic returns, social satisfaction, personal status, individual identity, and group power from their roles. And parents, most of whom have occupations providing similar rewards, have seen their educational role narrowed and redefined. It still involves early childhood education and help with homework in the elementary grades, but increasingly centers on insuring that children receive the right professional attention.

The growth of this division of labor had political consequences. In the early and middle 19th century, when public schools began, teachers had little status and less power: They were at the mercies of their communities. But the growth of a complex industrial division of labor weakened the bonds connecting work, family, school, and community, and eroded the forces that kept teachers in a subordinate and dependent position. Gradually, teaching—like many other occupations—has gained social definition, autonomy, and political power; community power over schools has correspondingly attenuated.

Since the imbalance in school power does not have political roots, political remedies may be marginal. Vouchers turned out so peculiarly in Alum Rock because the scheme fundamentally misconstrued the reason that power is so lopsidedly distributed in public education. As one might expect from such a misdiagnosis, the effects of the reform were perverse: Professionals gained power from an experiment in which they were supposed to lose it. Vouchers opened the door for power shifts, but they did not affect the ways in which work, authority, and child-rearing are apportioned in society. Because social realities were undisturbed by merely loosening up the political structure, the changes only enhanced the power of those who had it already.

Given this analysis, it is not surprising that all these changes occurred with little political conflict between parents and professionals. Predictably, most of the conflict was between professionals who advocated greater parent power and professionals who did not. That, after all, is what one would expect in an "expert society." The struggles were enough to make for several lively years in this small California city, but not enough to work basic changes in the distribution of political power.

More than meets the eye

At the same time, Alum Rock parents were more satisfied with their schools. This would seem perverse if one subscribed to the theory of parent power associated with vouchers: Why should parents' satisfaction increase if their power didn't? The answer, we think, is that vouchers in Alum Rock did offer benefits many parents desired, benefits that are consistent with the existing social division of labor. One of these was a somewhat greater range of educational alternatives. Some parents have strong views on the relative importance of language and culture, or on the balance among discipline, fundamentals, and individual discovery, or on the comparative significance of algebra and art. Although the mini-schools seemed to vary little in basic instructional patterns—most teachers spent about the same proportion of their time on reading and math—they did seem to offer diverse programs, thus more nearly corresponding with varieties of educational opinion. It is hardly surprising that parents with views hitherto unrepresented in the curriculum appreciated the new alternatives. Their appreciation may have followed from the substance of the new programs—or simply from being offered a choice. But whatever the reason, the opportunity to choose seems to have been welcomed.

Another benefit of the Alum Rock demonstration was that these alternatives were offered by professionals. Parents had the freedom to choose from a fairly conventional range of educational possibilities, but teachers defined, devised, and implemented them. The demonstration also tended to make professionals more visible and accessible to the parents. Most important, it did all this within the limits of established roles.

This helps to explain why parents in Alum Rock were more satisfied without being more powerful: They had more alternatives and more freedom to choose, but these were provided by professionals in authoritative and familiar ways—without much work for parents.

This points to a second lesson of the demonstration: It was hard to mount a voucher test because almost everyone ignored the considerable possibilities offered teachers. Instead, vouchers were advertised as a sort of radical social surgery to improve things for students and parents at the expense of the professionals. This approach to change was certain to flop unless a substantial proportion of teachers found vouchers attractive. But the project was promoted in such a way as to suggest that vouchers would punish professionals into better performance. So it is not surprising that OEO found few volunteers for a demonstration, or that professionals in Alum Rock responded with such caution. One political consequence of the social division of labor in advanced industrial societies is that the reform of social services is unlikely to succeed unless many professionals find it attractive. Because vouchers presented a rather threatening prospect, they had few takers.

The third lesson of the Alum Rock venture is that, ironically, there is more in the idea of choice for parents and professionals than the advertising suggested. Many teachers are strongly attracted by the prospect of choosing the sort of classroom they would work in, of shaping the curriculum they would use, and of working with students who find their style attractive. There is some evidence that when teachers exercise such choices—when they are able to create alternatives within the public schools—both parents and professionals are pleased with the results. Such efforts are underway in some cities (among them, Minneapolis and Cincinnati) and the reports seem encouraging. These professionally defined alternatives embody most of the main currents of thought about schooling and offer many of the specializations families desire—science, the arts, culture and language, and so on. If the voucher reform had been conceived and promoted differently, it might have met with somewhat greater enthusiasm among professionals.

Evaluating the scheme

This hardly exhausts the lessons of the voucher story, nor does it finish the tale itself. One fascinating item concerns the effort to evaluate vouchers effectively. A major justification for the federal program in the first place was the search for scientific results to support policy decisions about whether vouchers should be expanded or discarded. Large sums of money were spent in search of the answer, but the evaluation itself seems to have played no role in decisions about the future of vouchers. Experience provided more decisive and timely evidence. But the final evaluation does offer rich testimony concerning the difficulties involved in such scientific endeavors, and it might reveal something about their potential usefulness.

Similarly, there is still a question about the impact of the voucher program beyond Alum Rock. OEO and NIE tried to organize demonstrations in school districts all over the country; although all but one of these failed, promoting vouchers may have stimulated other efforts to increase choice and diversity. The prospect of government support for private schools may have stimulated attempts to promote diversity within the public schools, to show that alternatives were possible without resorting to nonpublic education. And all the publicity from Washington during the last five or six years may well have helped to legitimize diversity and choice, and create a climate of opinion in which they are more possible. It would be ironic if the primary impact of federal efforts to promote vouchers was indirect, but it would not be the first time in the history of social reform that unintended results were so significant.

Nor has this article fully probed some of the more programmatic issues raised by the voucher saga—for example, the federal role in school reform. There is certainly a need for reflection concerning how federal agencies might deal with reforms like vouchers that have more appeal than support. And what of the broader implications for participatory reforms? If, as we have argued, the sorts of participation most parents desire are different than those advocated by reformers, one wonders whether there are better ways to redress the imbalance of political power in education.

These and other questions are important, but must wait for a more detailed treatment of this fascinating episode in school reform. For now, it is enough to note that this scheme to promote parent power produced mixed results, and that several views are plausible. As an effort to reform the nation's schools, the voucher demonstration left much to be desired; it was an administrator's innovation, not a popular movement. Its only resources were its appeal and the ingenuity and money its advocates could produce. These were enough to keep the advocates busy, but not enough to foment a social experiment. Vouchers were intended to overturn the political power structure in local schools and put parents in the driver's seat, but the absence of popular support meant that there was really hope for success only when the opposition—the educational establishment—also liked the idea. There was only one actual test, and even there local forces tended to overwhelm federal priorities. The moral, we suppose, is that bright ideas, advice, and federal funds are no substitute for political power. Reforms spun from such political gossamer have similarly fragile prospects.

But vouchers can also be viewed as an attempt to change the balance of power within schools, and in this regard we think they produced both more and less than expected. As nearly as can be discerned, parents in Alum Rock have little more power now than before the test. The promise of parent choice and power rather unsettled teachers and principals, who promptly took steps to protect their interests. The ensuing story was enough to bring tears of joy to the eyes of the most hardened political observers: Professionals in Alum Rock emerged with undiminished and probably increased power—all this resulting from an innovation designed to boost the political fortunes of parents at the expense of professionals. The voucher idea was simply based on a serious overestimate of popular discontent and the demand for change in education. The moral is that reforms designed to "loosen up" school systems often succeed—but with perverse political effects. This is partly because the intended victims of reforms begin with much more organization and power than the intended beneficiaries; few of the beneficiaries have the time, energy, or resources to seize the opportunities presented by the reformers. The victims naturally use their superior power and organization not just to neutralize change but also to turn it to their own advantage. Similarly, the efforts of the Ford Foundation to loosen up the schools in New York through community control enhanced the political fortunes of the United Federation of Teachers. It often helps to loosen things up, but in the ensuing looseness, those with power get more.

From the perspective of promoting diversity, the story is less gloomy: The voucher demonstration in Alum Rock increased professionals' ability to choose and design their work settings, and made it possible for parents to select among alternatives. If choice and diversity are good, then schools in Alum Rock were better places.

Finally, the Alum Rock demonstration has provided an opportunity to learn a good deal about the possibilities for alternative programs, as well as helpful evidence concerning the likely roles of parents and professionals. Some of these lessons may be indirect and perverse, but they are instructive nonetheless. The experience with vouchers points to some ways in which diversity in education can be further explored and encouraged, even though it suggests other ways that seem barren. If the voucher plan is narrowly assessed in terms of its assumptions about political participation and school reform, it must be judged something less than a resounding success. But viewed as an exploration of educational alternatives, it may prove a source of suggestive ideas and lessons.

Contributors

William J. Bennett is Chairman of the National Endowment for the Humanities.

David K. Cohen is Professor of Education and Social Policy at Harvard University.

James Coleman is Professor of Sociology and Education at the School of Social Service at the University of Chicago.

Edwin J. Delattre is President of St. John's College in Annapolis, MD.

Martin Eger is Associate Professor at the City University of New York, College of Staten Island, where he teaches physics and philosophy and has participated in teacher education programs.

Eleanor Farrar is Senior Research Associate and Vice President of the Huron Institute, Cambridge, MA.

Nathan Glazer is Professor of Education and Social Structure at Harvard University. He is editor of *The Public Interest*.

Edward I. Koch is Mayor of the City of New York.

Daniel Patrick Moynihan is United States Senator from the State of New York.

Diane Ravitch is Adjunct Associate Professor of History and Education at Teacher's College, Columbia University.

Peter Skerry is a doctoral candidate in Government at Harvard.

Thomas Sowell is Senior Fellow at the Hoover Institution at Stanford University.

Jackson Toby is Professor of Sociology and Director of the Institute for Criminological Research at Rutgers University.